Law and Integration in the European Union

STEPHEN WEATHERILL

Professor of European Law
University of Nottingham

CLARENDON PRESS · OXFORD

1995

Oxford University Press, Walton Street, Oxford OX2 6DP
Oxford New York
Athens Auckland Bangkok Bombay
Calcutta Cape Town Dar es Salaam Delhi
Florence Hong Kong Istanbul Karachi
Kuala Lumpur Madras Madrid Melbourne
Mexico City Nairobi Paris Singapore
Taipei Tokyo Toronto
and associated companies in
Berlin Ibadan

Oxford is a trade mark of Oxford University Press

Published in the United States
by Oxford University Press Inc., New York

British Library Cataloguing in Publication Data
Data available

Library of Congress Cataloging in Publication Data
Data available
ISBN 0–19–876311–5
ISBN 0–19–876312–3 (Pbk.)

1 3 5 7 9 10 8 6 4 2

Typeset by Cambrian Typesetters, Frimley, Surrey
Printed in Great Britain on acid-free paper by
Biddles Ltd., Guildford and King's Lynn

Preface

England and Wales are about to follow where Scotland has led. EC law is on the brink of becoming a compulsory part of the undergraduate curriculum in England and Wales. Why has this decision been taken? Presumably there is some basic EC law information that all students now need. But this could be conveyed where it touches relevant English law subjects—in constitutional law, in a legal system course, in company law, and employment law. Of course, such integration properly occurs in our law schools. The case for exposure to EC law, taught separately from English law even though in a sense it *is* English law, is, as I see it, based on the perception that there is a distinctive quality to EC law that is liable to be obscured if it is taught only in the context of particular areas of English law. I have written this book in an attempt to distil what I see as the essential features of EC law of which a student should be aware. I believe that it is above all the dynamic, evolving character of EC law, rather than any particular chunk of subject matter, that needs to be grasped by the student. In the European Court and in the sphere of legislative activity, EC law has a different feel from English law.

This book has grown out of a curriculum restructuring undertaken at Nottingham in the light of the modularization of our undergraduate programme. For first-year students, it was agreed that there should be in their first semester a small, compulsory module. We call it *The Impact of the EC*. What we aimed to do was to expose students to *why* EC law was important to them as aspiring English lawyers. Most of all, we wanted to portray the dynamic and still-evolving character of EC law. We wanted to show how EC law changes as a system under pressure from legal and extra-legal influences. We wanted to show that it has become more multi-functional, thereby deepening its substantive impact and moving far beyond economic law, and (partly because of that spread) how it changes in its constitutional relationship with national law. We wanted to show how state structures have become blurred in modern economic and political conditions and how this affects power to make and enforce laws. We have tended to use case studies in class, and that is reflected here, but with a repetition of the warning that EC law is not a common law system. I owe debts to Nigel Gravells, Brian Wilkinson, and Thérèse Murphy, who have all played major roles in the development of the module, although the approach taken in this book is my responsibility alone.

The idea is that students will have a feel for EC law from the beginning of their legal education. It will not creep up on them subsequently as an awkward twist to the perceived 'normal' pattern of English law. The opportunity to pursue deeper study of particular aspects of EC law, such as internal market law, competition law, and environmental law, arises subsequently in their degree programme. I have an affinity for that pattern and I hope that compulsory EC law modules will in future permeate an undergraduate course rather than being stuck in one year only as a single block.

This book reflects the aspirations of our introductory module. It is intended to portray the evolution of EC law. It is not designed to provide detailed legal information (although it might stimulate a student to go and acquire that). It is lightly footnoted, with further reading lists at the end of each chapter. The book paints with a broad brush. It does not endeavour to find answers that fit every twist and turn of the Community legal order. My purpose will be served if I convey the impression that there are twists and turns, that a multiplicity of factors causes such undulation and that such trends are part of the continuing evolution of the Community. I make frequent reference to the intergovernmental conference (IGC) planned for 1996, which is already casting a shadow over the development of post-Maastricht EC law and policy.

I hope the book will stimulate anyone with an interest in how the law and policy of the European Community and the European Union have developed in the past and how they should develop in the future.

Contents

Table of Treaty Articles

EUROPEAN ATOMIC ENERGY COMMUNITY (EURATOM)

EUROPEAN COAL AND STEEL COMMUNITY (TREATY OF PARIS)

TREATY ON EUROPEAN UNION (MAASTRICHT)

Table of Directives and Regulations

Table of EC Cases

CASES BEFORE THE COURT OF HUMAN RIGHTS

Table of UK Cases

Opinions

I

From Community to Union

In the late 1980s the extraordinarily rapid disintegration of the Soviet Union and its effective sphere of influence placed sudden demands on the European Community. The Community was thrust into a leading role as a focus for securing the adjustment of the political and economic patterns of the former communist states in Europe. It is a matter of open debate whether the Community is performing this task creditably. But no other institution could conceivably have taken it on. The challenges facing the Community were entirely fresh, yet unnervingly familiar. They were novel in their detail. There was no blueprint for achieving the conversion of the former communist states into democratic market economies. Nor was there time to draw one up. The job simply had to be done in the shortest possible time. Yet these were old issues. Nearly forty years earlier, in 1952, the first of the European Communities had come into being as part of an ambitious scheme for securing the peaceful and prosperous reconstruction of the European continent after the devastation of the Second World War. Now, once again, after the collapse of Soviet Communism, the Community was a vehicle for the renovation of political and economic structures in Europe. Once again it was a source of optimism.

Although until recently it was possible to observe arguments about the economic role of the Community effectively obscure any recognition of its underlying political role, the changing shape of the continent since the decline of Soviet Communism forces a re-evaluation of the broader horizon. Snuffing out the threat of warfare has limited value as a contribution to the solution of detailed problems, but it is still the anchor for the Community's endeavours. Therefore no apology is offered for locating the first motivations for a European Community of a type recognizable today in the destruction wrought by the Second World War. The impulse to integrate reflected disillusionment with the repetitive pattern of bloody conflict between nation-states as a recurrent feature of European politics. Political elites were prompted to think afresh about political structures. Pursuit of the national interest could no longer be seen as a task capable of discharge by a single nation-state.

The post-war perception that political structures in Europe could beneficially be adjusted beyond the invidious nation-state pattern found an appealing echo in economic thinking. The limitation of markets to national territories fails to make the best of available resources. Exchange by import and export is mutually beneficial as states are able to take advantage of each other's strengths. states are able to expand production in areas in which they are strong and, where they are relatively weak, to rely on other states to fulfil needs. Such specialization improves the use of scarce resources in line with what economists choose to describe as the theory of comparative advantage. Producers gear up for a wider market and are able to cut costs by using production facilities more intensively. These are economies of scale. Consumer choice is restricted behind national tariff and quota walls, whereas integration offers wider availability of goods and services. Moreover, the integrated entity is able to use its greater muscle to obtain a favourable position on the international stage. This is naturally a brief distillation of a vast wealth of economic lore, but, on the most general model, a competitive cross-border market ought to operate to the general good.

This theoretical observation combines with the practical fact of technological advance. Recent decades have witnessed an extra-ordinary acceleration in the development of international trade in goods and services. The irresistible internationalization of commerce is a major factor in the decline of national markets. Moreover, that process is in turn a major factor in the decline of the independent state's ability to make and apply its own laws. To take a specific illustration, a state may choose a strict prohibition against particular types of pornographic films. The realization of the objective of maintaining morality standards is seriously undermined if citizens are able to tune their televisions to satellite channels with no direct link with the regulating state and watch such offensive material. The broadcaster might previously have been based in the regulating state, but may have chosen simply to move across a border to take advantage of a more favourable regime. Firms are mobile and can choose between regulators. Faxes, electronic mail, and the much-vaunted information super-highway are far more than exciting modern toys. They stand for the dismantling of the physical link between suppliers and consumers. This diminishes the state's capacity to define itself by its ability to mark out and defend its territory.

All this points to the growing drain of power from the state acting alone. In the modern economy, a state can in theory pass any law that appeals to its legislators. The coherent enforcement of those laws, too often seen as a mere technical matter by policy-makers, may be largely impossible. Worse, passing laws to control objectionable practices may simply drive firms away from the territory, causing job losses, but fail to suppress the practices.

This is state power in the modern world. In many sectors, effective regulation can be achieved only at international level. This dictates a need for individual states to involve themselves in international organizations equipped with power to respond to the strength of international commercial interests. This is not an instance of surrendering national powers to transnational bodies. Such a description makes the mistake of assuming that the content of national power occupies some definable, static shape. Instead the process is the creation of power at transnational level, transcending that held in aggregate by each state acting alone, in which each state then shares. These are both the political and economic motivations for European integration. The key point is that entry into a transnational organization is not the cause of declining national power. The cross-border structure is developed precisely because of a perception that national power is already illusory in a number of sectors.

This does not mean the disappearance of the state, still less of distinctive national identities. It means that states take different shapes and that a redistribution of functions occurs. It means a growth in transnational rule-making. This has occurred in the European Community over the last forty years. The idea that states alter shape under the pressure of political and historical development is nothing new. States have changed throughout history. Italy and Germany are nineteenth-century creations. Eighty years ago the territory of the British Isles was home to one state; there are now two. More fundamentally, the nineteenth century in particular witnessed wholesale changes in political institutions throughout Europe which caused radical change in the nature of every state's internal power structures.

A final point about national power in an international economy needs to be added. A state that has participated in the development of a transnational entity may wish to withdraw. This may be possible. It may then reclaim a power to regulate for its own territory. But this does not mean that a power of the same scope as that previously enjoyed will be repatriated. Once again, the idea that sovereignty can be disconnected from the transnational structure and taken back, like a beautiful rose planted in a fertile plot, misses the dynamic nature of markets and political structures. The rose, once uprooted, will look and smell quite different. Naturally it is a permissible political choice to cultivate one's own garden, however small, rather than to join a team cultivating a much larger field, but it is important that such choices are taken in the full knowledge that today individual gardens are smaller than they may have been in the past and that fences around them may in practice keep neither unwanted intruders out nor valued blooms in.

THE COMMON MARKET AND BEYOND

The sharing in economic power in the European Community is based on the elimination of barriers to trade across borders. State power to adopt or maintain measures that obstruct trade is constrained by the pattern of law that is part of the essence of Community membership. This means that EC law controls physical barriers at frontiers, but, more subtly, it also addresses the exercise of internal regulatory competence in so far as disparities between national rules may cause technical barriers to trade.

Article 2 of the Treaty of Rome, which brought about the creation of the European Economic Community in 1958, declared that:

The Community shall have as its task, by establishing a common market and progressively approximating the economic policies of Member states, to promote throughout the Community a harmonious development of economic activities, a continuous and balanced expansion, an increase in stability, an accelerated raising of the standard of living and closer relations between the states belonging to it.

This was a significantly ambitious statement. The common market referred to in Article 2 is more than a free trade area and it is more than a customs union.

A free trade area is based on the abolition of impediments to internal trade within the area. States retain independence over trading rules at their external borders. One of the consequences of this pattern is that free trade is envisaged only in goods produced within the free trade area. Goods produced in third countries and exported into the area are not then entitled to the benefits of free movement. This is essential to preserve the independence of the states to fix external trade policy. That independence would be fatally undermined were third country producers able to target imports on the state in the free trade area with the lowest import tariffs and then to supply the whole area from the territory of the weakest link.

The customs union adds the co-ordination of external trade policy that is missing from the free trade area. This gives the customs union the appearance from outside of a unified commercial block. The fact of a common external tariff allows the customs union to operate internally on the basis of free trade in all goods, not only those produced internally but also those produced externally that have paid the common price of market access. Internal controls to weed out goods entitled to free circulation from those not so entitled in accordance with their origin are unnecessary. The customs union is more ambitious in scope than the free trade area. It requires closer co-operation between participants in order to hammer out a common rule. And it envisages a greater surrender by states of power to act independently. That loss is judged to be outweighed by the economic advantage of participation.

The common market is more ambitious still. Common markets, as conventionally conceived, may take several different forms. On the European Community model, it is understood that the common market adds to the customs union pattern internal free movement of labour, services, and capital, as well as goods. It also envisages further co-ordination of policy-making in some sectors at least. For the EC, Article 2 places alongside each other 'establishing a common market and progressively approximating the economic policies of Member states'. It is controversial precisely how much common rule-making is required. Matters such as common economic policy-making, currency co-ordination, and ultimately monetary union are possible elements in a developed common market that is shading towards economic and political union. It will be elaborated in this book how the scope of the EC's activities has gradually expanded throughout its evolution. Such action in common plainly demands a well-developed structure for settling a common line. This, in turn, implies a significant loss of power to act unilaterally.

Such implications are part of the package bought by members of the Community. Giving up some apparent power that is in fact already lost to the internationalization of markets and giving up some power that may in fact still be exercisable is judged worthwhile because of the benefits offered by action in common. Politically, stability is the outcome within the territory of Europe occupied by the Community, coupled to a louder voice in global affairs. Internally the most obvious advantages are economic. The 'virtuous circle' of economic integration refers to increased competition, leading to wider consumer choice, higher quality goods and services, the realization of economies of scale, and lower prices. Firms shift their activities to a European level typically by building transnational distribution networks and/or relocating or expanding their places of production, perhaps in connection with a takeover strategy.

It is true that the explicit focus of Community activity throughout most of its lifespan has tended to be economic integration. The common market was its most widely advertised aspect. For many years in the United Kingdom, the Community was widely referred to as the 'Common Market', as if the two were one and the same notion. The emphasis was on free trade market economics. But a reading of Article 2 of the Treaty of Rome reveals this to be misconceived. Article 2 refers to a range of tasks, some of which are only loosely connected with the economy, most of all 'an accelerated raising of the standard of living and closer relations between the states belonging to it'. And, fundamentally, the establishing of a common market is not a Community task in itself according to Article 2, but rather a means to achieve these ends. Economic success is one part of a Community endeavour which was always planned with grander aspirations.

The Preamble to the Treaty of Rome referred to 'an ever closer union among the peoples of Europe'. Stronger still, the Treaty establishing the European Coal and Steel Community in 1952 expressed a resolve to create 'the basis for a broader and deeper community among peoples long divided by bloody conflicts'; peoples 'with a destiny henceforth shared'. Such explicit location of the nature of the Community endeavour beyond mere inter-state relations has inspired the European Court, in particular, to interpret the Treaties in a way that has diverged far from the normal assumptions of international treaty law. The Court's approach has greatly enhanced the position of the individual in EC law and has propelled EC law into the fabric of national legal systems.

THE INTERWEAVING OF POLITICS AND ECONOMICS

The political and economic scepticism about the desirability of an emphasis on the independent status of the nation-state were not simply two distinct impetuses pushing in the same direction. They were linked. In the immediate post-war years it was thought that deeper economic integration had of itself inevitable political repercussions.

This is well illustrated by the first of the three Communities that were created in the 1950s, the European Coal and Steel Community, created under the Treaty of Paris 1951 and coming into existence at the start of 1952. This was economically motivated in the sense that the coal and steel industries were capable of being run more efficiently on a European scale. More significant still was the role of these industries. At the time, these were the war-making industries. Placing them under common control was a means of providing an intensely practical assurance that war between France and Germany would not once again blight the continent.

Robert Schuman, the then French Foreign Minister, made the following immensely influential declaration on 9 May 1950:

Europe will not be made all at once, or according to a single plan. It will be built through concrete achievements which first create a *de facto* solidarity. The coming together of the nations of Europe requires the elimination of the age old opposition of France and Germany. Any action taken must in the first place concern these two countries. With this aim in view, the French Government proposes to take action immediately on one

limited but decisive point. It proposes to place Franco-German production of coal and steel as a whole under a common higher authority, within
the framework of an organization open to the participation of the other
countries of Europe. The pooling of coal and steel production should
immediately provide for the setting up of common foundations for
economic development as a first step in the federation of Europe . . . The
solidarity in production thus established will make it plain that war
between France and Germany becomes not merely unthinkable, but
materially impossible.

The linkage between economics and politics that is well illustrated
by the Coal and Steel Community lies in the notion that once
states are drawn to co-operate in one sector of the economy, there
will be an inevitable spillover into other areas. Such is the nature
of the modern economy. Economic integration begets economic
integration, and for some theorists it inevitably begets political
integration too, even without any explicit initiatives directed at the
political sector. For anyone who believed in the inevitable
momentum of such a process, the establishment of the European
Coal and Steel Community in 1952 was exciting enough in itself,
but its real importance lay in the impression that it was a snowball
launched into an unstoppable roll down a long hill.

Some observers came to emphasize the role of politics in
the process which robs economic integration of much of its
automacity. National political institutions were shown to be a good
deal more resistant to pressures for structural adaptation than was
initially predicted. It seemed that building 'supranational' institutions demanded an active approach and not an assumption of
natural growth. However, it remains central to the debate today
how much the Community is built on an inevitable integrative
process and how much depends on political planning—and where
the snowball, gathering up national functions into the body of the
Community, stops.

After the Second World War, the position of Germany was
critical politically and economically. Germany had to be
reconstructed, but in a European mould. The Coal and Steel
Community was a well-chosen starting point. It allowed the
rehabilitation of Germany in a technical setting to which no one
could object for grand political reasons. Germany was led by
politicians determined to refashion it in an outward-looking,
democratic image. Today the willingness of German politicians to

see the German interest as most effectively expressed as part of the European interest remains a regularly expressed orthodoxy both for internal and for external consumption. Germany is geographically and politically central to European integration and indispensable to the process.

THE THREE EUROPEAN COMMUNITIES AND THE LEGAL PATTERN

The European Coal and Steel Community, the creation of the Treaty of Paris, came into being at the start of 1952. The political and economic objectives were realized through the expression of a legal instrument. Law serves to realize political and economic aspirations.

The six states party to the Treaty of Paris, Germany, France, Italy, Belgium, the Netherlands, and Luxembourg, took two further steps in 1957 when they agreed to establish a European Atomic Energy Community (Euratom) and, most significant of all, a European Economic Community (EEC), both of which came into existence at the start of 1958.

By the end of the 1950s there were three European Communities comprising six members. These three Communities still remain constitutionally separate today, although for practical purposes they have been administered as one since the merger of the institutions in 1967.

The Communities through the 1960s seemed to be proceeding along a successful path. Political tensions did not disappear, but war between the Member states became an increasingly improbable occurrence. The economic indicators were highly favourable. Trade between the six had increased and not simply by shutting out former trading partners. The integrative process itself was creating trade, as envisaged by economic theory. In the middle of 1968 the abolition of customs duties on inter-state trade was completed eighteen months ahead of schedule.

The political and economic perceptions of the advantages of integration were expressed through legal rules. They involved a diminution in national states' ability to do as they pleased on their own territory. Membership of the Community involved acceptance of a fetter on national competence. The legal pattern had to involve the establishment of some transnational institutions able to make and enforce the rules. So the states were not simply giving up power; they were transferring it to the new European entity. Membership of the Community carried with it a curtailment of national power to act unilaterally, but it was done on the basis that independent national action taken by a single European state was at best fruitless in the modern world and at worst harmful, and that only action taken in common could be effective. The states acting together have more economic and political influence than the aggregate influence of each acting separately. EC law enforces that perception through the application of legal rules that stop states trying to stick only to the aspects of the process that suit them. The law requires that all states accept the rough with the smooth in the expectation that there is more smooth than rough for all participants.

The word 'supranational' was for many years employed to describe the nature of the Community as an independent entity to which powers had been transferred from national level. This indicated the contrast with the 'intergovernmental' nature of the traditional international institution, which operated as no more than a method of expressing the consensus view of its member states and which lacked the institutional sophistication of the Community. The word supranational has dropped from popular usage. It provides an insufficiently subtle description of the interplay between Member states and Community that has evolved over forty years. Nonetheless the basic, if unsophisticated, supranational/intergovernmental divide still usefully helps to begin to convey the distinctive nature of the Community. It has regained some of its descriptive value since the adjustments of the Treaty on European Union have created patterns akin to both supranationalism and intergovernmentalism within the European Union.[1]

THE TENSIONS OF ENLARGEMENT

The first phase of enlargement transformed the six into the nine from the start of 1973. The United Kingdom, Denmark, and the Republic of Ireland all joined the European Community, comprising, in technical terms, three Communities, EEC, ECSC, and

[1] 29 below.

Euratom. In part the countries concerned were attracted by the economic advantages which appeared to be on offer within the charmed circle of the Community. The new states were initially easily digested into the culture of economic expectation in the Community, although from 1979 severe differences over the question of how an economy should be regulated developed as the policies of successive Thatcher administrations developed in the United Kingdom. Politically, however, the new members had their differences with the original six. This was most apparent in the United Kingdom. It had chosen to remain outwith the integrative process in the 1950s. These were the days of the United Kingdom's lingering self-perception as a superpower. It looked to links with the United states and responsibilities to the Commonwealth as readily as to co-operation with continental Europe. The political impulse to abandon failed political institutions which prompted fresh thinking in most of Western Europe found a weaker echo in the United Kingdom, where, if anything, a contrary satisfaction with the successful outcome of the war prompted a desire to maintain existing institutions and to improve them, especially through the construction of the Welfare state. In the 1950s the United Kingdom was a leading actor in the European Free Trade Association, a bloc dedicated to free trade among its members (most of Western Europe outside the EC) and seen by the EC, probably correctly, as an attempt to dilute its own integrative efforts along the more intergovernmental lines preferred by the United Kingdom. To this extent, the United Kingdom followed the Soviet Union's path in recognizing the depth of the commitment involved in membership of the EC—and in staying outside. In the immediate post-war years, the United states-led Marshall Plan had been on offer to all the states of Europe. The Soviet Union perceived the integrative process as an attempt to establish economic dominance as a precursor to political control and was not prepared to permit the states of Eastern Europe to participate. The depth of ambition of the integrationists and the threat to national independence of the developing EC were already apparent and repellent to both Soviet Union and United Kingdom.

A combination of factors, such as waning global influence and economic performance, that compared increasingly unfavourably with the EC's six brought the United Kingdom to the position of seeking membership in the early 1960s. It was rebuffed twice and joined only in 1973. It is highly unlikely that the political elites of the United Kingdom accepted the full range of political objectives that had been latent in the Community process since its inception. Even in the early 1970s the general perception in the United Kingdom was not of the thorough reconstruction of political structures that had motivated the founders of the EC. There was no need at the time to thrash out such ideological differences about the Community's direction for, in their very nature, they remained concealed beneath the text of the Treaty. This is common to most international agreements and it is far from unknown in the Community. To an extent that cannot be calculated with any precision, the United Kingdom position differed from that of its new partners from the first day of 1973. Of course, it is no surprise that the aspirations of 1973 were different from those of 1951. The core six had undergone their own shifts in perception over that period as, for example, economic strength returned, Franco–German reconciliation deepened and the Cold War thawed. In any event the original six were themselves far from monolithic in outlook. The attitude of France under General de Gaulle in particular caused strains well before the United Kingdom joined.[2] However, the perception surfaces today that there is a core to the Community that involves a depth of commitment not assumed by later entrants. It affects the political climate and it is a thematic tension that is certain to influence decision-making about the future.

The accessions of Greece in 1981 and of Spain and Portugal in 1986 brought the number of members to twelve. Here, too, new and potentially divergent aspirations were fed into the Community structure. All three countries had relatively recently undergone transition to Western-style democracy. As recently as 1981, Spain had faced and defeated an attempted military coup. Much more than for the three new entrants of 1973, membership of the Community was an intensely political statement of commitment to democracy. All three new states also sought enhanced economic prosperity by participation in the wider market, but here, too, their ambitions were distinct from those of the 1973 trio. The economic performance of Portugal, Spain, and Greece fell well

[2] 62 below.

below the Community average. This posed problems for their economic absorption into the market that were more significant than those raised in 1973, where only Ireland, a relatively small country, slipped below the Community norm. The accessions of the 1980s brought forward questions about the role of the Community in securing equitable distribution of wealth among its members which remain unsolved. The enlargements of 1995, bringing the number of members to fifteen, were less problematic from the perspective of the identity of the newcomers. Austria, Finland, and Sweden were close to the Community's political and economic norm, although their above-average determination to defend the environment and their well-established commitment to state social welfare provision may cause some tensions. Yet there were strains based on the simple fact of enlargement. The number of members was now two-and-half times that of the original six. The institutional structure was placed under severe pressure.

Enlargement is in many ways the key issue for the Community. It is not simply a technical matter of adding numbers. The pursuit of peace and prosperity may serve as an enduring theme to the pattern of post-war European integration, but such objectives are achievable through many different methods. Once one abandons the broad brush and attempts to establish the detailed arrangements for integration, a multiplicity of factors intrude and the more members there are, *a fortiori* where they are politically, economically, and culturally heterogenous, the more difficult it is to achieve any consensus on the proper scope of future action.

The combined population of the Member states of the Community in 1995 is close to 400 million. 'Europe' and 'European Community' have too often in the past been used interchangeably as if countries outside the Community are not truly European. The stage has now been reached that nearly all the states of Europe are either members of the Community or aiming to join it in the medium-term. This still does not justify any notion that Norwegians or Swiss are not proper Europeans, but it does mean that the status of the entity acting as a bloc representing and acting for virtually the entire continent, imminently if not currently, is enormously enhanced. Those outside are dwarfed by the Community and in many respects live in its shadow. The point should be made that European states can decline to join the

Community and, although this is not explicitly provided for in the
Treaty, they may make the political choice to withdraw from
the Community. But they cannot withdraw from Europe. And this
means that any European state outside the Community is still
inevitably subject to its influence although unable itself to shape its
rules.

By 1986, the membership of the Community had doubled from six
to twelve without any formal Treaty revision of significance. This
changed in 1987. The Single European Act came into force at the
start of July 1987. It made a number of adjustments to the Treaty
of Rome.

   Additions were made to the Community's competence. Strictly,
it has only the competence conferred on it under its Treaty. It is
empowered to legislate only where a specific legal base can be
identified, and it then must use the procedures stipulated under
that base. In practice it had sufficiently broadly phrased bases to
permit action to be taken in a wide range of areas. This is
explained in Chapter 2. But the Single European Act provided the
first formal enhancement of the Treaty pattern of attributed
competences. Environmental protection, for example, found an
explicit place in the Treaty for the first time and the Community
became competent to legislate in the field. This was in many
respects a mere codification of pre-existing practice.[3]

   As is examined more fully in Chapter 3, procedures for voting in
Council were adjusted by the Single European Act. Harmonization of laws required to achieve the completion of the internal
market could in most areas be achieved by a qualified majority
vote in the Council, the Community's most powerful legislative
organ. This denied states the opportunity unilaterally to
veto proposals. This was a manifestation of the nature of the
Community as an autonomous entity to which powers have been
transferred from national level. States had accepted that they
would give up a power to oppose laws to which, on their own,
they would not have submitted. The higher profile conferred on
qualified majority voting on legislation in Council was a key

[3] Ch. 2, 50.

element in adjusting the formal constitutional structure of the Community in order to make it capable of achieving the political commitment to the completion of the internal market.

The Parliament obtained an enhanced role in the legislative procedure and, if the circumstances were right, it could block the adoption of legislation. More significantly, it was able to exert more effective informal influence. This is explored more fully in Chapter 3.

The Single European Act cannot be taken as a sustained attempt to address the problems caused by enlargement. Elements of the changes wrought represent attempts to stimulate decision-making, which is inevitably impeded by the presence of more people round the table. The shift towards qualified majority voting in Council may be assessed from this perspective. Yet that was not a radical rethinking. Rather, it was simply an attempt to move towards the type of pattern agreed in 1957 in the original Treaty of Rome.[4] In fact, the advantage of hindsight reveals that many of the questions about the future of the Community that were dodged at the time of the Single European Act have subsequently returned to the agenda with added force.

THE COMPLETION OF THE INTERNAL MARKET

The process of the completion of the internal market was ostensibly motivated by economic considerations. The internal market was defined in a new Article 8a EEC, inserted by the Single European Act, which became Article 7a EC after Maastricht. It provides that:

> The Community shall adopt measures with the aim of progressively establishing the internal market over a period expiring on 31 December 1992 . . . The internal market shall comprise an area without internal frontiers in which the free movement of goods, persons, services and capital is ensured in accordance with the provisions of this Treaty.

The Commissioner responsible for overseeing the development of the project, Lord Cockfield, was quite uncompromising in his public pronouncements on the impact of this provision. It meant, he wrote, 'the total abolition of internal frontiers and by necessary

---

[4] Ch. 3, 62.

implication the abolition of the frontier controls that go with internal frontiers'.[5] The United Kingdom has maintained that controlling third-country immigration and suppression of terrorism and drug trafficking continue to provide a justification for border checks, at least until such time as effective Community-wide policies in respect of these matters are put in place and, on some accounts, even beyond then. The United Kingdom, with one land border only, is in a rather different geographical situation from most states. Whether that indeed justifies its claim to a different legal status in the construction of the internal market will be tested. It will ultimately be for the European Court to rule authoritatively on precisely what is envisaged by Article 7a EC.

The 1992 project was first explained in detail in the Commission's White Paper of 1985,[6] which examines the economic and political advantages of completing the internal market and sets out an intensive programme of legislative action required to achieve that end. The Introduction to the White Paper emphasized the removal of physical, technical and fiscal barriers to trade. It explained that 'the reason for getting rid entirely of physical and other controls between Member states is not one of theology or appearance, but the hard practical fact that the maintenance of any internal frontier controls will perpetuate the costs and disadvantages of a divided market.' The White Paper was enormously influential. The notion of putting forward the programme was largely the brainchild of Lord Cockfield. The lifetime of two Commissions, 2 × 4 years, from publication of the White Paper, stimulated the choice of the end of 1992 as the date on which the mass of legislation that was required to make the internal market a reality should have been adopted. In June 1985 the Milan Council accepted the plan. '1992' promptly became a remarkably high-profile slogan, although in some countries, such as France, the reference was to '1993' as the magic date, reflecting the Treaty commitment to completion by the end of 1992.

The Commission funded a substantial investigation into the benefits that could be expected from the successful completion of the internal market. This was the Cecchini Report. Oddly, perhaps, this followed the publication and acceptance of the White

---

[5] Lord Cockfield, *The European Union: Creating the Single Market* (Chichester: Wiley Chancery Law, 1994), 66.   [6] COM(85)310.

Paper instead of preceding it. This may be explained in the light of the obvious economic good sense of the Internal Market package, which required no detailed proof in advance. It may also testify to the eagerness of the Member states to seize on some method for providing the Community with fresh momentum, even in the absence of extended demonstration of its value. By the early 1980s the first economic successes of the Community had given way to an increasing feeling of stagnation, both globally and in Europe. The political discussions of the Community were locked in bitter wrangles about matters such as the increasing budgetary drain of the Common Agricultural Policy and the British insistence on readjustment of its financial contributions. Vision and imagination were far from the agenda. In the light of such a gloomy background, the 1992 project was explicitly economic in motivation, but its implications for the reinvigoration of the ideals of the Community went much deeper.

The economic quantifications were summarized in precise figures in the Cecchini Report. The benefits of the internal market would vary sector by sector. They would accrue from the removal of the costs associated with border controls and from the creation of a more competitive economy within which resources could be employed to better advantage. Broadly summarized, Cecchini envisaged a 6 per cent increase in Community Gross Domestic Product, amounting to some £140 billion; the creation of five million new jobs; and a 6 per cent fall in the prices of consumer goods. Such gains would accrue in a relatively short period after the dismantling of barriers had been brought to fruition, but they would not be 'one-off'. The broad advantages of a more competitive economy would persist.

This analysis was close to the common market analysis of the 1950s. Consumer choice and economies of scale were not newly discovered phenomena. The empirical evidence of the early successes of the Community economy suggested that Cecchini was at heart well founded. Cecchini was valuable in its identification of specific areas where the market remained fragmented for reasons ranging from lack of political will to inadequate legal instruments. The '1992' project was in part a new start designed to capture public imagination and this places it beyond the sphere of mere economics.

The Cecchini Report attracted some criticism. It is certainly important to appreciate that integration brings with it economic and political risks. Bigger markets may breed bigger and more pernicious anti-competitive practices. Breaking down national barriers injects a blast of competition into previously protected markets, but the initial process of restructuring may be followed by the re-establishment of cartels, oligopolies, or monopolies at European level. The rationalization of the market will involve the disappearance of some industries in some areas with consequent job losses. Naturally the point of the process is that gains will outweigh such losses as switches occur to more efficient use of resources, including both raw materials and people. But some areas will gain more than others; some may not gain at all. Is the fact of wealth maximization enough justification in itself for the process or should the Community properly be engaged in questions of wealth distribution? And should the Community legislate for minimum standards of social welfare? These are questions that were left largely unresolved at the time the internal market process was unleashed. They continue to dog the Community today.

An additional element surrounds the question of the willingness of states and firms to play by the rules and the capacity of the Community to secure the enforcement of those rules. There are potential short-term gains to be won by not complying. Much of the pattern of the Community legal order is directed at shaping the rules and at striving to ensure adherence to those rules in order to protect the longer-term vision.

Perhaps most of all it is important to appreciate the psychological significance of the process. The market will be integrated only if traders and consumers treat it as such. The test of '1992' is in one sense the putting in place of hundreds of laws; in another sense it is the commercial decisions taken by firms and consumers about their practices. With that perception comes an appreciation that law is both central to the process and well-nigh irrelevant. The legal rules provide a framework within which commercial activity can be planned. The legal rules should breed confidence in the viability of the process. But commercial decision-making and consumer behaviour will make or break the internal market. And if resort to law to force open markets becomes anything more than the tip of the iceberg of cross-border trading then the costs are likely to prove sufficiently deterrent to frustrate the practical realization of the internal market. The effective management of the internal market involves a need for rather more thorough attention to choice of institutional support than is found in the Cecchini Report.

It was left obscure how the internal market was related to the common market. The absence of any reference to common policy-making in Article 8a EEC/7a EC suggested that it was a rather less ambitious project. For some this meant that the internal market was a mere staging post, after which further work would be directed at deepening other aspects of the Community's tasks and activities found in Articles 2 and 3. For others, notably the United Kingdom under Mrs Thatcher's leadership, the internal market was a deregulatory end in itself and a happy rejection of some of the more ambitious plans for re-regulating the European market in the field of, for example, social policy and for developing political institutions at European level. The ambiguous relationship between internal and common market was left unresolved at the time of the adoption of the Single European Act. It was doubtless thought better to proceed with such agreement as there was rather than to haggle over perhaps abstract points of political and economic theology. Indeed, the success of 1992 seems to be in the main attributable to keeping grand political solutions out of the prescription and sticking to the basic idea of a territory that is border-free in economic terms. Unsurprisingly, these are issues that have returned to haunt the policymakers. The basic difference of opinion on the status of the internal market has led subsequently to ferocious differences of opinion on the appropriateness of deeper spheres of competence for the Community after the end of 1992 and the consolidation of the internal market. The process of the completion of the internal market was ostensibly motivated by free market economic considerations, but in fact it concealed a necessity to make such significant decisions about the institutional support required to sustain that market. It also delayed the inevitability of addressing the proper scope for Community action in the several areas referred to in Articles 2 and 3 of the Treaty that go beyond the economy.

THE EUROPEAN ECONOMIC AREA AND
THE WIDER EUROPE

The 1992 project created an impression of an enormously powerful entity ready to compete on equal terms in the global market with Japan and the United states, itself prompted to pursue the integrative path through the North American Free Trade Area, NAFTA. The fear of exclusion and the attraction of inclusion drew the EFTA rump into negotiation with the predominant EC. What emerged was the European Economic Area. This involve the extension of most of the basic pattern of the EC Treaty to five of the former EFTA countries. It was not achieved without problems. The European Court ruled a draft Agreement incompatible with the EC legal order, forcing renegotiation.[7] Once this hurdle was surmounted, the Swiss people sprung a surprise by voting in a referendum against their country's participation. A further re-adjustment was necessary. But the EEA entered into force at the start of 1994. It did not last long in that form. It had been hailed as a second-tier Community and as a training ground for would-be members. Austria, Finland, and Sweden did not choose to spend long on the training ground. They were full members of the Community only twelve months later.

If the process of the completion of the internal market and even the EEA could be examined primarily in terms of economics, the same could not be said for a cascade of other dramatic events in the early 1990s. The Soviet bloc crumbled with extraordinary speed. The states of Eastern Europe quickly sought linkage with the European Community, achieved initially in the shape of a pattern of association agreements, and most of these states asserted that Community membership was a medium-term objective. This was a political statement reflecting a determination to join the Western-style democracies as much as a perceived method for constructing workable economies.

Meanwhile, Yugoslavia fragmented into violent racism. War in the European Community had become unthinkable, but war in Europe plainly had not. The response of the EC to the conflict in former Yugoslavia has attracted widespread criticism for its ineffectual nature, although some critics have underestimated a

---

[7] See Ch. 6, 186 below, for further details.

historical background that breeds scepticism about the ability of any mediator to bring peace to that part of the continent. More fundamental still, the perceived inadequacy of the EC response is capable of attracting two quite opposite conclusions; either that the EC cannot cope with such political matters and should withdraw to the economic realm, or that the EC structure must be strengthened in order to provide it with the power to play an effective role in such circumstances. The Treaty on European Union has opted for a course which contains traces of both perceptions. It prepares the institutional and constitutional ground for closer co-operation between the Member states, but outwith the familiar EC pattern. This is examined below.

The combination of the queue of would-be new members in former Eastern Europe, the unification of Germany and the horrors occurring in the former Yugoslavia has transformed the focus of the Community. It is no longer essentially West European in outlook. It is more truly European. As Central Europe re-emerges on either side of the old post-war East–West divide and as Eastern Europe disappears as a recognizable political concept, attitudes among most of the Community Member states have changed. The Community's centre of gravity has moved eastwards. It is far from clear whether the message has been heard in Britain, which is geographically more remote from the heart of Europe. The consequences of failing to appreciate this shift include a remoteness that is more than geographic.

The general role of the EC as a focus for the reconstruction of the continent has suddenly reemerged after decades of sub-ordination to more detailed matters. A pattern of what might be termed concentric circles is taking shape, although the shapes are rather more irregular than is suggested by that metaphor. The Community is the core, but outside it lies first the Union, which comprises the same membership as the Community, then the European Economic Area, and then the pattern of association agreements. At a global level, the World Trade Organization, on which agreement was reached in late 1994, provides a still wider framework.

The question whether the Community itself might fragment into circles of varying diameters is for the future, as is the completion of a balance sheet of advantages and disadvantages that might flow from such internal change.

THE TREATY ON EUROPEAN UNION

In December 1991, at Maastricht in the Netherlands, the next step forward for the Community was agreed. This was its transformation from European Community into European Union, enshrined in the Treaty on European Union. This Treaty could come into force only once each Member state had ratified it in accordance with domestic constitutional requirements. There was fierce opposition in several Member states, especially in Denmark where an initial 'no' vote in a referendum in 1992 was overturned a year later by a narrow positive vote in a second referendum. Public disquiet was evident in several Member States. In late 1993 the Treaty was finally ratified by the twelfth and last state, Germany, after a favourable ruling by its Constitutional Court, and the Treaty on European Union came into force on 1 November 1993. The opposition can be summarized as arising from insecurity and confusion about the path the Community had been taking and that which the Community, and now the Union, were planning to take. Many lurking disagreements about the scope of the project came to the fore at Maastricht and afterwards. Some were resolved; many were not.

According to Article A, the Union Treaty 'marks a new stage in the process of creating an ever closer union among the peoples of Europe'. This accords with the insistence of the Treaties of the 1950s that people, not simply states, are the explicit focus of the process.

The Treaty on European Union is best assessed from two separate standpoints. The first allows a survey of the changes wrought to the EC. The second allows an examination of the nature of the 'European Union' that has been created in a mould quite distinct from the established EC.

The Pattern of the European Community

The Treaty on European Union leaves in place the existing three European Communities, but renames the most high-profile of the trio the 'European Community'. The EEC is now officially the EC. The loss of the word 'economic' from the title may be taken as a symbol of the rather more extensive ambitions of the organization. The EC Treaty is substantially amended by Title II, Article G, of the Treaty on European Union. A flavour of the new depth may be tasted from comparing the newly amended Article 2 EC with its predecessor reproduced on page 5 above, Article 2 EEC. Article 2 is now much enhanced:

> The Community shall have as its task, by establishing a common market and an economic and monetary union and by implementing the common policies or activities referred to in Articles 3 and 3a, to promote throughout the Community a harmonious and balanced development of economic activities, sustainable and non-inflationary growth respecting the environment, a high degree of convergence of economic performance, a high level of employment and of social protection, the raising of the standard of living and quality of life, and economic and social cohesion and solidarity among Member States.

The use of the phrase 'Common Market' as synonym for the Community is now an even more blatant blunder than previously. Those who prefer the phrase are seeking to confine the Community to a free market economic focus which has never been its sole domain and which in future is even more clearly simply one component of Community activity.

Like the Single European Act before it, the Treaty on European Union tinkers with the pattern of the original EEC Treaty, now the EC Treaty. The voting rules in Council undergo shifts. The Parliament obtains a higher profile. The scope of Community competence is widened by the inclusion in the Treaty for the first time of titles dealing with matters such as culture and consumer protection. The Treaty creates a status of Citizen of the Union. Perhaps the centrepiece of the Treaty lies in the new Articles 102a–109m, which put in place the procedures for aligning economic and monetary policy and for establishing a single currency. This is a step which offers scope for greater price stability and control of budget deficits. But even though it may be grounded in theory as a method of improving economic performance, its political resonances for national power are loud. It involves further location of power at European level and a diminution in unilateral national power.

The present pattern of the EC Treaty deserves an overview. Many of the elements mentioned here are examined in more depth in the course of this book. However, this portrayal of the framework will make plain the remarkably broad scope of current Community competence.

Part One of the EC Treaty covers Articles 1–7c and is entitled

Principles. It includes Article 2's list of tasks, followed by a list of Community activities in Article 3. Article 3a refers to the introduction of a single currency. Article 3b provides that, in areas that do not fall within its exclusive competence, the Community shall take action in accordance with the principle of subsidiarity. This involves an assessment, *inter alia*, of whether objectives are better achieved by state or Community action.

Articles 4–4b establish the Community's institutions. Article 5 commits states to take all appropriate measures to ensure the fulfilment of Treaty obligations. This is the duty of Community solidarity. Article 6 establishes a prohibition against discrimination on grounds of nationality within the scope of application of the Treaty. Nothing is closer to the core of the Community's objectives and ideals than this principle.

Article 7 deals with the progressive establishment of the common market. Articles 7a–7c deal with the progressive establishment of the internal market by the end of 1992 and first appeared in the Treaty as a result of the amendments of the Single European Act.

Part Two of the Treaty covers Articles 8–8e and is wholly new to the Treaty after Maastricht. It creates the status of Citizenship of the Union, which is conferred on all persons holding the nationality of a Member state.

Part Three of the Treaty is entitled *Community Policies*. It stretches from Article 9 to Article 130y and includes within it seventeen separate Titles. An appreciation of the range of these policies is critical to a grasp of the modern multi-functional face of the Community. Free trade is a part of the Community's policies, but a part only. The original Treaty of Rome contained versions of seven of these titles. Ten may be traced in the Treaty as amended by the Single European Act. That there are now seventeen is eloquent testimony to the Community's spreading influence.

The first Title has always been a major element in the Community structure. It is the *Free Movement of Goods*, Articles 9–37 EC. Article 9 declares that the Community 'shall be based upon a customs union'. Articles 12–17 deal with the abolition of customs duties between states; Articles 18–29 with the setting up of the common customs tariff; Articles 30–37 with the elimination of quantitative restrictions between Member States. This third category of provisions has generated a great deal of litigation pitting commercial interests against state regulations that tend to impede free trade in goods across national borders. Article 30 has always been one of the most visible means for the penetration of national systems by Community law obligations.

Title II, Articles 38–47, is entitled *Agriculture*. For France, above all, putting in place this regime (and funding it through the Community) was a precondition for the whole Community enterprise. The sector has retained its place as an indispensable part of the Community's activities and, in budgetary terms, it is highly significant. It is also based on a set of rules of fiendish complexity.

Title III, Articles 48–73h, cover the free movement of persons, services, and capital. At one level, these provisions belong alongside Title I, governing the Free Movement of Goods. The liberalization of the market for goods, together with those for workers, services, and capital, is a cornerstone of common market theory. The frequent reference in Community jargon to the 'four freedoms' refers to free movement of goods, persons, services, and capital. However, these provisions have a deeper impact than the mere creation of a more economically efficient trading area. They concern people. Article 48 confers a right of free movement on workers; Article 52 grants the same right to the self-employed; Article 59 contains a parallel entitlement for a more temporary migrant, the provider of services. Accompanying rights, for example to move with a family and to enjoy aspects of social welfare in the host state, ensure that these provisions have impacts that run far deeper than the mere restructuring of the economy on a European scale. Community trade law already has a developed pattern of individual rights and the insertion into the Treaty of the new status of Citizenship of the Union is, in part at least, no more than a consolidation of existing patterns. These provisions apply not only to natural but also to legal persons. Companies are able to take advantage of the wider market by relying on these rights. The final part of this Title, that dealing with capital mobility, languished largely unregarded for most of the first thirty years of the Community's activity. It has now been resuscitated by the commitments undertaken in the fields of economic and monetary policy at Maastricht. These are outlined below.

Title IV deals with *Transport*. It has kept a relatively low profile, in stark contrast to Title V, which stretches from Articles

85 to 102. Title V is entitled *Common Rules on Competition, Taxation, and Approximation of Laws*. It is split now, as it always has been, into three Chapters. The first covers Articles 85–94, and it contains provisions that remain virtually unchanged from the original Treaty of Rome. These are the competition rules, which serve to guard the integrating market against anti-competitive practices. Article 85 governs cartels; Article 86 monopolies. Article 90 provides a special regime to control public undertakings and undertakings to which Member states grant special or exclusive rights. Articles 92–94 provide a special system for controlling state aids. The second Chapter of Title IV contains tax provisions, including a prohibition in Article 95 on discrimination against imported goods and providing in Article 99 for the possibility of tax harmonization. The third Chapter is entitled *Approximation of Laws*, although the phrase harmonization has become more normal. It is envisaged that divergences between national laws will act as obstacles to the establishment of common market conditions throughout the Community's territory. This Chapter provides power for the Community to introduce harmonization measures that will replace divergent national rules with a common Community regime. The primary instrument in the original Treaty of Rome was Article 100. For reasons largely connected with the need to accelerate the adoption of such harmonized rules, Article 100 has been superseded in practice by Article 100a, a provision inserted into the Treaty by the Single European Act. Article 100a, in contrast to Article 100, allows such laws to be made by the Community even where a minority of states oppose the initiative.

Title VI, *Economic and Monetary Policy*, is in some respects the centrepiece of the Maastricht amendments. The provisions, Articles 102a–109m, go far beyond the relatively thin provisions on economic policy in the pre-Maastricht Treaty, which they replace. These provisions, in conjunction with several important Protocols to the Treaty, provide the framework for the establishment of economic and monetary union, of which the most visible manifestation will be a single currency. Three stages are timetabled during which convergence in economic and monetary policy is planned. A European Central Bank is to be established in accordance with the provisions of the Treaty. The third stage is timetabled for the start of 1999, although it may be advanced by

Council action. It is then that a single currency will come into being. The name and appearance of the currency are undecided, but the conditions for its birth are clearly mapped out. The states that will participate in the single currency must meet defined convergence criteria based on price stability, budgetary balance, conformity with exchange rate margins, and interest rates. States that fail to meet these criteria may be able to join the system subsequently. The United Kingdom is not obliged to proceed down this route and a Protocol allows it to make its choice whether or not to join subsequently. Denmark, too, is not tied to the timetable.

At the end of 1991, when the Treaty was agreed in Maastricht, the likelihood that a significant number of states, including most importantly France and Germany, would satisfy the criteria seemed strong. Turbulence in international money markets in 1992 and 1993 changed the prospects. It seemed unlikely that sufficiently close convergence could be achieved and political commitment to the single currency appeared to waver. Moods change rapidly. By 1995 the possibility that at least some states would meet the criteria seemed realistic and, more important, the political attraction of the single currency had been recaptured. Further fluctuation in the economic and political climate is inevitable and subsequent Treaty revision may yet adjust the legal timetable. Once the single currency comes into being among some, though inevitably not all, states, there will be a strong impression of a 'core' Community, surrounded by a satellite ring. In fact, the satellite metaphor is compelling. As a matter of economic reality, European states outwith the single currency will be deeply affected by it, although they will be unable significantly to affect it. Their policy-making independence will be more apparent than real.

Title VII deals with the *Common Commercial Policy* in Articles 110–115. In essence this provides for action to secure the necessary common external aspect of the customs union to which the Community is committed by Article 9 EC.

Title VIII is entitled *Social policy, Education, Vocational Training, and Youth*. Amid the furore of recent years about the desirablity of social policy-making at European level, it is easy to lose sight of the fact that social policy has *always* featured on the Community's legal and political map. Certainly the current scope of these provisions extends beyond those in the original Treaty of Rome. But social policy was firmly rooted in the text of the Treaty that came into force in 1958 and therefore the current debate is properly seen as one about the appropriate reach of the Community's activities, rather than their very existence. The Title comprises social provisions in Articles 117–122; the European Social Fund in Articles 123–125; education, vocational training, and youth in Articles 126–127. The pattern must also take account of a Protocol to the Treaty agreed at Maastricht. The parties to the Treaty agree to authorize all the Member states with the exception of the United Kingdom to make use of the Treaty structure to develop a deeper range of social policy on the basis of an Agreement annexed to the Protocol. The United Kingdom remains bound by existing and future social policy legislation made under the Treaty, but it will not participate in Council deliberation and voting on proposals falling under the Protocol/ Agreement, nor will those acts be applicable to the United Kingdom.

The next five Titles are all new to the Treaty since Maastricht. In substantive terms they have no single linking thread. However, all represent the expanding scope of the Community's influence. Titles IX–XIII cover *culture* (Article 128), *public health* (Article 129), *consumer protection* (Article 129a), *trans-European networks* (Article 129b–129d), and *industry* (Article 130). The three Titles that follow are all substantially reworked versions of Titles originally inserted into the Treaty by the Single European Act. They are *Economic and Social Cohesion* (Title XIV: Articles 130a–130e); *Research and Technological Development* (Title XV: Article 130f–130p); *Environment* (Title XVI: Articles 130r–130t). The final Title in the Treaty's lengthy Part Three is Title XVII, *Development Co-operation*, Articles 130u–130y. This is another Maastricht innovation. Member States, too, are active in these fields. Making the best of the distinctive contributions made by Community and stated in these areas is a key issue.

Part Four of the Treaty includes Articles 131 to 136a and is entitled *Association of the Overseas Countries and Territories*.

Part Five of the Treaty governs the *Institutions of the Community*. Five institutions are dealt with successively in Articles 137–188c. They are the Parliament, the Council, the Commission, the Court of Justice, and the Court of Auditors. Three further institutions are dealt with subsequently; the Economic and Social Committee (Articles 193–198) and the Committee of the Regions (Articles 198a–198c), both of which have advisory status, and the European Investment Bank (Article 198d–198e). Articles 189 to 192 appear under the title *Provisions common to several institutions* and focus on Community legislative procedure. They are fundamentally important to the practical implementation of the several policies in respect of which the Community possesses competence. Articles 199 to 209a are *Financial Provisions*.

Part Six of the EC Treaty appears under the title *General and Final Provisions*. Several will be discussed individually in the course of this book. One that is not present is any explicit provision for withdrawal by a Member State.

Under Article 236 EEC amendments to the Treaty could be made by common accord only. Under Article 237 EEC unanimity in Council was required to accept an application for membership. Both provisions are now repealed and corresponding provisions are located in Articles N and O respectively in the Treaty on European Union. Unanimity remains the rule for both procedures. Joining the Community alone is no longer possible. New entrants join the Union, the structure of which is examined below.

The Pattern of the European Union

By far the longest Article in the Treaty on European Union is Article G, which forms Title II, and which contains the amendments to the EC Treaty. The examination of the EC Treaty above is of that Treaty as it stands after absorption of the Article G alterations. Titles III and IV of the Treaty on European Union, Articles H and I, amend the European Coal and Steel Community Treaty and the European Atomic Energy Community Treaty respectively. The three European Communities remain in place, their provisions duly amended.

The major structural innovation achieved by the Treaty on European Union lies in the creation of two areas of co-operation which are not covered by the established pattern of the EC. These are in the areas of common foreign and security policy and justice and home affairs. The former field of co-operation is planned in Title V, Article J, of the Union Treaty. The latter is found in Title VI, Article K.

Article J.1 provides that 'The Union and its Member States shall define and implement a common foreign and security policy.' For justice and home affairs, Article K.1 provides a list of matters that Member States shall regard as matters of common interest. It includes asylum policy, immigration policy and policy regarding nationals of third countries, judicial co-operation in civil and criminal matters and, for some purposes, police co-operation.

This is *not* an expanded EC. The two new 'pillars' are distinct from the institutional and constitutional pattern that has developed in the EC over thirty-five years. The provisions make it clear that the key actors are in fact the Member States and the Council/European Council, both of which are composed of representatives of the Member States. Article D declares that the European Council 'shall provide the Union with the necessary impetus for its development.' Unanimity is the norm for both Titles, with limited exceptions only.[8] The combination of the domination of the institutional pattern by the Member States and the requirement of consensus to proceed gives a strongly intergovernmental flavour to the two non-EC pillars of the Union.

The European Court is denied a power to review activity conducted under Articles A–F of the Union Treaty. It is also denied a role under both the two intergovernmental pillars, Articles J and K, with one small exception only.[9] Litigation before the International Court in respect of the two non-EC EU pillars is a possibility lurking in the background, although it seems politically inconceivable that the Member States of the EU would submit disputes for resolution in that forum.

The European Parliament and Commission are not completely ignored in the text of Articles J and K of the Treaty on European Union. However, their position, though vague, is clearly weak in comparison with their status under the EC Treaty. The Parliament is to be consulted and kept informed.[10] It cannot impose its views. Nor is any sanction made explicit in the event of failure to consult. The Court has no jurisdiction to offer protection to the Parliament.

Under Article J.9 the Commission 'shall be fully associated with

---

[8]   Arts. J.8(2), K.4(3).
[9]   Art. L TEU; exceptionally it has jurisdiction in respect of the 3rd para. of Art. K.3(2)(c).   [10]   Arts. J.7 and K.6. Cf also Art. D.

the work carried out in the common foreign and security policy field'. Article K.4 employs the same phrase in relation to work in the areas referred to in the justice and home affairs Title. Again this is imprecise and apparently incapable of judicial enforcement. Article C adds that the Council and the Commission shall be responsible for ensuring the consistency of its external relations. This is not supported by any detailed elaboration of how the Commission shall fulfil such responsibility, save only that implementation shall be in accordance with its powers. Its exclusive power of initiative under the EC Treaty, which grants it significant leverage, is not taken over into the wider EU. Commission portfolios have been allocated in the areas of both foreign and security policy (Santer/van den Broek) and justice and home affairs (Gradin), but it remains to be seen how much influence the Commission is able to wrest from the hands of the Member States.

The two new intergovernmental pillars are testimony to the perception among the Member States that closer co-operation has become essential in order effectively to pursue policy interests in the areas concerned. The need to pursue co-operation in justice and home affairs, especially in relation to policing, is driven at least in part by the elimination of borders as part of the 1992 internal market project. Attempts to co-ordinate defence and foreign policy flow in part from the perception that in the Gulf War, most prominently, the Member States failed to pull their weight for want of an effective common decision-making framework. To an extent the construction of these two new pillars fits into the expectation that states that work together in one area will be driven to work together in other areas, too. However, the pattern chosen for the Union suggests a determination among at least some of the states to keep at bay the EC pattern and, especially, the two most evidently Community-minded institutions, the Parliament and the Commission.

It has become common to describe the Union as a structure built on three pillars, first, the well-established ECs, second, co-operation in justice and home affairs and, third, co-operation in foreign and security policy matters. The Union Treaty itself describes the Union as 'founded on the European Communities'.[11]

[11] Art. A TEU.

It further declares that the Union 'shall be served by a single institutional framework which shall ensure the consistency and the continuity of the activities carried out'.[12]

None of this is convincing. It is rather misleading. The pillars are quite distinct, judged by their institutional patterns and by the nature of the law that they produce. The institutions of the EC have a relatively well-developed interrelation in the pursuit of EC policy. Under the two non-EC EU pillars, the patterns, though as yet immature, are quite different and concentrate power overwhelmingly in the hands of the Member States, albeit acting in Council and/or European Council. The thematic development of the EC as an entity possessing autonomous institutions to which the Member States have transferred power cannot be transplanted to the EU experience. The nature of EC law, nurtured as a constitutional legal order by the European Court over four decades, is not that of EU law. In fact there is no coherent corpus of law that deserves the name 'EU law'. The intergovernmental pillars produce traditional international law, whereas EC law has long been regarded as *sui generis*, neither typical international nor typical national law. Nor does the Union have legal personality, in contrast to the EC.[13]

This breeds scepticism about the claim of the Union Treaty to have established a single institutional framework. However, this, although a criticism of presentation, need not be a criticism of substance. It would be incorrect simply to assume that the EC pattern is appropriate for all forms of common action in Europe. Institutional diversity is not of itself necessarily damaging. It would probably be widely accepted that foreign policy matters should be handled through different channels from some traditional EC activities. The problem is less the fact of divergence than the manner in which it is achieved. It is important that the different shapes that are chosen are identifiably distinct forms of common action. Absent such transparency, confusion will follow that is likely to impede coherent policy implementation. The EU suffers in this respect. Moreover it may prove impossible properly to explain what has been created to the people supposed to benefit from it. This final inadequacy is arguably the gravest in the Treaty on European Union structure. At Maastricht concern to achieve

---

[12] Art. C TEU.   [13] Art. 210 EC.

transparency seemed to be furthest from the minds of the heads of state and government of the Member States as they struggled to agree a text that could be brandished as proof of a successful conclusion to their negotiations.

Some aspects of the Union Treaty suggest that attention has been paid to the question of coherent demarcation between the policy areas covered by the different pillars. For example, a corridor is deliberately placed between the justice and home affairs pillar and the EC Treaty, although traffic may travel along the corridor in one direction only. The Council is empowered to transfer some of the matters in the Article K(1) list across to Article 100c EC. A unanimous vote is required.

However the overwhelming impression is of lack of coherent, planned fit between the pillars. Economic sanctions imposed on third countries touch commercial policy, an EC matter, and foreign policy, an EU but non-EC matter. Article 228a EC recognizes this potential overlap. But it seems that, depending on the precise circumstances, both pillars could or must be used, yielding their fundamentally different types of law. Article B provides that the objectives of the Union shall be achieved as provided in this Treaty while respecting the principle of subsidiarity as defined in Article 3b EC. Is this to apply subsidiarity throughout the Union Treaty? If so, why is its explicit definition to be found only in the EC Treaty?[14] And how is it to be enforceable outwith the EC Treaty, given that the European Court is denied that wider role?

Citizenship of the European Union is a status that exists under the EC pillar. Union Citizens are plainly likely to be affected by action in the environment of intergovernmental co-operation in justice and home affairs. Yet both European Court and Parliament lack formal jurisdiction outwith the EC pillar. National systems offer limited protection, because practical control has been shifted to European level and effective national control is not feasible. Union Citizenship has generated a suspicious response. This was especially apparent in Denmark and part of the effort made at Edinburgh in December 1992 to assuage Danish fears in advance of the second referendum in that country involved the 'clarification' that Union Citizenship in no way replaced national

---

[14] Ch. 5, 169 below.

citizenship. The lawyer who read the text of the Union Treaty would not have doubted that. Lawyers have rightly commented on the dynamic and rather exciting potential for developing the shape of Union Citizenship beyond the pedestrian terms of Articles 8–8e.[15] For all that, it was scarcely surprising that most people were left simply confused by a status that sounded immensely significant coupled to a legal pattern giving shape to the notion of Union Citizenship that was obscure and incapable of reasonably simple elaboration. What was 'Citizenship'—and what was the 'Union'?

The Treaty on European Union, like the Single European Act before it, does not represent a sustained attempt to address the problems caused by both the functional and the geographical enlargement of the EC. The intergovernmental pillars may be taken as mistrust of the application of the EC structure to a wider Union. The states have taken matters of common concern beyond the EC structure. They have done this quite deliberately and rather incoherently.

1996—THE INTERGOVERNMENTAL CONFERENCE (IGC)

The Treaty on European Union provides for a conference of representatives of the governments of the Member States to be convened in 1996.[16] This intergovernmental conference (IGC) will be the next major forum in which further Treaty revision will be planned. Some matters are explicitly due for revision,[17] but doubtless much else besides will be added to the agenda.

Treaty amendments are to enter into force only after ratification by all the Member States in accordance with their domestic constitutional procedures. Some states require referenda, others depend on Parliamentary decisions; the pattern varies. Probably one can anticipate that 1997 will witness wrangles over ratification that will be at least as high profile as those that accompanied the post-Maastricht ratification procedure during 1992 and 1993.

---

[15] C. Closa, 'The Concept of Citizenship in the Treaty on European Union' (1992) 29 CMLRev. 1137, D. O'Keeffe, 'Union Citizenship' in D. O'Keeffe and P. Twomey (eds.), *Legal Issues of the Maastricht Treaty* (Chichester; Wiley Chancery Ltd, 1994).   [16] Art. N.   [17] Art. N(2) TEU.

Much will depend on the content of the Treaty that emerges from the intergovernmental conference. Ireland will hold the Presidency of the European Union in the second half of 1996 and the European Council for late 1996 is to be held in Dublin. The next historic milestone on the tortuous road might be the Treaty of Dublin; alternatively the IGC process may drag on deep into 1997.

The requirement that Treaty amendments can be made only by unanimity confers a veto power on each state. Practical politics dictate that the position is less clear-cut. States that find themselves in a minority are aware that obstruction of the majority may cost them much political capital at European level. They may judge that domestic gains justify the adoption of an attitude that some would call cautious, others sceptical. Compromise solutions are a common result in such finely balanced international negotiation. The Maastricht Treaty, as explained, bears the marks of such compromise. However, the Community and, less so, the Union, have developed a sufficient momentum that it is unlikely that any state can effectively veto further development.[18] The United Kingdom discovered at Maastricht that its solitary opposition to deeper social policy-making was insufficient to deter the other eleven states from finding a way to proceed.[19] In 1996, a state that refused to agree to further deepening of the process in particular areas and, *a fortiori*, at the general level would probably find that agreements were struck between the remaining states to give effect to deepening. The minority would be excluded, perhaps willingly. This is the road marked 'variable geometry' or 'differentiated integration'—the two- (or more) speed Europe.

There was much overt and covert manœuvring in 1991 in the run up to Maastricht. As early as 1994, only months after the entry into force of the Treaty on European Union, the approach to the 1996 IGC was already plainly under way. Plans are being aired; alliances are being struck. Any serious student of modern affairs should follow developments.

This survey of the Treaty on European Union has taken the rather easy option of criticizing the seizure of a grand label, the European Union, which is not underpinned by a constitutional blueprint. Yet criticism is deserved. The three-pillar structure is intransparent. In fact it is possible to view the Union as even more

[18] With the possible exception of Germany.   [19] Ch. 5, 174 below.

unstable than the three-pillar metaphor suggests. The arrangements for economic and monetary union possess an institutional character all of their own and have some claim to be regarded as a fourth pillar. The Social Policy Protocol-plus-Agreement, which envisages that Community institutions will be placed at the disposal of the eleven (now fourteen) Member States without Britain, is also far enough removed from the normal arrangements to be viewed as, if not a fifth pillar, then at least a prominent splinter from the EC pillar.

Perhaps, in the world of *realpolitik*, into which clear-cut decisions rarely intrude, a fudged solution is preferable to nothing. But the compromises are stored up and it seems probable that, sooner rather than later, a sustained attempt will have to be made, first, to address the scattered pattern of accumulated Treaty revision and, secondly, to draft a forward-looking plan for an enlarged Union which takes in most of Europe. It will be harder to accept incremental drift in 1996.

Over-use of the architectural metaphor might usefully be abandoned for 1996 lest it, with its echoes of Maastricht, induce preconceptions about the task ahead. But to retain it for the moment; solutions need not involve insistence on a single pillar. The pursuit of rigid legal, constitutional, and institutional uniformity is a fruitless objective. More, such purism may be damaging to the modern Community/Union where some strength lies in some diversity. Yet to loosen the structure without having first identified an inalienable core runs the risk of complete fragmentation. Perhaps the main issue now is identifying and protecting that core and building upon it. This is an issue to which this book will return after looking more closely at how the building blocks of the Community and Union have developed.

FURTHER READING

Bieber, R., Dehousse, R., Pinder, J., and Weiler, J. H. H., (eds.), *1992: One European Market* (Baden-Baden: Nomos, 1988).

Bogdanor, V. 'Britain and the European Community', Chapter 1 in Jowell and Oliver (eds.), *The Changing Constitution* (Oxford: OUP, 1994).

Booss, D., and Forman, J., 'Enlargement: Legal and Procedural Aspects' (1995) 32 *CMLRev*. 95.

COCKFIELD, LORD, *The European Union: Creating the Single Market* (Chichester: Wiley Chancery Law, 1994).

CREMONA, M., 'The Dynamic and Homogenous EEA: Byzantine Structures and Variable Geometry' (1994) 19 *ELRev.* 508.

CURTIN, D., 'The Constitutional Structure of the Union: A Europe of Bits and Pieces' (1993) 30 *CMLRev.* 17.

DEHOUSSE, R., (ed.), *Europe after Maastricht* (Munich: Law Books, 1994).

GEORGE, S., *Politics and Policy in the European Community* (Oxford: OUP, 1991).

HARMSEN, R., 'A European Union of Variable Geometry: Problems and Perspectives' (1994) 45 *NILQ* 109.

HEUKELS, T.,and DE ZWAAN, J. W., 'The Configuration of the European Union: Community Dimensions of Institutional Interaction' in Curtin, D., and Heukels, T., (eds.), *Institutional Dynamics of European Integration* (Dordrecht: Martinus Nijhoff, 1994).

MACCORMICK, N., 'Beyond the Sovereign state' (1993) 56 *MLR* 1.

McGOLDRICK, D., 'A New International Economic Order for Europe?' (1992) 12 *YEL* 433.

MESTMÄCKER, E.-J., 'On the Legitimacy of European Law' (1994) 58 *RabelsZ* 615.

MORAVCSIK, A., 'Preferences and Power in the European Community: A Liberal Intergovernmentalist Approach' (1993) 31 *JCMS* 473.

NICOLL, W., and SALMON, T. C., *Understanding the New European Community* (Hemel Hempstead: Harvester Wheatsheaf, 1994).

O'KEEFFE, D., 'The Emergence of a European Immigration Policy' (1995) 20 *ELRev.* 20.

—— and TWOMEY, P., (eds.), *Legal Issues of the Maastricht Treaty* (Chichester: Wiley Chancery Law, 1994).

PEERS, S., 'An Ever Closer Waiting Room?: The Case for Eastern European Accession to the European Economic Area' (1995) 32 *CMLRev.* 187.

SWANN, D., *The Economics of the Common Market* (London: Penguin, 1992).

URWIN, D., *The Community of Europe* (London: Longman, 1991).

2

The Competence of the Union

THE EC'S 'ATTRIBUTED COMPETENCE'

The European Community does not enjoy a general competence. It is competent only in the areas in which its Treaties attribute competence to it.

Therefore the principles of Community law are not of universal relevance. They apply only in areas that fall within Community competence. A further consequence of the rule of limited, attributed competence is that it is necessary to identify in the Treaty a specific legal base authorizing action before Community legislation is constitutionally valid. The absence of an adequate legal base in the Treaty means that the Community is not competent to act. Any act adopted in areas where the Community is not competent will be susceptible to annulment as an invalid trespass on to areas of national competence.

This is the theory of competence attributed to the Community by its Treaty. In practice the principles of Community law exert a remarkably wide influence. The European Court has never annulled a Community act on the basis that the Community (as opposed to an individual institution) lacked competence. Community competence seems rather flexible, even, at times, open-ended.

In practice, areas where the Community is arguably without competence are remarkably few and far between. The corollary of the incremental growth in the Community's sphere of influence is that areas where the Member States are able to claim that they hold exclusive competence, untouched by Community membership, are rather less extensive than might be expected. A vast range of areas is within Community competence, although this is not to say that it is not also within national competence. Competence is shared in very many areas. To this extent a rigid, legalistic view of competence demarcation has given way to a widespread infusion of Community law into national law.

Nevertheless, there have been more recent signals that a

sensitivity is felt in some Member States about the apparently unchecked outward drift in the Community's competence. Such concerns are especially keenly felt where Community competence ousts national competence in a particular field, *a fortiori* where the Community may act without the unanimous support of the Member States. National reactions, which may be traced in both the political and the judicial spheres, will be examined later, especially in Chapters 5 and 6.

This Chapter picks out two related areas that have made a major contribution to the expansion in Community competence. The first is the spreading impact of the general principles of the Community legal order. The second is the dynamic expansion in practice of Community legislative competence.

THE PRINCIPLE OF NON-DISCRIMINATION ON GROUNDS OF NATIONALITY

The influence of Community law principles is extraordinarily far-reaching and cannot be appreciated by a simple textual analysis of the Treaty. Trade law reflects this feature of Community law. The drive to secure an integrated market has allowed the invocation of Community law in some areas of national activity that one might have supposed would be untouched by Community law. In particular, national measures bearing no relation on their face to cross-border trading have been subjected to control under Community law where they have been shown to exert an effect that is prejudicial to the interpenetration of national markets. Illustrations of these developments provide much of the subject matter of Chapters 7 and 8. However, of even more general impact has been the deep penetration into areas of apparently exclusive national competence of the general principles of Community law. Some of these principles have their explicit source in the Treaty. Others have been developed by the European Court. All exercise an often surprisingly extensive control over national action. In theory, they apply only in areas within the scope of application of the Treaty. In practice, that limitation is of less significance than might be supposed.

The prohibition against nationality discrimination is fundamental to the Community's endeavours in the fields of economic equality of opportunity and individual protection.

Article 6 EC, which was Article 7 EEC prior to the Maastricht amendments, provides that 'Within the scope of application of this Treaty, and without prejudice to any special provisions contained therein, any discrimination on grounds of nationality shall be prohibited.' So in *Cowan* v. *Le Trésor Public* Mr Cowan, a British tourist, was mugged in Paris.[1] He was refused compensation under the French equivalent of the British Criminal Injuries Compensation Scheme, on the basis that he was neither a national of nor resident in France. The European Court ruled that, as a tourist, he was receiving services and, as an economically active cross-border migrant, he fell within the scope of application of the EC Treaty. That then triggered a right under Article 6 EC to be treated no less favourably than a French national. He was therefore entitled to compensation. Opinions could reasonably differ on whether the Community enjoys competence to establish its own criminal injuries compensation scheme, but once a Member State chooses to set up its own scheme, it may find that principles of Community law fasten on to and control its administration.

The critical notion within Article 6 that defines the outer limits of the spread of Community competence is the opening phrase, 'Within the scope of application of this Treaty'. It is the indeterminate location of the outer boundaries and the European Court's predilection for finding that matters fall within rather than without them that has led to the remarkable development in the scope of Article 6. Occasionally, however, the limits of Community law surface in case law. In *Walrave and Koch* v. *Union Cycliste Internationale* the Court ruled that, in so far as sport constitutes an economic activity, it is subject to the rules of Community law.[2] This brings it within the range of application of the rule against nationality discrimination. However, the Court ruled that this prohibition 'does not affect the composition of sport teams, in particular national teams, the formation of which is a question of purely sporting interest and as such has nothing to do with economic activity'. *Walrave and Koch* concerned the rather esoteric sport of pacing. To bring this principle within the sporting mainstream, the French national football team's understandable preference to make its selection from the pool of French nationals, rather than the ranks of Citizens of the European Union, is

---

[1] Case 186/87 [1989] ECR 195.   [2] Case 36/74 [1974] ECR 1405.

discriminatory on grounds of nationality. Yet the policy is not outlawed by Article 6 EC because, as a choice made for reasons of purely sporting interest, it does not fall within 'the scope of application of the Treaty', which is an essential prerequisite to the invocation of Article 6. The ruling in *Walrave and Koch* exposes an area in which equal treatment irrespective of nationality is not required. However, as is often a feature of European Court rulings, the restrictive flavour was more than matched by the expansionist impact of the ruling. Of much wider significance than the concession to the permissibility of representative sporting teams was the Court's insistence that the prohibition on nationality discrimination 'does not only apply to the action of public authorities but extends likewise to rules of any other nature aimed at regulating in a collective manner gainful employment'. The Court thereby created a broadly applicable source of anti-discrimination employment law.

The Italian railway service, like many others, offers different types of trains to which apply different types of ticket categories. Iorio, an Italian national, boarded a Rome–Palermo 'rapido' train. The rules stated that he was obliged to hold a ticket for a journey of at least 400 kilometers. He did not have the correct ticket and he was fined. He argued that conditions limiting his access to the train violated the free movement rights conferred by Article 48 of the Treaty. The matter reached the European Court in *Paolo Iorio* v. *Azienda Autonoma delle Ferrovie dello Stato*[3] when an Italian court asked in the context of the Article 177 preliminary-ruling procedure whether any violation of Community law had occurred. For Advocate General Mancini 'the answer is no' and the Court was only a little less curt. This was an Italian national travelling in Italy under conditions laid down with general effect by the Italian authorities and there was no connection with Community law. It is submitted that the same would have been true had Iorio been British or French. There, too, the rule would have been an expression of national regulatory competence. There would have been no collision with general principles of Community law nor with the principles of market access that drive Community trade law. Yet it still misleads simply to assert that such matters fall within the exclusive competence of the Member State. Had the

---

[3] Case 298/84 [1986] ECR 247.

passenger been a British or French national living and working in Italy who found that Italian rules drew a distinction between cost or conditions of travel in accordance with nationality, then Italy would certainly have violated its Community law obligations.[4] In this way the basic rule of non-discrimination spills over into the social sphere of the worker's lifestyle and converts EC law into a method for securing that the migrant enjoys the type of benefit that a citizen of the host state would look to his or her government to provide. The status of Citizenship of the Union that is created by the Treaty on European Union takes individual rights on to a different constitutional plane, but it would be an error to suppose that pre-Maastricht rights arose only in the economic sphere.

THE WIDER SWEEP OF GENERAL PRINCIPLES

In other areas, too, it has proved crucial to locate the outer bounds of the application of Community law. This determines to what extent the validity of national actions may be tested against the general principles of Community law. Article 6 EC enshrines one such principle, but there are a number of other important principles, some of which are not found in the Treaty and which are instead the creations of the European Court. Respect for fundamental rights is one such principle. Community institutions must certainly abide by those principles, but the same is true of national authorities in so far as they act within the sphere of Community law. This immediately dictates the vital need to define the outer limits of that sphere. Beyond the margin, national competence prevails and there is no obligation to respect principles drawn from Community law. *Cinéthèque* v. *Fédération Nationale des Cinémas Français*[5] involved questions concerning the compatibility with Community law of French rules preventing the release of films on video until the expiry of one year from the date of the cinema performance certificate. The European Court considered that the system obstructed trade in goods, but was nonetheless justified under Community law. Almost certainly today it would reach that same result by the rather different route of finding that there was no adequate impact on inter-state trade

---

[4] e.g. Case 32/75 *Cristini* v. *SNCF* [1975] ECR 1085.
[5] Cases 60 & 61/84 [1985] ECR 2605.

such as to require the state to show justification.[6] The alleged incompatibility of the rule with the provisions of the European Convention on Human Rights dealing with freedom of expression had also been canvassed before the Court, which ruled that, although 'it is the duty of this Court to ensure observance of fundamental rights in the field of Community law, it has no power to examine the compatibility with the European Convention of national legislation which concerns, as in this case, an area which falls within the jurisdiction of the national legislator'.

By contrast, national legislation that implements Community law should be applied in conformity with Community fundamental-rights standards.[7] Furthermore, national derogations from the principles of free movement in Community trade law must be compatible with fundamental rights. This approach led the Court in *Elliniki Radiophonia Tileorassi (ERT)* v. *Dimotiki*[8] to refuse to accept that Greek rules that had the effect of impeding market access by broadcasters could be justified, given their damaging effect on freedom of expression.

Where such general principles of the Community legal order are shown to control the exercise of powers at national level, they are in one major respect of greater significance than the basic right to non-discriminatory treatment under Article 6 EC. The right to non-discriminatory treatment achieves no more than the equalization of the rights of the migrant with the host-state national. There is no absolute Community law right. Cowan was able to secure compensation, not because Community law required compensation of victims of such attacks, but rather because French law made such provision. He was then able to take a piggyback ride on the French system. But, had French law offered no protection to anyone, he would have been without a claim. He would have been forced to await the rather distant possibility of Community legislation intervening to provide such an entitlement. By contrast, principles such as protection of fundamental rights involve the establishment of a system of protection for any individual whose situation falls within the scope of Community law. These rights lay a common floor of individual protection under Community law that is in no way dependent on national choices. In fact, it is

---

[7] Case 5/88 *Wachauf* [1989] ECR 2609.   [6] Ch. 8, 226.
[8] Case C–260/89 [1991] ECR I–2925.

possible that the migrant worker able to draw on this reserve will be in a better position than the national of the host state who will typically be unable to bring him- or herself within the scope of application of Community law. The national of state A living and working in state A and who has never worked other than in state A appears unable in the eyes of the Court to look to Community law for such protection.[9] This is a matter of exclusive national competence, because of the identity of the individual, not because of the subject matter at stake.

Konstantinidis v. *Stadt Altensteig*[10] provides a valuable insight into the implications for control of national acts that flow from the fixing of the outer margins of Community competence. Kostantinidis was a Greek national wishing to work in Germany. German law required his name to be registered according to the Latin alphabet. Added to the injury of obligatory transliteration was the insult that the German method rendered his first name as 'Hrestos', rather than 'Christos' a name that Konstantinidis owed to the day of his birth, 25 December. The German laws were distasteful to Konstantinidis, but were they incompatible with EC law? Advocate General Jacobs found it easy to conclude that an interference with fundamental rights had occurred, but more problematic was the question whether, assuming them to be non-discriminatory, the national laws at stake could as a matter of Community law be tested against such norms. He believed that they could. He viewed the migrant worker as entitled to a set of fundamental rights under Community law that were in effect portable and inalienable. They protected that person as an individual and were not limited to those necessary to facilitate economic activity. However the European Court adopted a much narrower approach. It considered that the scope of Community law extended only so far as the economic aspects of the treatment to which Konstantinidis was subjected. A violation of Community law would be established only where the spelling he was forced to use distorted the pronunciation of his name and thereby exposed him to the risk of confusion on the part of his clients.[11] The Court

---

[9] Cf Case 298/84, n. 3 above, and Case 175/78 *R.* v. *Saunders* [1979] ECR 1129.
[10] Case C–168/91, judgment of 30 Mar. 1993.
[11] The Court did not address the question whether the German system discriminated against Greeks.

identified a limit to the spread of the Community's constitutional order.

Nevertheless the formal limits of application of Community law principles should not be taken to signal a clean, sharp division, beyond which national lawyers may work undisturbed by troublesome imports. First, Community competence is not static. There is no bright line which it may not cross. Where it takes in new areas, those areas become subject to the general principles of Community law. Second, *even where it is acknowledged that Community law is formally inapplicable*, it is increasingly plain that the influence of Community law analogies cannot simply be ignored. The infiltration of Community principles into national systems even where this is not obligatory is a key feature of modern European law. Chapter 6 addresses these issues.

ARTICLE 5 AND COMMUNITY SOLIDARITY

Article 5 EC is commonly known as the duty of Community solidarity or fidelity. It provides that:

> Member States shall take all appropriate measures, whether general or particular, to ensure fulfilment of the obligations arising out of this Treaty or resulting from action taken by the institutions of the Community. They shall facilitate the achievement of the Community's tasks. They shall abstain from any measure which could jeopardise the attainment of the objectives of the Treaty.

At the simplest level, Article 5 is no more than a general statement of the duty to abide by specific Treaty provisions, such as Article 30 in the field of the free movement of goods. However, Article 5 has been used to impose obligations on Member States in a variety of situations in which it was initially far from clear that the fact of Community membership involved any legal consequences or, at least, any legal consequences that were capable of being given concrete shape at Community level. Article 5 has yielded some highly surprising implications.

The general policy around which may be grouped the several types of fact pattern in which Article 5 has been applied may be summarized as the determination by the European Court to give effective support to the development of Community policy. It has used Article 5 to tie states down more securely than is explicitly envisaged in the Treaty.

The Court has tended typically to use Article 5 initially as a means of making clear that Community membership entails responsibilities and then subsequently as a basis for developing explicit obligations in specific areas. The applicant in *Thieffry* v. *Conseil de l'Ordre des Avocats à la Cour de Paris*[12] held a Belgian legal qualification that had been recognized by relevant French authorities as equivalent to a particular French qualification, yet he was refused entry to the French bar on the basis he did not hold a French qualification. His right to work in France was plainly within the scope of objectives of the Treaty. The Court commented that 'in so far as Community law makes no special provision, these objectives may be attained by measures enacted by the Member States, which under Article 5 of the Treaty are bound to take all appropriate measures'. The absence of directives governing qualification requirements in a particular profession did not absolve national authorities of the obligation under Article 5 to permit the exercise of freedoms envisaged by the Treaty. In Thieffry's case the recognition of equivalence made it unlawful for him to be refused access to the French market simply because he did not hold the French diploma but only one recognized as equivalent. The Court went considerably further in *Vlassopoulou* v. *Ministerium für Justiz, Bundes- und Europaangelegenheiten Baden-Württemberg*,[13] where the element of prior cross-recognition that was so helpful to Thieffry was missing. Vlassopoulou had a Greek legal training, but wanted to work in Germany where she was not fully qualified. The Court was not content to rule that a state could maintain market access rules based on obtaining national qualifications or those recognized as equivalent. Such a stance would impede Treaty-conferred rights of establishment. Article 5 was then deployed by the Court to oblige Member States to take into account qualifications obtained in other Member States and to compare the level of knowledge and ability thereby certified with the standards demanded under national rules. This does not oblige the receiving Member State to set aside its qualification rules, but it requires that state to assess the quality of the migrant's training, rather than merely its origin. Article 5 is in this way a means of requiring national authorities to set up some

---

[12] Case 71/76 [1977] ECR 765.
[13] Case C–340/89 [1991] ECR I–2357.

kind of system that will provide a means of hearing the case of the migrant who is from the national perspective under-qualified. None of this is explicit in the Treaty nor in Community secondary legislation, but Article 5 builds specific obligations out of the framework of policies mapped out.

Article 5 expresses obligations that are part of a general framework for securing effective institutional supervision of Community obligations. An even more vivid proof of the Court's readiness to convert Article 5 beyond its literal terms into a general principle whereby institutional patterns may be shaped in the Community is provided by the imposition in *Zwartveld*[14] of obligations on the Commission despite the reference in Article 5 only to the duty of the Member States. *Zwartveld* arose out of Dutch investigations into allegations of fraudulent practices connected with fish quotas. The judge wished to obtain Community documents concerned with fisheries and to question Community fishery inspectors. The Commission did not accede to his request. Perhaps it was genuinely doubtful about the propriety of its involvement. Perhaps it hoped to provoke litigation that would lead to a breakthrough in patterns of institutional co-operation. The Dutch judge asked the European Court to order the Commission to provide assistance. This fell outside the scope of any procedure for institutional co-operation recognized by the Treaty. The Court nevertheless made the requested order, envisaging only that the Commission might be able to show to the Court imperative reasons relating to the need to avoid any interference with the function and independence of the Community that might justify refusal. This was, in the Court's assessment, an element in the overall structuring of a system of judicial supervision appropriate for a constitutional legal order. The justification was drawn from the overall pattern and spirit of the Treaty, reflected by the very broad provisions of Articles 5 and 164. Article 5 was treated as no more than a specific expression of a general principle requiring collaboration in pursuit of the success of the Community's endeavours. *Zwartveld* is powerful evidence of the Court's unwillingness to treat attributed Community competence as a rigid, textual matter.

National laws governing remedies and procedure provide a

---

[14] Case C–2/Imm. [1990] ECR I–3365.

high-profile area in which to illustrate how Article 5 has come to the fore in placing Community obligations on Member States independently of explicit legislative rules that make specific the obligations of national authorities. This is examined in depth in Chapter 4 of this book, but it deserves summary here for the light shed on the phenomenon of blurred competences. Although the Court's conception of Community law has, since the 1963 ruling in *Van Gend en Loos*,[15] envisaged enforceability before national courts and tribunals, it was initially assumed that the methods by which those enforceable rights would be vindicated rested with national systems. This expectation of national procedural autonomy has been significantly eroded. The European Court has insisted that Article 5 obliges national courts, as part of the state structure, to act in support of the Community's objectives, which means in specific terms that they must ensure the effective protection of rights under Community law. This means that they must go beyond established national techniques where this is necessary to ensure effective protection for the litigant basing him- or herself on Community law. In *Factortame*[16] the European Court ruled that the United Kingdom courts were competent to award interim relief against the Crown, although the House of Lords had in the course of the litigation determined that, as a matter of English law, such a power was unavailable. The European Court left unclear, probably deliberately, the issue whether Article 5 EC here obliged national courts to re-shape existing national remedies or to create new remedies. The vigour of Article 5 was even more vividly apparent in *Francovich*.[17] The European Court insisted that national systems must be prepared to award damages in some circumstances where Community law was violated. The Community pedigree of the remedy was plainly demonstrated by the European Court's willingness to specify conditions that are essential to a finding of liability. Article 5 provided the basis for remarkable judicial activism. In this evolution the Court has gone beyond a basic requirement of non-discrimination between

---

[15] Case 26/62, *NV Algemene Transport en Expeditie Onderneming Van Gend en Loos* v. *Nederlandse Administratie der Belastingen* [1963] ECR 1.

[16] Case C–213/89, *R.* v. *Secretary of State for Transport, ex parte Factortame Ltd.* [1990] ECR I–2433.

[17] Case C–6, 9/90, *Andrea Francovich* v. *Italian State* [1991] ECR I–5357.

national litigants and those basing themselves on Community law, and has instead created a floor of Community rules in the area.

Article 5 is a major element in the permeation of Community law into national systems which has occurred in a way that would be baffling were a literal approach to the Treaty taken. National courts and administrative authorities are expected to act as Community institutions and to pursue in good faith the objectives of the Community. What if they prove unwilling? What if they decide that the European Court has taken to exaggerating those objectives beyond the justified scope of the Treaty? Article 5 works splendidly as a means of developing the Community legal order while the co-operation which it envisages is forthcoming. It is not simply the job of the national courts to provide that support. It is for the European Court, too, to wield Article 5 with care. This is further explored in Chapter 6.[18]

LEGISLATIVE COMPETENCE

The Court's expansionist approach to the scope of Community competence embraces both its outer limits, which have tended to be pushed ever wider, and the applicable principles within it, which have become ever more elaborate.

A further element critical to a grasp of the practical scope of Community competence lies in the unexpectedly broad use made of legislative competence. It remains unavoidable to identify a legal base in the Treaty as a prerequisite to the valid adoption of Community legislation. But in practice this has often proved rather easy, even in areas of activity that at first sight seem far removed from the purposes of the Community. The main 'culprits' in this broad approach to legislative action are Articles 100 and, since the entry into force of the Single European Act, 100a and, most of all, Article 235.

Article 100 provides that 'The Council shall, acting unanimously on a proposal from the Commission, issue directives for the approximation of such provisions laid down by law, regulation or administrative action in Member States as directly affect the establishment or functioning of the common market.' Article 100a was introduced by the Single European Act with the objective of

---

[18] 210 below.

accelerating the adoption of laws required to complete the internal market.[19] To this end it alters the applicable voting rules in Council;

The Council shall, acting by a qualified majority on a proposal from the Commission in cooperation with the European Parliament and after consulting the Economic and Social Committee, adopt the measures for the approximation of the provisions laid down by law, regulation or administrative action in Member States which have as their object the establishment and functioning of the internal market.

These provisions, both altered in detail since Maastricht, are explicitly designed to secure the adoption of laws that are necessary to realize an integrated market. They have been been used as the base for Community laws that seem rather remote from that process. The Community legislative record under these provisions includes, for example, laws dealing with the protection of workers on collective redundancies[20] and the consequences for consumers of contracts concluded away from business premises, the phenomenon of 'doorstep selling'.[21] The competitive distortion that is alleged to flow from legislative diversity between Member States in such areas has provided the rationale for Community action.

Article 235 provides the broadest base for Community action. 'If action by the Community should prove necessary to attain, in the course of the operation of the common market, one of the objectives of the Community and this Treaty has not provided the necessary powers, the Council shall, acting unanimously on a proposal from the Commission and after consulting the European Parliament, take the appropriate measures.'

The growth of environmental policy serves as a valuable example of the ease with which Community activity is capable of being nurtured despite an apparently barren constitutional background in the Treaty. For many years neither the political institutions nor the Court have felt much exercised by the limitations of the theory of attributed competence nor by respect for areas of exclusive national competence into which the Community could not trespass.

The Treaty of Rome conferred no power on the Community to legislate in the field of environmental protection. One can explain

---

[19] Ch. 1, 15 above.   [20] Dir. 75/129 [1975] OJ L48/29.
[21] Dir. 85/577 [1985] OJ L372/31.

this by reference to the limited awareness of the march of environmental degradation during the 1950s. Once environmental protection assumed a higher profile in society, there was a growing appreciation that Community action was desirable and, at a general policy level, essentially uncontroversial. However, the translation of that notion into a specific legal response would have seemed in theory to be blocked by the absence of a Treaty base. Nothing could be done, short of Treaty amendment. However, such rigidity was not reflected in practice. The presence of a will to act allowed the finding of a way to act, even absent an explicit Treaty base. In 1973, the first Environmental Action Programme was agreed. This did not constitute binding Community law within the meaning of the Treaty, but as 'soft law' it took the Community beyond the constraints of its Treaty. More significantly still, formal legislative action followed.

A directive concerning the quality of bathing water, adopted in December 1975 (and subsequently amended),[22] 'concerns the quality of bathing water, with the exception of water intended for therapeutic purposes and water used in swimming pools'. This was adopted on the basis of Articles 100 and 235. The Preamble to the measure explains that there exist in the area national measures 'which directly affect the functioning of the common market'. This seems hard to believe. It is not elaborated. What was really at stake was environmental protection, and this motivation underlies the bulk of the Preamble. The link to the Treaty is found in the claim that surveillance of bathing water is necessary in order to attain the Community's objectives as regards the 'improvement of living conditions, the harmonious development of economic activities throughout the Community and continuous and balanced expansion'. These are phrases drawn from the original text of Article 2 of the Treaty of Rome.[23] The validity of the measure was not challenged before the European Court. It had been adopted by unanimous vote, as required under Articles 100 and 235.

Spurious reasoning such as that found in the Preamble to the Bathing Water Directive makes it hard to take seriously the notion that Community competence is limited by anything other than the need to secure unanimous support in Council. The concluding recital is especially illuminating. It declares that 'whereas public

---

[22] Dir. 76/160 [1976] OJ L31.   [23] Ch. 1, 5 above.

interest in the environment and in the improvement of its quality is increasing'. Apparently the Community is capable of legislating when there is pressure for it to do so. Textual limitations drawn from the Treaty seem to be of no account.

By 1985 the Court felt able to declare in *Procureur de la République* v. *Association de Défense des Brûleurs d'Huiles Usagées* that environmental protection counted as 'one of the Community's essential objectives'.[24] This was unjustified on the literal terms of the Treaty. But it reflected practice.

It was explained in Chapter 1 that the Single European Act brought about an expansion in Community competence. One of the new elements was Environmental Protection. Articles 130r–t, a new Title XVI, conferred explicit competence on the Community in the field. This removed any lingering doubts that there might have been about the validity of Community initiatives in the environmental field. It did, however, create a new problem, endemic to the pattern of attributed powers to which different legislative procedures are attached. It became necessary to choose whether a measure harmonizing laws in the environmental sphere was validly adopted under Article 100a (which in practical terms took over the harmonization role from Article 100 after the entry into force of the Single European Act) or the new provisions, Article 130r–t. This issue of demarcation has generated complex constitutional litigation, examined below.[25] Subsequently, the Treaty on European Union brought about a further expansion of the environment title.

The critical point is that in practical terms the Treaty list of explicit enumerated powers is not closed. Activity in unexpectedly wide areas may occur via the broad legal bases found in Articles 100, 100a and 235. So the dividing line between Community and national competence—which must in theory exist—is in practice hard to discern and, critically, is not static. It shifts under the influence of Treaty amendment, legislation invading unexpected areas, and also because of the Court's own activism. And that shift has essentially been in one direction only—in favour of enhanced Community competence, cutting down the realms in which

[24] Case 240/83 [1985] ECR 531.
[25] 'Titanium Dioxide', Case C–300/89 *Commission* v. *Council* [1991] ECR I–2867, 88 below.

the Member States retain an exclusive national competence. Lenaerts asserts with vigour that '[t]here simply is no nucleus of sovereignty that the Member States can invoke as such against the Community'.[26] So, according to the Court in its major constitutional rulings of the early 1960s participation in the Community means that 'the Member States have limited their sovereign rights, *albeit within limited fields*'.[27] By the early 1990s, the Court had changed its choice of phrase to refer to a limitation of sovereign rights *'in ever wider fields'*.[28]

At the political level, this competence drift matters little in practice where unanimous voting in Council is the rule. States have a political veto. Each state is able to prevent the making of legislation of which it disapproves. It has no need to test questions of competence by challenging legislation before the Court once it is made. The rise in qualified majority voting in Council, triggered by the Single European Act and taken further by the Treaty on European Union, radically changes the picture. The Community's own competence and its relationship with that of the Member States is currently the critical issue in the development of the Community. It is addressed from this perspective in Chapter 5. In assessing these tensions it is as well to remember that the history of dynamic growth of Community competence, largely unrelated to strict adherence to the text of the Treaty, is a product not simply of judicial activism but also of the attitude of the Member States in Council.

Competence is inextricably linked to legal base. To find competence to legislate one must look for a specific legal base in the Treaty. So the Bathing Water Directive could not simply be made by the Community under the powers conferred by the Treaty without a more specific reference to the Treaty provision conferring competence, Articles 100 and 235 in that instance. The legal base will then provide for a specific legislative procedure. That, then, will determine how the legislation is to be made; but tactically it may also determine whether or not it can be made at

---

[26] K. Lenaerts, 'Constitutionalism and the Many Faces of Federalism' (1990) 38 *AJCL* 205, 220.

[27] Case 6/64 *Costa* v. *ENEL* [1964] ECR 585; Case 26/62 *Van Gend en Loos*, n. 15 above, both examined below.

[28] Opinion 1/91 on the draft agreement on a European Economic Area [1991] ECR I-6079.

all. Choice of legal base is not the most immediately compelling area of study of EC law, but in fact it is critical in assessing what is the scope of Community action in practical terms. One of the least edifying aspects of the debate about what the Community should or should not do is the tendency of national politicians or commentators to fail to appreciate that the Community, although an autonomous entity, has only limited competences conferred on it and, of more practical significance, can legislate only where stipulated requirements are satisfied, which may involve the assembly of adequate support among the Member States in Council. It is not unheard of for national politicians to wring their hands before national audiences bemoaning their inability to act without Community authorization while diligently voting against Community action in Council. Nor, by the same token, is the Community immune from being cast as a scapegoat for meddling intervention by politicians who have voted in Council in favour of the very rules that, for domestic consumption, they choose to criticize. Such tactics were especially tempting in the years before December 1993 when all Council votes remained secret. Recent moves towards greater transparency in the proceedings of the Council have gone some of the way to reducing the opportunity for such economy with the truth, but, even if complete openness in Council were to become the rule, the mythology that surrounds what 'Brussels' can and cannot do will be dispelled only through a prolonged campaign of education.

Even where an explicit Treaty base for legislative action is lacking, the Court has made use of the idea of 'implied powers' to extend the reach of competence. *Germany, France, Netherlands, Denmark, and United Kingdom* v. *Commission*[29] provides an example of the Court's technique, although it is a ruling concerned with implications of extended powers for the Commission in particular, rather than than for the Community in general. Article 118 refers to the Commission's task of promoting close co-operation between Member States in the social field, but omits any reference to legislative power. A Commission Decision requiring the Member States to consult with it and to supply it with information relating to immigration into the Community from third countries was challenged by several Member States which

[29] Cases 281, 283–5, 287/85 [1987] ECR 3203.

were alarmed at the Commission's attempt to seize power beyond that stipulated in the Treaty. But the Court upheld most of the Decision, annulling as beyond the Commission's reach under Article 118 only parts relating to cultural integration. The conferral of a specific task carried with it an implication of conferral of powers that are indispensable in order to carry out that task. Here Article 118 would remain a dead letter were the Commission denied power to set up consultation and information mechanisms.

The field of external relations has been an especially fruitful area for the Court's assertion of a broad approach. The Community has some external powers that are expressly granted by the Treaty. Article 113 governs the implementation of the common commercial policy; Article 238 the power to conclude association agreements. The Court has gone further and has held that the Community possesses the external powers that are necessary in order effectively to develop the activities of the Community listed in Article 3. External powers are defined with reference to the scheme of the Treaty not its explicit provisions.[30] This is important as an expression of the dynamic growth of Community competence, a consistent theme, and the consequential impact that this has on the competence of the Member States.

Expanding Community competence has inevitable implications for national competence. Such judicial activism is therefore directed at sensitive areas. The notion that internal power breeds external power may prompt some reluctance among Member States to develop internal Community powers lest it be discovered subsequently that external power has shifted unseen into Community hands. Member State nervousness may also translate into responses not simply in the Community legislative process, but also in the intergovernmental conferences that are becoming regular features of the Community/Union process. At Maastricht, the crafting of new intergovernmental pillars that lie outside the established EC framework reflects a healthy appreciation of the depth of the political and legal shift involved once a matter falls within Community competence.

There is every likelihood that the approach towards competence

---

[30] Initially, Case 22/70 *Commission* v. *Council* [1971] ECR 263.

taken by both the Court and the Member States will in future become a great deal more rigorous. This diagnosis is explained more fully in Chapters 5 and 6.[31] Much depends on the nature of the competence that is transferred to the Community; or, to approach the problem from the opposite direction, the extent to which Member States find that their scope of action is inhibited by the assumption of Community competence. The political sensitivity of exclusive Community competence is a great deal more acute than a competence shared by both Community and Member States. These issues of the nature of Community competence, rather than simply its scope, are addressed further and more specifically in Chapter 5, after an examination of legislative process (Chapter 3) and the nature of the legal system (Chapter 4).

THE COMPETENCE OF THE UNION

This Chapter has focussed on Community competence, rather than the competence of the Union more generally. In part this reflects the limited experience gained in the development of practice under the two new intergovernmental pillars. However, it also reflects the fact that unanimity is required virtually through-out the two pillars dealing with justice and home affairs and with foreign and security policy.[32] Although both relevant Titles of the Treaty contain lists of matters falling within the Titles, it is unlikely that textual limits will provoke overt debate, given that in any event action can be taken only with the agreement of all the Member States. In practice, competence is likely to be what the Member States make it. In this sense questions of competence in the non-EC Union are likely to remain submerged beneath political negotiation among the Member States, much as they remained obscured in earlier times in the Community by the practice of unanimity in the Council.

However, the area in which problems are highly likely to arise lies in the demarcation between the EC pillar and two new pillars. The subject matter of the litigation in *Germany, France, Netherlands, Denmark, and United Kingdom* v. *Commission*,[33]

---

[31] 147, 210 below.   [32] 30 above.
[33] Cases 281, 283–5, 287/85, n. 29 above.

mentioned above, might conceivably be fitted within EC competence via a generous interpretation of the scope of Article 235, but would arguably be more properly scattered throughout all three pillars. These issues of demarcation are the subject of further study in the next chapter.

FURTHER READING

DEHOUSSE, R., 'Community Competence: Are there Limits to Growth' in R. Dehousse (ed.), *Europe After Maastricht* (Munich: Law Books, 1994).

JOERGES, C., 'Social Regulation and the Legal Structure of the EEC' in B. Stauder (ed.), *La Securité des produits de consommation* (Zürich: Schulthess Verlag, 1992).

KOOPMANS, T., 'The Quest for Subsidiarity' in Curtin, D., and Heukels, T., (eds.), *Institutional Dynamics of European Integration* (Dordrecht: Martinus Nijhoff, 1994).

LENAERTS, K., 'Constitutionalism and the Many Faces of Federalism' (1990) 38 *AJCL* 205.

LANE, R. C., 'Alternative Approaches to Constitution Building: The Judicial Committee of the Privy Council' in Curtin, D., and Heukels, T., (eds.), *Institutional Dynamics of European Integration* (Dordrecht: Martinus Nijhoff, 1994).

TEMPLE LANG, J., 'Community Constitutional Law: Article 5 EEC Treaty' (1990) 27 *CMLRev.* 645.

—— 'What Powers Should the European Community Have?' (1995) 1 *Eur. Pub. L* 97.

USHER, J., 'The Development of Community Powers after the Single European Act' in Smythe, B., and White, R., (eds.), *Current Issues in European and International Law* (London: Sweet and Maxwell, 1990), Chapter 1.

3

Union Legislation

INSTITUTIONAL ARRANGEMENTS IN THE
EUROPEAN UNION

The purpose of this Chapter is not to provide a comprehensive account of the composition or activities of the institutions of the Union. Instead, it sketches the roles of and, especially, the relationships between the institutions. The objective of this inquiry is to identify where the power lies in the Union. An appreciation of the allocation of power and responsibility to the different institutions is critical to an understanding of the potential scope of Union action. An awareness of where power lies is also essential to an understanding of how the aspirations of the founders of the European integration process are reflected in the institutional arrangements.

The Treaty of Rome established three principal political institutions for the European Community, a triumvirate that remains today at the core of the Community's political architecture. The three are commonly known as the Council, the Commission, and the Parliament, although by their own preference they are the Council of the European Union, the European Commission, and the European Parliament.

The structure of the European Union is quite distinct. As explained in Chapter 1, the EC is but one of three pillars of the European Union. The institutional pattern of the EC does not cover the whole EU. The only genuinely Union-wide institutions, spanning the three pillars, are the Council and the European Council. The Commission and the Parliament are not wholly excluded from the two non-EC EU pillars, but their roles are much confined in comparison with the sophistication of their input into the EC. Beyond the political institutions, the Court is an EC body alone and the terms of the Union Treaty almost completely exclude it from the two non-EC pillars.[1]

---

[1] 30 above.

This pattern seems uneven. As already suggested in Chapter 1, it is a major reason why the nature and purpose of the EU is so difficult to grasp. It would have been well-nigh impossible to write a book accurately entitled 'Maastricht made easy'. Yet the Member States made a deliberate choice to structure the EU on three pillars and to reject the EC pattern as a general model. The public mystification that followed during the ratification process was a well-deserved consequence. The newly created Citizens of the Union were perfectly entitled to adopt a rather curmudgeonly attitude to their new status when comprehensible explanations of precisely what they had become were not forthcoming and, worse, scarcely possible. In Denmark, indeed, a major impetus towards the initial 'no' vote appears to have been fears about obligations of European Citizenship. This prompted the Edinburgh European Council in December 1992 to insist on the non-threatening nature of Citizenship and, specifically, on the fact that it does not replace national citizenship. Widespread bewilderment was natural. Even the observer of the Maastricht process who was familiar with the nature of EC law was left puzzled by, *inter alia*, the positioning of Citizenship of the *Union* in the European *Community* Treaty.

It remains to be seen whether the lesson that transparency is an indispensable factor in inducing a positive public reaction will be learned in time for the 1996 intergovernmental conference.

THE POLITICAL INSTITUTIONS OF THE EC

The original pattern of the Treaty envisaged the Commission as the motor of integration. It holds the strategically important power of initiative. In most instances, legislative proposals have their source in the Commission. It is also responsible for administration and it supervises the observance of Community law. It is staffed by individuals who are nationals of the Member States, but who are expected to show loyalty to the Community, not to individual states. This is made explicit in Article 157(2) EC: 'The members of the Commission shall, in the general interest of the Community, be completely independent in the performance of their duties. In the performance of these duties, they shall neither seek nor take instructions from any government or from any other body.' The Member States undertake, in the same Treaty provision, 'not to seek to influence the members of the Commission in the performance of their tasks'. It is common to see or hear reference to the 'British Commissioner(s)' or even to 'our Commissioner(s)'. As a reference to nationality this is correct, but in so far as it is a suggestion that such individuals represent their country and seek to protect its interests at the expense of others, it reflects a quite incorrect grasp of the Community institutional patterns mapped out by the Treaty.

The Parliament, directly elected since 1979, is, like the Commission, typically perceived as a Community-minded institution. Its members represent local interests, but they must operate within the wider European context if they are to prove effective. In the Parliament's chamber, MEPs sit by political affiliation, not nationality. The Parliament's formal role in the legislative process remains limited, although that role has been expanded by successive Treaty revisions.[2] The Treaty of Rome conferred on it, at most, a right to be consulted in some areas of legislative activity. Since the entry into force of the Treaty on European Union, the Parliament has had at its disposal a veto power in some areas of legislative activity.

The Parliament and the Commission are typically seen as allies in support of the broader Community interest. This has often pitted them against the institution in which the national interests of the Member States are expressed, the Council. According to Article 145 EC, the Council 'shall, in accordance with the provisions of this Treaty: ensure coordination of the general economic policies of the Member States; have power to take decisions; confer on the Commission, in the acts which the Council adopts, powers for the implementation of the rules which the Council lays down.' Each of the Member States has a seat in the Council, which is occupied in accordance with the subject matter debated. National agricultural ministers sit in Council where agricultural affairs are on the agenda; finance ministers where budgetary questions are up for discussion. A great deal of preparatory work is carried out by the highly influential Committee of Permanent Representatives, 'COREPER'.[3] COREPER provides a link with national bureaucracies and it keeps in close touch with the Commission during policy formulation. In practical, though not formal, terms its approval of

---

[2] 71 below.   [3] Art. 151 EC.

a proposal is frequently sufficient guarantee of full Council approval.

COREPER contributes to bringing a degree of consistency to the work of the Council. However, this element of consistency is undermined by the pattern of the Presidency of the Council, which is held for just six months by a Member State before being passed on to the next state on the list.[4] This rapid handover is not conducive to long-term management nor to the accumulation of *communautaire* expertise among national officials.

EC LEGISLATION—VOTING IN COUNCIL

It is the legislative process that provides the clearest insight into the functions of the European Community's political institutions relative to each other.

Overall, the Council is by far the most powerful element in the Community's legislative machinery. In limited circumstances the Commission enjoys legislative powers. Since the entry into force of the Treaty on European Union, some legislation is adopted jointly by Council and Parliament. But in the main the Council is the institution holding predominant responsibility for the adoption of Community legislation.

The pattern of interaction between the three institutions is rather complicated. It does not correspond to the traditional notions of separation of powers. In particular, the identification of a distinct legislature and a distinct executive is scarcely feasible.[5] This regrettable intransparency contributes to public misperception of what the 'Community' is and what it can and cannot do. The following discussion concentrates on the legislative process as a means of exposing the institutional balance of power.

Voting under the Treaty of Rome

Combining, first, the perception that the Council reflects primarily national interests whereas the Parliament and the Commission act as Community institutions and, secondly, the realization that the

---

[4] Art. 146 EC.
[5] K. Lenaerts, 'Some Reflections on the Separation of Powers in the European Community' (1991) 28 *CMLRev.* 11.

Council wields the most power in the actual process of adoption of legislation leads to an awareness of the vital importance of voting rules in Council. For if the Council operates on the basis of unanimity—the norm in international institutions—then each state will hold an effective veto. In such circumstances the notion of the Community as an autonomous entity to which the Member States have transferred powers will be seen to be rather seriously undermined. The Community's momentum will be no more than that permitted by the most cautious participating state.

The original Treaty of Rome displays a full awareness of the need to establish voting rules that allow the Community to move faster than the pace of the slowest member. Indeed, the Treaty of Rome went so far as to declare in Article 148(1) that 'Save as otherwise provided in this Treaty, the Council shall act by a majority of its members.' This apparently rather remarkable dilution of the blocking power of individual Member States was affected by the fact that it *was* widely elsewhere provided in the Treaty that higher hurdles had to be crossed before a measure was validly adopted. Nonetheless Article 148(1) serves as a demonstration of the awareness at the dawn of the Community that the legislative procedure ought to encourage the development of momentum at Community level even in circumstances where unanimous agreement among the Member States was lacking.

With this in mind, the original Treaty put in place a timetable according to which gradual moves away from unanimity would occur. It planned a series of transitional periods. This would include a shift from unanimity to varieties of majority voting, already available in some areas in 1958, but planned to increase as the transitional periods expired. Under a majority voting system one state alone is not able to block the adoption of laws that bind all Member States, which seems vital to the potential of the Community to develop independently of its Member States. This pattern of voting was also fundamental to the Community's aspirations to develop beyond the more traditional type of international organization that commonly, though not invariably, preserves veto powers for each participant.

However, the planned shift towards variants of majority voting was abruptly halted in 1965. France, led by General de Gaulle, was not prepared to accept the consequences for its power to control the Community of the shift away from unanimity towards majority voting that was planned for the end of the second transitional period. Its refusal to accept the loss of its veto was dramatic. France simply declined to participate in meetings of Community institutions for several months—the so-called *politique de la chaise vide*. In January 1966 a solution was reached in Luxembourg that was sufficient for the French chair thereafter once again to be filled.

The basic bone of contention remained outstanding. The 'Luxembourg Compromise' was essentially an agreement to disagree. Where negotiations touched 'very important interests' of one or more Member States, the 'Compromise' states that in the case of decisions capable of adoption by majority vote on a Commission proposal, Council would endeavour, within a reasonable time, to reach solutions which could be adopted by all the members of Council. This was enough to persuade all six states to re-start the day-to-day activities of the Community. That formulation does not address the basic question whether majority voting would operate once those Council endeavours proved inadequate to secure consensus. The 'Compromise' simply records the French view that it would not and implies the contrary view held by the other five Member States. This was the lurking agreement to disagree.

The 'Compromise' had not followed the stipulated procedure required to convert it into a formal Treaty revision, but it came to affect practice in Council. Difficult decisions were increasingly postponed, rarely because of a formal assertion of veto power, but frequently because of an atmosphere in which it came to be assumed that individual states expressing strong reservations would not be forced into a corner by a move to a formal vote. The capacity to paralyse proposed Community initiatives by whispers of vital national interests permeated even rather low level preparatory meetings and the whispers were not only in French.

As the following account explains, the Luxembourg Compromise as such has no practical relevance to the modern operation of the Community. Yet it is of much more than historical interest. Concern about vital national interests has not today disappeared. They are still a necessary part of the Community policy making process. Their expression occurs today via different channels. A single state could not walk away as France did in 1965 and confidently expect to see the Community structure grind to a halt until such time as the dissentient's objections are met.[6] Subtler issues of accommodating sensitive national interests within the basic fact of participation in Community activities are now at stake. In fact, the issue of respect for national interests becomes ever sharper as both the membership and the activities of the Community enlarge and survival of the Community's ambitions is shown to be impossible where movement occurs only at the pace of the slowest member. The Community today is a great deal more heterogeneous than it was in 1966.

The Community legislative process in the period between the mid-1960s and the mid-1980s was conducted under the shadow of the Luxembourg Compromise and the lurking threat of the national veto. Apart from areas of essentially technical interest, the Community had largely retreated to consensus-based inter-governmentalism in its legislative procedures. The Council held ultimate power to adopt legislation, but under this regime the Council, as an independent Community institution, could do no more than was agreed by *all* the Member States. The Commission retained the power of initiative and the Parliament held certain rights to be consulted and some practical power to exert influence, but both Commission and Parliament were confronted by the naked political fact that their best endeavours to promote significant new initiatives were capable of being blocked by a single Member State.

One consequence of the focus on the Council was the rise to prominence of the 'European Council'. Heads of state or Government tended to use the Council as a forum for general discussion of policy. On a formal constitutional level, this undermined the right of initiative vested by the Treaty in the Commission. However, the Commission right of initiative had already been stripped of much of its vitality by the practice of unanimity in Council. The rise of planning within the Council was an inevitable consequence of the Luxembourg Compromise. The Commission was at least able to secure the position of its President as a member of the European Council. The European Council was first officially recognized in the Community Treaties by the Single European Act, although it was not there made clear precisely what its institutional role was designed to be. Its rise to prominence

---

[6] Unless, perhaps, the dissentient was Germany.

continued in the Treaty on European Union, which declares that 'The European Council shall provide the Union with the necessary impetus for its development and shall define the general political guidelines thereof.'[7] The European Council is required to meet at least twice a year and has in recent years occasionally met more often. It is chaired by the head of state or government of the Member State holding the Presidency of the Council. It has become normal for the end of a six-month Presidency to be marked by a high-profile European Council at which attempts are made to secure major policy breakthroughs and—sometimes, it appears, more importantly—at which the host state and the host city are able to present themselves for public consumption in the most glamorous light possible.

The concentration of power in the hands of the Council amounted to a major shift away from the institutional pattern mapped out in the Treaty towards the predominance of Member-State control. The Community seemed to be losing much of its momentum and many of its ambitious institutional and constitutional features.

The rise of intergovernmentalism sounds terribly damaging. In a sense it was. The development of new areas of activity was largely stifled. But the thwarting of the capacity of the Community to adopt decisions against the will of a minority of members ran alongside the judicially-inspired development of a legal system that secured the primacy of law that *was* agreed at Community level over conflicting national laws, combined with the conferral on individuals of rights to invoke Community law in national proceedings. The Member States could be taken to have viewed with equanimity the Court's construction of these cardinal notions of supremacy and direct effect precisely because each state retained a veto over the acts that would attract these profound constitutional characteristics.[8] More positively, states had incentives to encourage the attachment of such characteristics to the legal rules in order to secure the enforceability of hard-fought compromise agreements in Council. 'Normative supranationalism' held together 'decisional intergovernmentalism' in a dynamic

[7] Art. D TEU.
[8] Influentially developed by J. Weiler in 'The Community System: The Dual Character of Supranationalism' (1981) 1 *YEL* 273.

balance. So, from this perspective, the unanimity rules (relating to Treaty revision and to the making of legislation) allowed the Member States to see the scope of Community as ring-fenced *by them*; so within that ring-fence an active Court was welcome.

This is an attractive portrayal of the harmony between the interest of the Member States in Council in suppressing decisional supranationalism and the interest of the Court in elaborating normative supranationalism. Nevertheless, the pattern of Community lawmaking has changed significantly in recent years, especially since the Single European Act's reassertion of a relatively wide scope for qualified majority voting in Council. It is necessary to assess what the consequences for the Court's approach to the constitutional principles should be as decisional supranationalism takes hold. Moreover, it has become increasingly apparent that the 'ring-fence' is not static and that the European Court has involved itself in widening the areas of Community activity within which its constitutional principles operate. If the acquiescence of Member States in the Court's activism collapses, what implications may follow?[9]

Treaty Amendment of the Voting Rules

By the 1980s it was becoming increasingly widely accepted that the paralysing effect on legislation of the practice of unanimity demanded a response. The enlargement of the Community was one contributory factor. As new members joined, especially those holding different aspirations from those of the core six, the oppressive effect of the veto was more widely and more often felt. Another factor was economic downturn. The damaging effect of the veto was concealed for a number years by the largely satisfactory performance of the Community's economy. By the early 1980s no such equanimity was possible. Other elements, such as persisting disquiet at the immense budgetary demands of the Common Agricultural Policy, contributed to the impression of a Community bereft of momentum and vision.

The Community needed to recapture its flair. A clutch of initiatives at the political level was floated, for example the draft Treaty on European Union championed by a leading federalist Altiero Spinelli, and approved by the Parliament in 1984. But

---

[9] Ch. 6, 210 below.

these initiatives evoked little enthusiasm and some opposition among the governments of the Member States. The plan to complete the internal market by the end of 1992 proved to be the scheme that formed the basis for the reinvigoration of the Community. As was observed in Chapter 1, the internal market project attracted the unanimous support of the Member States, largely because of its overt emphasis on economic regeneration and its avoidance of overt political commitment.[10] The belief among some Member States that '1992' was confined to market economics—or that it could be so confined—was probably essential to the plan's universal popularity. However, the suppression of the collision between that minimalist view of the 1992 initiative and the belief that 1992 was simply a new stage in the process towards an ever closer Union lies at the heart of many of the Community's current disagreements about future direction.

The technical core of the internal market process was the adoption of some 300 legislative measures directed at the elimination of persisting obstacles to trade. For this reason, if for no other, it was essential to tackle the impediments to the making of legislation caused by the practice of unanimity in Council. Goals of substantive integration dictated a need for constitutional and institutional amendment.

The Single European Act, the first major formal revision of the original 1957 Treaty of Rome, injected a qualified majority voting rule for the Council into a number of provisions permitting the Community to legislate. Of direct relevance to the '1992' process, it inserted a new Article 100a into the Treaty. This allowed the Council to act by qualified majority to 'adopt the measures for the approximation of the provisions laid down by law, regulation or administrative action in Member States which have as their object the establishment and functioning of the internal market'. Article 100, by contrast, had allowed harmonization of laws 'as directly affect the establishment or functioning of the common market', but imposed a requirement of unanimity in Council. Here, then, the unanimity constraint was firmly lodged in the Treaty, and was not even a consequence of practice that had evolved in the wake of the Luxembourg Compromise. The Member States, in agreeing the Single European Act reforms, had

---

[10] 19 above.

committed themselves to ensuring the Community could move more quickly than the pace of the slowest member. States could be bound by measures with which they disagreed and against which they had voted in Council.

The surrender of the veto was vital to the practical realization of the aspirations of the internal market project. The drive to adopt the mass of legislation that had to be put in place before the end of 1992 would have been fatally stalled were it to have been necessary to secure unanimous support in Council for every measure. The Single European Act did not formally abolish the Luxembourg Compromise. That had evolved outwith the formal Treaty structure and remained in that political netherworld. In practical terms the commitment shown to the reinvigoration of the Community by the formal acceptance of qualified majority voting in the Single European Act was sufficient to push the Luxembourg Compromise to the furthest margins of the Community's operation. Although it remained theoretically capable of invocation, its pervasive effect was banished.

The details of qualified majority voting (QMV) are fixed by the Treaty. In the Community of twelve, it was provided that for a measure to pass under the QMV rules, fifty-four votes must be cast in favour out of a total of seventy-six. So twenty-three votes were required to prevent the assembly of a qualified majority. Ten votes each are held by France, Germany, Italy, and the United Kingdom; eight by Spain; five each by Portugal, Greece, the Netherlands, and Belgium; three each by Denmark and Ireland; and two by Luxembourg. This is not one-state-one-vote. Each state is not treated equally, to the apparent detriment of smaller states. However, judged by population, the smaller states enjoy favourable treatment under this formula at the expense of the more populous.

Changes to the figures were required as the Community increased its membership from twelve to fifteen at the start of 1995. These changes were not mere technical adjustments. They went right to the heart of the sensitivity of the QMV rules and their vital role in the balance between state and Community powers. Plainly, entrant states must receive their own weighted vote. This was fixed as four for Austria, three for Finland, and four for Sweden. It is then a matter of acute controversy how the new tally should be reflected in the threshold to achieve a QMV. If the figure required for adoption of a proposal is not adjusted upwards, then it becomes significantly easier to force measures through Council despite opposition. At the other extreme, if all the new votes are added to the figure required for adoption, then the Council process will have been stalled; the same number of votes will be required to block a proposed measure, yet there will be more scope for gathering those votes. At Ioannina in Greece in March 1994 a fierce debate was conducted about the changes to the QMV figures appropriate once the 1995 accessions had occurred. The debate illuminated the range of expectations about the state/Community relationship. The United Kingdom loudly argued in favour of the stalling option; that the figure required for a blocking minority should not rise above twenty-three. Spain, too, expressed support for this position. The majority of Member States and the new entrants were in favour of raising the threshold required for a blocking minority to reflect the higher number of votes in the pool. In principle the support of all the Member States was required, for it was a constitutional matter of accession to the Union.[11] Yet, politically, neither the United Kingdom nor Spain felt able to insist on its veto over change and a compromise was struck, albeit one that had to be adjusted again once it became clear late in 1994 that Norway would not after all accede. The result is that the QMV rules for the Community of fifteen are based on a total of eighty-seven votes; the number required for a qualified majority is sixty-two, and therefore twenty-six acts as a blocking minority. The sole concession to the grudging minority was that where twenty-three to twenty-five votes are cast against a measure subject to QMV a reasonable period will be allowed within which the Council will do all within its power to reach an agreement capable of attracting sixty-five votes in support, reflecting the old blocking figure of twenty-three. That is a formulation which has something in common with the Luxembourg Compromise's reference to devoting a reasonable time to finding a text capable of unanimous support. The Luxembourg Compromise came to be applied until the 1980s in such a way that voting never interfered with the running of the reasonable time period, which became in practice infinite. It is highly improbable that such an attitude will prevail in respect of

[11] Art. O TEU.

the Ionannina Compromise. The reason does not lie in the gulf between Felipe Gonzalez' or John Major's personal magnetism and that of General de Gaulle, wide though some might reckon that to be. It is simply the case that the Community has a great deal more momentum today and the objections of a single state will not hold it back indefinitely.[12] It is probable that resort to majority voting under the new figures will be delayed little by the compromise formula agreed at Ioannina.

Plainly such constitutional matters are fertile areas of debate at time of future accession. They also deserve re-examination quite separately from accession as part of the debate about the autonomy of the Community from its Member States. Both the QMV figures themselves and the allocation of votes state-by-state are probable agenda items for the 1996 intergovernmental conference.

The present pattern of weighted voting means that thirteen states are always able to secure the adoption of a measure by QMV. Three states, at least, must oppose a measure for there to be any chance of blocking. Depending on the identity of the states concerned, more may be required. In extreme circumstances a measure could be adopted with the support of only eight states, where the dissenting seven are at the small end of the spectrum.[13] One should not lose sight of the fact that many Community measures are agreed with the full support of all the Member States, but there is scope for political horsetrading in Council as attempts are made to construct coalitions adequate to cross the QMV threshold or to block adoption by QMV.

Member States' willingness to accept the possibility of being outvoted is explained by their interest in acquiring the opportunity to outvote other states. The advantages on offer in an internal market act as a sufficient inducement to enter into a kind of package deal where the benefits in the shape of agreed legislation favoured by that state (and a sufficient majority) outweigh the costs of agreed legislation unwanted by that state (and an inadequate minority). This is the basis of the EC generally, outlined in Chapter 1. Acting together, the states can wield more

[12] Except Germany? See n. 6 above.
[13] Except that on the rare occasions when the Council can act *without* a Commission proposal at least 10 states must vote in favour.

power than the aggregate that they would exert acting separately. Giving up power is a means of sharing in more power.

The Single European Act came into force at the start of July 1987. The next major Treaty process of revision occurred at the end of 1991 in Maastricht and yielded the Treaty on European Union. Here, too, the pattern of voting in Council was affected by an extension in the areas subject to qualified majority. Once the Treaty on European Union came into force on 1 November 1993, qualified majority voting had become the norm in the EC. There remained residual areas of unanimity only, largely those of core constitutional importance such as new accessions and the sensitive area of harmonization of taxation. The fact that not all measures are adopted under the same legislative procedure has some troubling consequences. Some areas demand unanimity, others only qualified majority. As is discussed below, different procedures attract different Parliamentary inputs. It is therefore vital for an EC lawyer to know his or her way round the Treaty, in order to be able to identify precisely which Treaty Article provides the correct 'legal base' for a proposal and therefore which legislative procedure must be chosen in support of a particular proposal. This will be especially tricky where a proposal touches more than one area of Community activity, yet where the possible legal bases follow different legislative procedures. This is examined below. Reform, particularly simplification, of the Community legislative procedure is a pressing need.

EC LEGISLATION—THE ROLE OF THE PARLIAMENT

The previous section explains how the voting rules in the Council dictate the extent of the autonomy of the Community legislative process from its constituent Member States. The other major historical shift in the Community legislative process has involved the position of the Parliament.

The Parliament is frequently viewed (not least by itself) as the democratic element of the Community institutional structure. To some extent this is true, but the Council, too, is able plausibly to claim democratic legitimacy. After all, members of Council represent democratically elected governments in the Member States. Choices of appropriate forms of democratic accountability, and judgements about their effectiveness, will radically affect one's notion of proper power distribution among the Community's institutions. However, it is submitted that as a general thesis both Council and Parliament are necessary players in future reorganization of democracy within the Community and within the Union.

It should be stated simply and clearly that the European Parliament has no independent legislative powers. This remains unaltered even by the Treaty on European Union. The position of the Parliament has nevertheless been strengthened by successive Treaty revisions.

The Treaty of Rome conferred on the Parliament no veto in any area of legislation. Its role was limited to consultation. Its peripheral status in the original Treaty may be gauged by its designation therein as an 'Assembly', not a Parliament. In practice it quickly restyled itself the Parliament and this was widely, though not universally,[14] copied. However, the change was conclusively confirmed only in the Single European Act.

The Parliament is able to enforce its right to be consulted. In *Roquette Frères* v. *Council*[15] the Court annulled a measure because of the Council's failure to provide the Parliament with an adequate opportunity to express its opinion. The Court made much of the Parliament's right to be consulted within the framework of the democratic process. It declared that consultation of the Parliament as part of the legislative procedure 'reflects at Community level the fundamental democratic principle that the people should take part in the exercise of power through the intermediary of a representative assembly'.

Stirring though those sentiments may be, their practical impact was undermined by the severe limitations placed on the Parliamentary role by the Treaty itself. It could not oblige the other political institutions to adopt its view once it had been expressed. The Parliament had no effective means of requiring the Council to do more than go through the formality of requesting its view.

The Single European Act raised the Parliament's profile and provided it with enhanced powers. The Member States resisted the conferral of a formal power to legislate. The summit of

---

[14] Preference for the term 'Assembly' tended in the United Kingdom to be favoured by those who employed 'common market' in preference to 'Community'; Ch. 1, 7, 23 above.   [15] Case 138/79 [1980] ECR 3333.

the Parliament's role was the co-operation procedure. In the areas to which it applies, the Council considers a proposal and may reach a common position by qualified majority vote. The proposal is accepted after a second 'reading' in Council if the Parliament approves. If the Parliament rejects the common position, the Council can adopt the original proposal only by unanimity. There is no Parliamentary veto, but the Parliament is able to block laws adopted under legal bases to which the co-operation procedure applies (of which Article 100a was one) provided it can find an ally in at least one Member State. This is hardly an authentic democratic control system. It was really the product of a political compromise at the time of the drafting of the Single European Act between the perceived need to involve the Parliament more closely in the legislative process and the determination of the Member States to retain the core of effective political power in the Council.

The Parliament's power has on occasion proved to be of real practical value. The Parliament found an ally in Denmark which allowed it to block the adoption of a legislative proposal relating to emission standards for cars below a certain size. The common position set standards lower than the environmentally conscious Parliament considered appropriate. It rejected the common position. The Council was unable to return to its original draft because unanimity could not be achieved. Denmark, traditionally environmentally conscious,[16] sided with the Parliament. That might have meant that the initiative would have failed altogether, with the result that *no* standards would have been set, which might have been even worse than low standards. But the Parliament had astutely judged that the Council was subject to sufficient political pressure to be unprepared to abandon the matter. The Council, faced with the choice of no action or action of a type that would attract Parliamentary support, opted for the latter.[17] When circumstances are propitious the Parliament enjoys leverage. But take away the supportive state from this saga; or the political imperatives that foreclosed Council abandonment of the plan; and the weakness of the Parliament's position is exposed.

The breakthrough to a Parliamentary veto was achieved in the Treaty on European Union. At Maastricht, the Member States

---

[16] Cf Ch. 7, text at n. 13 ff.   [17] Dir. 89/458 [1989] OJ L226/1.

created a legislative procedure which, like the co-operation procedure, draws the Parliament and the Council into a type of process of negotiation, but, unlike the co-operation procedure, provides that at the end of the process the Parliament retains the power to reject the proposed measure. So the Parliament lacks legislative powers of its own, but under the legal bases to which this new procedure applies (of which Article 100a is one), it is able to prevent the Council exercising its powers. The Parliament enjoys this blocking power even where the Council is unanimously in favour of a proposal. This is likely to yield the Parliament an informal influence rather more extensive than the formal power of veto, which is likely to play a role more as threat than execution. The Parliament is, after all, a largely Community-minded institution. It might block acts that it thinks too weak; it might block acts in respect of which it has no particular axe to grind, but where it perceives that, by exercising that formal power, it could obtain some advantage in another area where it lacks effective formal power.

The increase in Parliamentary input into the legislative procedure in, first, the Single European Act and, secondly, the Treaty on European Union suggests that in 1996 further enhancement of the Parliament's role will be an important agenda item. This might involve an increase in its veto power. It might involve endowing it with independent legislative powers, in some areas at least. Yet these are controversial areas. The Single European Act and the Treaty on European Union did not provide a coherent plan for democratizing the Community through Parliamentary participation. Both represented an incremental and rather grudging drift towards growth in Parliamentary influence. It remain to be seen whether the 1996 review will take the process on to a higher plane by attempting to address directly the question of where democratic accountability ought to reside in the Community. The European Parliament is plainly entitled to a role. The Council, too, has serious claims to democratic legitimacy. And, moreover, it is appealing to consider the role of more localized expressions of popular will. Perhaps national parliaments ought to be allowed or encouraged to have a more direct link with the Community process than their current input via domestic procedures and indirect and often haphazard pressure on those who form the Council. National parliaments and the European

Parliament could fruitfully deepen co-operative structures rather than maintain the current notion that national parliaments express their view through the Council. Even in states where this is not in political practice a fiction, the absence of national veto under the QMV procedures undermines the value of an input by national Parliaments. Already Declarations attached to the Treaty on European Union state that the 1991 Maastricht intergovernmental conference 'considers that it is important to encourage greater involvement of national parliaments in the activities of the European Union'; and the conference 'invites the European Parliament and the national parliaments to meet as necessary as a Conference of the parliaments'.

Apart from or in addition to building on existing national institutions, the Community may be able to secure input from a local level within its own institutional structure. The Committee of the Regions was created by the Treaty on European Union, but its powers are advisory only.[18] In this respect, its status bears comparison with the place of the Parliament under the original Treaty of Rome. The Committee, like the Parliament, merits an increase in its role as it evolves and it could usefully provide a further channel for feeding expressions of local opinion into the Community structure.

There remains a great deal to be done. It is wearying to hear debates barely rising above a level at which national politicians overtly and covertly dismiss arguments in favour of enhanced Parliamentary powers by reference to the alleged low quality of European Parliamentarians, to which the typical Parliamentary response is denial of this quality assessment combined with a demand for more power so that true worth can be measured. The only proper way forward lies in a comprehensive re-examination of power and responsibility in the European Union; yet another challenge for the 1996 IGC.

THE EVOLVING RELATIONSHIP BETWEEN THE PARLIAMENT AND THE COMMISSION

The role of the Parliament extends beyond its participation in the legislative process. Its relationship with the Commission has come

---

[18] Arts. 198a–c.

under increasing scrutiny. The Parliament, as an elected body, has some democratic claim to exercise a supervisory function over the unelected Commission. Pre-Maastricht, this notion was seriously underdeveloped. The Parliament could vote to remove the entire Commission. But it could not vote to remove individual Commissioners. The power was therefore blunt and it was never used. The Treaty on European Union brought a little more sophistication to the Parliamentary supervisory role. The Parliament and the Commission run on parallel five-year terms from the start of 1995, which offers at least a framework through which effective co-operation and supervision may be developed. However, the details of effective supervision remain inexplicit in the Treaty and must be hammered out through practice.

The Parliament has devoted energy to acquiring a more sophisticated influence than is granted by the Treaty. Practice has rapidly overtaken the detailed pattern mapped out in Article 158 EC. Under that provision, the governments of the Member States nominate the person they intend to appoint President of the Commission by common accord after consulting the Parliament. No provision is made for the consequences of an unfavourable Parliamentary reaction. In July 1994 the nomination of Jacques Santer as Commission President in succession to Jacques Delors was the subject of much criticism within the Parliament. Santer himself found his capacity to provide dynamic leadership questioned; more generally, many MEPs saw an opportunity to express frustration at their lack of input into a procedure settled behind closed doors by the representatives of the Member States. In the event, Santer eventually won Parliamentary approval by a small majority. Had he been rejected, it seems that on a strict application of the letter of the Treaty, the Member States could still have secured his appointment. As a matter of practical politics this would have been difficult and would certainly have soured relations between the Member States/Council and the Parliament. It seems difficult to defend the Treaty position that allows individual Member States to reject possible candidates for the Presidency, as the United Kingdom did in 1994 when refusing to agree to the nomination of the Belgian Jean Luc Dehaene, while refusing that veto power to the European Parliament. The incoming President of the Commission, Jacques Santer, who endured the rigours of Parliamentary scrutiny, has suggested that in future candidates for the Presidency of the Commission could be proposed to and elected by the Parliament. This shows a remarkable spirit of personal generosity, and, of wider significance, it offers an imaginative means of contributing to the development of a formal constitutional relationship between Parliament and Commission.

Once the intended President is identified, the governments of the Member States then consult with him or her and nominate the other intended appointees as Commissioners. The Parliament has no explicit role. The whole body is then subject to a vote of approval by the Parliament. This provides the Parliament with the opportunity to block the formal appointment of the whole package, but it cannot isolate and reject individuals whom it deems unsatisfactory.

The existence of a formal requirement for a favourable Parliamentary vote before the Commission may assume office allowed the Parliament to carve out for itself a role unforeseen in the text of Article 158 EC. The Parliament used this power to persuade each of the incoming twenty Commissioners to appear and answer questions before the Parliament's vote. This occurred in a series of high-profile sessions in January 1995. This practice, which the Parliament could not claim as of right, seemed to raise its profile as a forum in which accountability is ensured. However the Parliament remained armed with an all-or-nothing power; it could reject all twenty or accept all twenty. Criticisms of varying severity were directed at five—Flynn, Bjerregaard, Thibault de Silguy, Gradin, and Liikanen—but the Parliament was not competent formally to strike out selected names. It chose to vote in favour of the package of twenty.

The Treaty on European Union has effected some adjustment of the institutional balance in favour of Parliamentary control of the Commission. It is at the informal level that Parliamentary power is more significantly on the rise. The hearings were opportunities for Parliament to attain a profile far higher than that which one might have expected from a purely textual reading of the Treaty. This is an important pointer to the capacity of practical politics to adjust power relationships and to open up channels of influence in ways that would be obscured by mere poring over the text of the Treaty. The Commission and Parliament appear to be developing an ever more fruitful collaborative co-existence.

The European Court too has acted to protect the position of the Parliament. It is aware of the Parliament's claims to democratic legitimacy within the Community based on the rule of law. This was manifested by its comments in *Roquette Frères* v. *Council*, mentioned above.[19] At a more general level, this is examined more fully in Chapter 6 of this book, where it will be seen that part of the Court's commitment to securing the constitutionalization of the Treaty has involved some adjustment of the institutional patterns apparently planned by the Treaty. The Parliament was given a right to seek annulment of acts where its prerogatives were threatened which was absent from the Treaty until the Maastricht amendments. This was an instance of the Court choosing to up-date the Treaty in one area in order to buttress the advances in Parliamentary participation made in others. Moreover, the Court has decided disputes about choice of legal base for Community legislation in part by reference to a determination to protect the rights of participation held by the Parliament.[20]

DEMOCRACY IN THE EUROPEAN UNION

Within the two non-EC pillars of the European Union, the power relationship is significantly more heavily weighted in favour of the Council/European Council and away from the European Parliament than under the EC pattern. The Parliament's opportunity to be consulted illustrates the problem. The Parliament's position in the non-EC EU, though vague, is clearly weaker than its status under the EC Treaty. Parliament is to be consulted and kept informed.[21] It cannot impose its views. Nor is any sanction made explicit in the event of failure to consult. It has no formal leverage. Article D requires the European Council to submit to the Parliament a report after each of its meetings, which must occur at least twice a year, and a yearly written report on the progress achieved by the Union. This pattern initially sounds analogous to the Parliament's limited role under the original Treaty of Rome, but in fact it is much weaker. Failure to consult could there lead to

---

[19] N. 15 above.   [20] '*Titanium Dioxide*', n. 35 below.
[21] Arts. J.7 and K.6, 31 above.

annulment of the act in question by the Court.[22] The Court lacks jurisdiction in the two intergovernmental pillars, so the Parliament is not able to seek the European Court's protection in the event that it considers that its interests have been disregarded by the Member States.

As practice has evolved since the agreement of and, especially, the entry into force of the Treaty on European Union, the Parliament has endeavoured to carve for itself a more significant role in the practical operation of the new areas of intergovernmental co-operation. It has, in particular, made strong representations in support of its perception that it should legitimately be involved in the development of policy under the Title of the Treaty on European Union dealing with justice and home affairs. Action agreed by the Member States is capable of exerting a significant impact on the position of individual citizens. The theoretical chain of accountability in the non-EC European Union runs from Council/European Council back to national Parliaments. Whether this is realistic is, for many, questionable. The secrecy that pervades the process is notorious. It is by no means uncommon for national Parliaments to find their scrutiny impeded by explanations that the matter is confidential as a European matter; yet Parliamentary responsibility at European level has been effectively excluded. Less conspiratorially, developments at European level are simply more difficult to track even where no deliberate veil of secrecy has been drawn across intergovernmental activity. This seems remote from the claim made by Article A of the Treaty on European Union that it 'marks a new stage in the process of creating an ever closer union among the peoples of Europe, in which decisions are taken as closely as possible to the citizen.' The European Court, too, is almost completely excluded from a supervisory role in the two non-EC EU pillars. This is the democratic deficit; a disturbing 'black hole' into which responsibility vanishes. Action is taken, yet neither national nor European institutions are able to exercise any effective control on behalf of individuals.

It remains to be seen whether the Parliament proves capable of securing an effective role through political persuasion. Its Committee on Civil Liberties and Internal Affairs has reported

---

[22] Case 138/79, n. 15 above.

with distaste on the institutional patterns of the justice and home affairs pillar. It recommended that strenuous efforts be made to maximize Parliamentary involvement.[23] In the United Kingdom, too, the House of Lords Select Committee examined the institutional pattern and declared itself convinced that control by national Parliaments of the intergovernmental pillar on justice and home affairs was essential. It argued, too, in favour of liaision with the European Parliament.[24] Non-governmental organizations with interests in civil liberties are also conspicuously attempting to respond to these developments by building trans-border networks.

The tensions that are emerging as a result of the strain placed on the institutional framework of the European Union by its assymetric architecture are likely to grow stronger. The Parliament, in particular, has been stimulated by the enhancement of its powers under the EC pillar and it is not likely meekly to acquiesce in a role of interested observer in the non-EC EU pillars. The potential impact on the individual citizen of action taken under the justice and home affairs pillar represents an especially cogent argument in favour of the legitimacy of active Parliamentary involvement. It should be added that it would be quite wrong to see this in simplistic terms as the Parliament waging a valiant but lonely battle against the dark forces of the intransigent Member States. There are plainly very significant differences of opinion among the Member States, ranging from those implacably opposed to the involvement of the European Parliament or the Court to those determined to open up channels of co-operation among the several interested institutions at European level.

For the present these debates will be played out against the background of the three-pillar Treaty on European Union. They are further compelling agenda items for the 1996 IGC. From the perspective of aligning Union processes of accountability to elected representatives with those that are normal in the Member States, there are strong arguments for collapsing the justice and home affairs pillar into the EC pillar. As part of this renovation the role of Parliament could be enhanced. The common foreign and security pillar retains a stronger claim to separate treatment as a matter for the European Council alone.

[23] PE Doc. A 3–215/93 (July 1993).
[24] House of Lords scrutiny of the inter-governmental pillars of the European Union (1992–3), HL Paper 124.

TYPES OF LEGISLATION

The list of types of Community legislation is found in Article 189. This describes three binding Community acts—regulations, directives and decisions—and two more that have no binding force—recommendations and opinions.

According to Article 189, '[a] regulation shall have general application. It shall be binding in its entirety and directly applicable in all Member States.' The characteristic of direct applicability, unique to regulations, is that once the act is duly made and published in accordance with the constitutional requirements of Community law, it becomes law in all the Member States. There is no need for transposition into national law. Indeed there is in principle a prohibition on national transposition.[25] Only in exceptional cases where national implementation is permitted by the regulation may the state intervene. So once a state becomes a member of the Community it has signed up for regulations as directly applicable laws emanating from the Community legislative machinery. Such laws are in principle capable of pre-empting national competence in the field, a matter examined more fully in Chapter 5. Regulations are sources of national law within the Community legal order and their penetration of the national system is a major feature of the deepening interdependence of Community and national legal orders.

The directive, in contrast to the regulation, does not form an automatic part of the national legal order. It depends on national implementation. According to Article 189 the directive 'shall be binding, as to the result to be achieved, upon each Member State to which it is addressed, but shall leave to the national authorities the choice of form and methods'. Directives set out objectives. Article 5 EC requires Member States to take all measures necessary to guarantee the effective achievement of those objectives in the national system. The choice of precise method rests with the national system and therefore the precise pattern whereby rights and obligations envisaged under a directive are vindicated will vary state by state, albeit within an overall framework shaped by the common goals envisaged by the

---

[25] Case 34/73 *Variola* v. *Amministrazione delle Finanze dello Stato* [1973] ECR 981.

directive. Some states will, for example, enforce standards drawn from a directive by criminal penalties; others will prefer administrative control. Provided only that the (admittedly vague) obligation of effective enforcement is met, such different choices are equally permissible. In order to allow Member States the opportunity to select the appropriate method of implementation, a directive includes a deadline by which time implementation must have occurred.

The directive as a Community act is separated by national implementing measures from the parties who are intended as ultimate beneficiaries and from those intended to be subject to obligations. Directives are a creative type of measure. They act as a bridge between Community and national law. Once implemented, they are in effect both. They allow the objectives of the Community legal order to be harnessed to the established patterns of national law.

The distinction between regulations and directives may be assessed as an expression of the principle of subsidiarity. Where an objective is capable of achievement through national implementing measures, without a need for a single Community structure, there is no call to preclude such national-level choices, sensitive to the practical realization of the relevant objectives. A directive, rather than a regulation, is appropriate. Equally, where the variation inherent in (and a strength of) the directive inhibits the establishment of the required common regime, subsidiarity points in favour of a regulation. This distinction between the regulation and the directive is useful as an analytical tool. It is not here suggested that it is a model that has been followed rigorously in Community practice in the past. It may be that it will have to be followed more carefully in future. In surveying the Council's approach to the application of the subsidiarity principle, the Conclusions of the Presidency emanating from the Edinburgh European Council in December 1992 stated that, other things being equal, directives should be preferred to regulations, and framework directives to detailed measures. Article 190 EC combined with Article 3b EC might now mean that where regulations are preferred to directives, the choice must be adequately reasoned.[26] Another intriguing twist may be that if

[26] Cf Ch. 5, 172.

states persist in failure to implement directives, this might constitute an argument for preferring regulations. This is a point touched on by the Sutherland Report into the management of the internal market after the end of 1992, which is considered more fully in Chapter 9.

By 'implementation' much more is involved than putting the law in place on paper. Effective implementation involves empowering agencies, providing budgets, and securing willing support from responsible national officials who should be prepared to regard laws deriving from Community law as no less a source of law than 'purely' national law. Directives are peculiarly vulnerable forms of Community law because of their dependence on national and local structures and attitudes, which, moreover, are often incapable of thorough monitoring. The Commission has been guilty of preparing 'league tables' of implementation in which points are scored for mere paper implementation and where no inquiry into practical implementation has been undertaken. Admittedly, it is not feasible for the Commission to track the practical application of laws emanating from directives at every stage in the national system. This highlights the need for active co-operation at national level. It also underlines the role of individuals in policing the proper application of Community law through reliance on the phenomenon of, in particular, direct effect, examined in the next chapter.

The regulation and the directive are essentially legislative in nature. Their adoption engages the complex legislative machinery discussed at page 61. The Community's primary formal administrative act is the decision. According to Article 189 '[a] Decision shall be binding in its entirety upon those to whom it is addressed.' The addressee may be a Member State or a private party. There are procedural preconditions that must be observed in the making of a Decision, but the formal and complex interrelationship of the political institutions typical of the making of a regulation or directive is not engaged.

Article 189 declares that recommendations and opinions 'shall have no binding force'. This by no means deprives such Community 'soft law' of legal effect. In *Grimaldi* v. *Fonds des Maladies Professionelles*[27] the Court accepted that a national court

[27] Case C–322/88 [1989] ECR 4407.

is able to make a preliminary reference regarding the interpretation of a recommendation. At the very least a recommendation
may have relevance to the interpretation of national law prompted
by the EC recommendation. In *GB-INNO* v. *Confédération du
Commerce Luxembourgeois* the European Court was concerned
with the compatibility with Article 30 EC of a law that restricted
marketing techniques involving the provision of price information
to consumers.[28] The European Court found that the law exerted
an unjustifiable restriction on the development of cross-border
marketing campaigns. It referred to the 1981 Resolution adopting
a Consumer Protection and Information Policy for the Community.
The Court drew on this 'soft law' instrument, outwith the list of
binding Community acts in Article 189 EC, in ruling that there is a
close connection between consumer protection and consumer
information.

The expansion of the institutional apparatus of the Community
increasingly means that activities of the institutions affect third
parties. The Court has shown itself willing to review acts even
where not formally within the Article 189 list, provided they have
legal effects. It is therefore recognized that legally relevant acts of
the Community are not restricted to the Article 189 list.[29]

THE IDENTIFICATION OF LEGAL BASE AND VARIATION BETWEEN LEGISLATIVE PROCEDURES

It has already been outlined in Chapter 2 that Community
competence to legislate is dependent on the identification of a
specific legal base in the Treaty. The Bathing Water directive
could not simply be made by the Community under the powers
conferred by the Treaty without a more specific reference to the
Treaty provision conferring competence; Articles 100 and 235 in
that instance.[30] The legal base will then provide for a specific
legislative procedure. That, then, will determine how the legislation is to be made.

The plea was made in Chapter 2 that, although choice of legal
base is not the most immediately compelling area of study of EC

---

[28] Case C-362/88 [1990] ECR I-667.
[29] E.g. Case 22/70 *Commission* v. *Council* [1971] ECR 263.
[30] Ch. 2, text at n. 22.

law, it is critical in assessing the practical scope of actual and
potential Community action. That plea is here repeated and its
justification is elaborated below.

The Different Legislative Procedures

The European Community has no single legislative procedure. It is
necessary to identify which Treaty Article provides the legal base
for a Community legislative initiative and then to apply the
legislative procedure applicable under that base. The variation
between the detail of different legal bases is the source of dispute
both among Community institutions and between the Member
States. The choice of legal base dictates, for example, which of the
acts mentioned in Article 189 are available. But the fiercest
disagreements have arisen in relation to, first, the level of
Parliamentary input—which, crudely though regrettably largely
accurately, the Parliament aims to increase, the Council to
decrease; and, secondly, the applicable voting rules in Council—
which, crudely though, again, largely accurately, the United
Kingdom in particular attempts to fix as unanimity while the other
Member States increasingly regard QMV as the desirable norm in
most areas.

Piris identifies no fewer than twenty-two different procedures
from which the Council selects under the post-Maastricht EU
Treaty.[31] Most involve at least elements of the rough traditional
pattern of Commission initiation, Parliamentary involvement, and
Council power of adoption. But the precise patterns are a great
deal more complex.

It is risky to attempt to obtain an overview of the pattern given
this diversity. Each legal base must be carefully checked in order
to identify the applicable procedure. This should be borne in mind
in the following discussion. But the three procedures sketched
below are arguably the most important. Contrasting the trio also
helps to provide an appreciation of the way that Parliamentary
involvement in the procedure has developed. The first was the
norm under the original Treaty of Rome and is still applicable in a
number of areas today. The second is the creation of the Single
European Act. The third is the creation of the Treaty on European
Union. All three were mentioned above in connection with

[31] J.-C. Piris, 'After Maastricht, are the Community Institutions more
Efficacious, more Democratic and more Transparent? (1994) 19 ELRev. 449.

assessment of the Parliament's place in the legislative procedure, but they deserve separate consideration here for the light they shed on the legal base issue.

Consultation

The Commission proposes; the Parliament is consulted on that proposal; the Council adopts the act as law. This was the norm in the original Treaty of Rome. Consultation of the Parliament provides the Parliament with the opportunity to influence decision-making. However, although consultation is obligatory, no consequences of that consultation are made explicit. The Parliament's views are not binding. Formally the Council could simply reject the Parliament's objections out of hand. This happens. Informally the working relationship of Parliament and Council, although on occasion frosty, has been a little more fruitful. This is suggested by the Council's informal practice of consulting the Parliament even in those areas where the Treaty continues to envisage the adoption of measures by the Council without even the formality of consultation. But the consultation procedure itself gives the Parliament minimal formal leverage.

The Co-operation Procedure, Article 189c

This procedure was introduced by the Single European Act and it is now found in Article 189c of the EC Treaty after the entry into force of the Treaty on European Union. The Parliament enjoys no right of veto except where it is able to align itself with at least one Member State. This enhances its influence while leaving it distant from any real legislative role. The Commission proposes and the Parliament is consulted. The Council then adopts a common position under QMV, instead of moving directly to adoption of the proposal. This common position is transmitted to the Parliament. It may approve it or it may take no decision, in which case the Council moves to formal adoption. It may propose amendments which then leads to Commission re-examination in accordance with the procedure laid down in Article 189c. Or—the test of its veto power—the Parliament may reject the common position. The Council may then adopt the common position only if unanimity can be assembled. The Parliament has no legislative powers on its own, nor any veto power on its own. But where it has at least one supporter among the Member States it may block adoption.

The Article 189b Procedure

This was introduced into the EC Treaty by the Treaty on European Union. Its major novelty is the invention of a Conciliation Committee which brings together the Parliament and the Council in a forum in which a mutually satisfactory compromise may be found. However, ultimately, the Article 189b procedure confers a veto power on the Parliament in the areas to which it applies. A common position is reached, in the same way as under the co-operation procedure. If the Parliament decides by an absolute majority that it intends to reject the act, the Council may then convene the Conciliation Committee. This comprises representatives of Council and Parliament and it is charged with the task of trying to agree a joint text. The Parliament is entitled thereafter to confirm its rejection of the proposal and the proposal falls. If the Parliament proposes amendments, the Council is able to adopt the act including those amendments by QMV.[32] If the Council demurs, the Conciliation Committee is convened. Ultimately, however, where agreement cannot be reached both Council and, in accordance with the specific provisions of Article 189b, Parliament are empowered to prevent the making of the act. Conciliation and veto is a helpful label for this process. The term co-decision is also widely used, although it was excluded from the Treaty, apparently because of fears that it overstated the Parliament's place relative to the Council. Strictly the Parliament's power is negative only. It has no independent legislative powers. Yet a successful outcome under the Conciliation Committee framework envisages a melding of Parliament and Council views in a final text. At least in these circumstances, co-decision seems apposite and by no means an inflation of the Parliament's position.

These three procedures are closely associated with the Treaty of Rome, the Single European Act, and the Treaty on European Union respectively. So will the intergovernmental conference in 1996 add a further distinct procedure? This would not be desirable—or at least it would not be desirable unless a new procedure were developed as part of a campaign to clarify the whole process rather than as yet another addition. The current

[32] Except that unanimity is required where the Commission's opinion on the amendments is unfavourable.

chaotic mess is the price paid for the incremental growth in the Parliament's powers in successive Treaty revisions. The time is ripe for rational consolidation.

The Treaty on European Union created the Article 189b procedure and shifted a number of Articles previously subject to the Article 189c co-operation procedure across to Article 189b. Article 100a, the provision central to harmonization of laws in pursuit of the completion of the internal market, is one example. Clarification could helpfully be achieved by transferring all Article 189c bases to Article 189b and by abolishing Article 189c altogether. The range of other procedures could be rationalized with a view to leaving as few as possible from which to choose. Conciliation and veto could become the standard legislative procedure for the Community. A window on this prospect is found in Article 189b(8), which states that the scope of the procedure may be widened on the basis of a report to be submitted to the Council by the Commission by 1996 at the latest. This is clearly a worthwhile agenda item for the 1996 IGC.

Prioritizing the conciliation and veto procedure is one possible solution only. To some extent the detail of the solution matters less than the pressing need that the matter be addressed. The chaotic state of the Community's legislative procedure has reached a level of such incomprehensibility that comprehensive reform is urgently required, provided only that the hard-won input of the Parliament is not reduced.

Identifying the Correct Legal Base

It is necessary to make the choice between legal bases to discover which legislative procedure is appropriate. The European Court's task of identifying the correct legal base has been discharged in relation to a number of different Treaty provisions. The Court insists that these questions are a matter of law. It has consistently ruled that choice of legal basis has to be made according to objective criteria amenable to judicial review.[33]

It must be welcomed that the political institutions are denied a free choice of legal base. Were it otherwise, it would be possible for tactical choices to be made on political grounds that might

---

[33] E.g. Case 45/86 *Commission* v. *Council* [1987] ECR 1493; Case 68/86 *UK* v. *Council* [1988] ECR 855.

allow the Council, in particular, to push other institutions, particularly the Parliament, to the sidelines. The Court has wisely ruled that Article 235—requiring unanimity in the Council and mere consultation of the Parliament—should not be tacked on to a measure as an additional legal base, where other more specific Treaty provisions (with different procedures) supply an adequate legal base.[34] But in a number of sectors the European Court's task is severely hampered by the problem of choosing a single legal base for measures which are multi-functional. It is forced to make choices with fundamental implications for the allocation of political power in the Community where different bases attract different procedures.

The Court's role under the pattern of the Treaty pre-Maastricht is forcefully illustrated by its ruling in the so-called 'Titanium Dioxide' case, *Commission* v. *Council*.[35] Legislation in the sphere of the internal market belongs under Article 100a. Legislation with the objective of environmental protection is properly made under Articles 130r–t. The question that arose in the case was how one distinguishes between the two objectives. Directive 89/428 approximated national programmes for reducing and eventually eliminating pollution caused by waste in the production of titanium dioxide. The Council had adopted it on the basis of Article 130s. The Commission, supported by the Parliament, sought its annulment on the ground that it should instead have been based on Article 100a. It is hard to deny that the measure touched both objectives. It contributed to environmental protection by setting controls over pollution. But it also set common Community-wide rules which had the effect of equalizing competitive conditions in the market in question. Yet it was not possible to take the easy option of simply basing the Directive on both Articles. Article 130s required unanimity in Council and mere consultation of the Parliament, whereas Article 100a involved QMV in Council and the co-operation procedure. To use both would defeat the whole purpose of the co-operation procedure, because the need for unanimity in any event would deprive the Parliament of any effective leverage.

The Court therefore felt a choice between legal bases to be

---

[34] Case 45/86 *Commission* v. *Council*, n. 33 above.
[35] Case C-300/89 [1991] ECR I-2867.

constitutionally necessary. Article 130r(2) declares that 'environmental protection requirements shall be a component of the Community's other policies'. This prompted the Court to conclude that the fact that a measure pursues the objective of environmental protection does not automatically place it within Article 130r. The Court then observed that harmonization of national rules on production conditions contributed to the realization of the internal market and proceeded to identify Article 100a, the internal market base, as the correct provision. This led it to annul the Directive for incorrect choice of legal base.

It is hard to see how a measure such as that at stake in *Titanium Dioxide* can coherently be pinned down to the realm of internal market-building rather than environmental protection. It has an impact on both. In fact the Court's need to choose is driven by the constitutional eccentricities of the Treaty itself. The applicability of the co-operation procedure to internal market legislation, but not to environmental legislation, made it unavoidable for the Court to make a choice about which legal base should prevail. The Court has to take to itself this choice, by insisting that it is a matter of law, or else the Council will be able to shut out the Parliament, in particular, from the legislative process. It will be noted that the Council's initial preference for Article 130s over Article 100a diminished the influence of the Parliament, which in turn explains the Parliament's support for the Commission in the *Titanium Dioxide* case.

Once the Court had satisfied itself that it could not avoid making the choice between Articles 100a and 130s, it was drawn into discussion of the function of the Directive. As analysed above, the Court's preference for one function—internal market building—over another—environmental protection—does not seem convincing. The strong impression is that the Court was driven to select the basis that maximized the Parliamentary role, thereby reflecting the judicial identification of the Parliament as a key democratic element in the Community that is deserving of protection. The preference for Article 100a was driven by the Court's own perception of institutional balance in the Community. But since the Court was forced to make the choice because of the basic Treaty failure to provide a coherent pattern to the legislative process, it is hard to accuse the Court of undue activism in this instance.

The apparent priority accorded to Article 100a was called into question by subsequent decisions relating to apparently dual-function legislation that suggested different priorities by preferring Article 130s as the proper legal base.[36] These rulings dispelled the impression that the *Titanium Dioxide* ruling had undermined the vitality of Article 130s in relation to legislation touching conditions of competition, but, overall, they left the constitutional picture, if anything, yet more confused. The precise implications of these rulings were adjusted by the amendments effected by the Treaty on European Union. Article 100a now attracts the Article 189b legislative procedure, which is variously referred to as conciliation and veto, negative assent, and co-decision, whereas Article 130s(1) uses the Article 189c co-operation procedure. The basic difficulty of demarcation remains and there are a great many areas in which such demarcations have to be made in order to establish appropriate institutional consequences. Perhaps the Court's preference for bases that maximize Parliamentary involvement, apparent in *Titanium Dioxide*, will tempt it towards a preference for bases attracting the Article 189b procedure, which reserves a veto power to the Parliament, over those offering a more limited expression of the Parliament's view. If this proves correct, Article 100a's prominence is assured.

Fundamentally, the Treaty on European Union has not solved the legal base conundrum. It simply invites further litigation. In a number of areas the problem is accentuated by the Treaty on European Union.

The pattern of Article 130s itself, as amended by the Treaty on European Union, encapsulates the chaotic, fragmented pattern of legislative procedures under the Treaty. The first paragraph provides a basic power for the Community to act in order to achieve the environmental objectives referred to in Article 130r EC. This engages the Article 189c procedure, accompanied by consultation of the Economic and Social Committee. Article 130s(2) contains a derogation from this. Unanimity in Council, following a proposal from the Commission and consultation of the Parliament and the Economic and Social Committee, is required for the adoption of provisions primarily of a fiscal nature; and

---

[36] Case C–155/91 *Commission* v. *Council*, judgment of 17 Mar. 1993; Case C–187/93 *Parliament* v. *Council* [1994] ECR I–2857.

measures concerning town and country planning, land use with the exception of waste management, and measures of a general nature, and management of water resources; and measures significantly affecting a Member State's choice between different energy sources and the general structure of its energy supply. It is open to the Council to transfer any of these matters to the realms of QMV, but unanimity is required to achieve this. According to Article 130s(3), in other areas general action programmes setting out priority objectives to be attained are to be adopted by Council action in accordance with the Article 189b procedure and after consulting the Economic and Social Committee. The measures necessary for the implementation of the programmes are to be adopted by the Council acting under either Article 130s(1) or (2) as appropriate. So the Parliament is able to veto general action programmes but not, acting on its own, specific implementing measures.

This would create a complicated enough pattern on its own. The exasperating realization that in addition the demarcations between these different procedures are far from clear suggests that Article 130s may serve as a microcosm of the intransparency that disfigures the EC legislative process.

The Demarcation between the Three Pillars of the Union

Of even wider significance in the Treaty on European Union are the problems of demarcation between the three pillars. It has been explained that the law which emerges from the two distinct mechanisms is not merely subject to different procedures; it is a fundamentally different type of law, EC or international, treated quite differently by national courts. So choosing the correct pillar for dealing with a particular subject matter is critically important. Yet is it really possible coherently to judge whether, for example, action to develop co-operation in policing, which has a direct impact on individual rights of movement within the Union, is properly achieved within the EC Treaty or a matter falling within the non-EC EU pillar on co-operation in justice and home affairs? Are not both involved? Comparable problems arise in placing action in the field of, for example, trade sanctions within the correct Union 'pillar', EC or common foreign and security policy. Litigation to choose between pillars may be predicted. Member States and/or Community institutions have incentives to pursue such a path in order to protect their distinct prerogatives under the different pillars.

The European Court would find itself required to resolve such disputes. The European Court's jurisdiction over matters falling within the two non-EC EU pillars is almost entirely excluded by Article L of the Treaty of European Union.[37] Presumably, however, the Court is competent to rule on the limits of its own jurisdiction by policing the boundaries of the EC pillar. Article B of the Treaty on European Union refers to maintenance in full of the *acquis communautaire*. Article M provides that the EC Treaty is *not* amended by the two new intergovernmental pillars. The former Article falls outwith the scope of the Court's jurisdiction, but Article M is within it. The Court is therefore competent to rule whether or not measures are properly treated as EC matters. It is competent to rule against attempts by the Member States to nibble away at the existing EC edifice.

Severe potential tensions lurk beneath such litigation. As explained, placing subject matter into the 'correct' pillar has fundamental institutional and constitutional consequences. Acute problems could arise were the European Court to adopt a more expansive view of the scope of EC competence than one, some, or all of the Member States judged appropriate. Perhaps, in such circumstances, the Member States would receive just desserts for their failure at Maastricht adequately to demarcate the three pillars. But there could develop damaging tensions between the Court and the institutions of the Member States, both political and judicial. The peril that disregard of Court rulings would follow cannot be discounted. Opposition is capable of jeopardizing the whole basis of the Community. It might, therefore, emerge that the Court will tread delicately at the margins of EC competence. It is plausible that its characteristic predilection for presiding over dynamic growth in Community competence will diminish, especially where it touches matters of common foreign and security policy and justice and home affairs. Further attention is devoted to these questions of competence in Chapters 5 and 6.[38]

Reorganizing Legal Bases

The eccentric combination of several voting rules and varying

---

[37] 30 above.   [38] 166, 210 below.

institutional roles lacks constitutional respectability. It is hard to persuade the Citizen of the Union of the dignity and honour of that status when the Union itself is a structure lacking in transparency and architectural elegance. It should also be appreciated that some fundamental political and economic questions about the development of an appropriate regulatory structure for the Community lie hidden beneath these opaque institutional and constitutional issues.

The lesson of these conundrums is that a rigorous reshaping of the Union constitution is urgently required. The Court in *Commission* v. *Council*[39] expressed unease about the rationality of some of the choices it is called upon to make: 'Under the system governing Community powers, the powers of the institutions and the conditions on their exercise derive from various specific provisions of the Treaty, and the differences between those provisions, particularly as regards the involvement of the European Parliament, are not always based on consistent criteria.' In *Titanium Dioxide*[40] the Court's deliberate maximization of the Parliament's role shows that it is perfectly well aware of the institutional in-fighting that generates these constitutional cases.

In part, the issue of identfication of legal base is no more than the consequence of the Treaty pattern of attributed competences. The Community must show competence and it does that by pinning down a legal base, to which is attached a particular legislative procedure. But it does not follow from this that there should be such an absence of coherence between different but related legal bases and their attached legislative procedures. The Treaty needs cleaning up with a single legislative procedure; or, at least, there should be developed transparent reasons for use of different procedures and a coherent categorization of bases under the different procedures. Furthermore, as the Court implied in its *Titanium Dioxide* ruling, that base or bases must involve a democratic input that is at least no weaker than is presently provided.[41]

There is also much to be said in favour of an overhaul of the type of laws that the Community may make. A Declaration attached to

---

[39] Case 242/87 [1989] ECR 1425, para. 13.
[40] Case C–300/89, n. 35 above.
[41] Cf para. 20 of the Court's judgment in Case C–300/89, *ibid*.

the Treaty on European Union stipulates that the 1996 Conference 'will examine to what extent it might be possible to review the classification of Community acts with a view to establishing an appropriate hierarchy between the different categories of act'. It might be possible, for example, to set up a structure that would place key policy making instruments at the top of the hierarchy and more technical matters lower down the list. Different legislative procedures would be attached to different levels in the hierarchy in a clear and transparent manner. It is submitted that considerations of effective democratic control dictate that 'laws' at the top of this scale ought to attract full Council and Parliament involvement.

FURTHER READING

BOGDANOR, V., and WOODCOCK, G., 'The European Community and Sovereignty' (1991) 44 *Parliamentary Affairs* 481.

BOYCE, B., 'The Democratic Deficit of the European Community' (1993) 46 *Parliamentary Affairs* 458.

BRADLEY, K., 'The European Court and the Legal Basis of Community Legislation' (1988) 13 *ELRev.* 379.

BRITTAN, SIR LEON, *Europe: The Europe We Need* (London: Hamish Hamilton, 1994).

BUNYAN, T., (ed.), *Statewatching the New Europe: A Handbook on the European State* (London: Statewatch, 1993).

CROSBY, S., 'The Single Market and the Rule of Law' (1991) 16 *ELRev.* 451.

EMILIOU, N., 'Opening Pandora's Box: The Legal Basis of Community Measures before the Court of Justice' (1994) 19 *ELRev.* 488.

HARLOW, C., 'A Community of Interests? Making the Most of European Law' (1992) 55 *MLR* 331.

FINK-HOOIJER, F., 'The Common Foreign and Security Policy of the European Union' (1994) 5 *EJIL* 173.

FIJNAUT, C., 'International Policing in Europe: Present and Future' (1994) 19 *ELRev.* 595.

LENAERTS, K., 'Some Reflections on the Separation of Powers in the European Community' (1991) 28 *CMLRev.* 11.

MÜLLER-GRAFF, P.-C., 'The Legal Bases of the Third Pillar and its Position in the Framework of the Union Treaty' (1994) 31 *CMLRev.* 493.

PIRIS, J.-C., 'After Maastricht, are the Community Institutions more Efficacious, more Democratic and more Transparent?' (1994) 19 *ELRev.* 449.

RAWORTH, P., 'A Timid Step Forwards: Maastricht and the Democratisation of the European Community' (1994) 19 *ELRev.* 16.

RESS, G., 'Democratic Decision-Making in the European Union and the Role of the European Parliament' in Curtin, D., and Heukels T., (eds.), *Institutional Dynamics of European Integration* (Dordrecht: Martinus Nijhoff, 1994).

WEILER, J., 'The Community System: The Dual Character of Supranationalism' (1981) 1 *YEL* 273.

4

Characteristics of Union Law

The Nature and Purpose of Direct Effect

The principle of direct effect is a key component of the *sui generis* constitutional nature of EC law. 'Direct effect' refers to the capacity of EC law to be invoked by individuals in proceedings before national courts. Were direct effect not to form part of the constitutional pattern of the EC legal order, the dynamic development and practical significance of EC law would be immeasurably reduced.

Yet direct effect is nowhere identified in the Treaty as a characteristic of EC law. Article 189 states that direct applicability is a characteristic of regulations. Direct applicability secures the status of regulations as law within the domestic legal orders of Member States once made in conformity with the Community procedures. But direct effect, unmentioned in the Treaty, is of far wider significance than direct applicability. Direct effect is a characteristic capable of attaching to any type of Community legal provision. A provision, once declared by the European Court to be directly effective, confers legally enforceable rights on individuals within the national system. Directly effective rights offer a source of protection against action in violation of EC law.

The establishment and development of direct effect as a cornerstone of the EC Constitution represents a classic case study in the European Court's teleological approach to legal interpretation. Direct effect might not have been found in the explicit terms of the Treaty, but the European Court regarded its task as dictated by the need to secure the realization of the overall objectives of the Treaty. And, reasoned the Court, without direct effect those objectives could not effectively be achieved. The Court established the place of direct effect in the Community legal order at a relatively early stage in the Community's evolution.

In 1963, in *Van Gend en Loos*, the Court observed that:

The objective of the EEC Treaty, which is to establish a common market, the functioning of which is of direct concern to interested parties in the Community, implies that this Treaty is more than an agreement which merely creates mutual obligations between the contracting states . . . the Community constitutes a new legal order of international law for the benefit of which the states have limited their sovereign rights, albeit within limited fields, and the subjects of which comprise not only Member States but also their nationals. Independently of the legislation of the Member States, Community law therefore not only imposes obligations on individuals but is also intended to confer on them rights which become part of their legal heritage.[1]

The notion of direct effect places the enforcement of Community law on two levels: the so-called notion of *dual vigilance*. State violations of EC law may be challenged not only at the 'supranational' level, whereby the Commission may initiate Article 169 proceedings leading to a European Court ruling against a defaulting state, *but also* at national level by an individual able to rely on the principle of direct effect. For the individual prejudiced by a violation of Community law it is possible both to alert the Commission to the alleged infraction and seek to persuade it to investigate and also to make use of national procedures in order to secure protection and/or redress through his or her own efforts. For the alleged violator of Community law, there is the risk of challenge both by the Commission and by private initiative.[2] By virtue of dual vigilance, it should be extremely difficult for a state to violate Community law with impunity.

Direct effect makes a significant contribution to the effective policing of EC law. Enforcement is not simply a transnational matter, subject to the inevitable vicissitudes of at least some quasi-political negotiation between Commission and defaulting Member State. Enforcement is also driven by individuals with a direct interest in the vindication of their Community law rights. Enforcement is placed in the hands of national judges. This is of the highest importance. The temptation that may exist to disregard a court that can, however mendaciously, be presented to national electors as 'foreign' does not exist when it is the courts of the state

---

[1] Case 26/62 *NV Algemene Transport en Expeditie Onderneming Van Gend en Loos* v. *Nederlandse Administratie der Belastingen* [1963] ECR 1.

[2] Art. 170 allows Member State to bring Member State before the Court; this is very rare.

in question that are the authors of a ruling of violation requiring remedial action. In political terms, once the European Court has acquired loyal allies in the national courts it has done much to quell practical possibilities for state revolt against Community law.

This in turn sustains more than the bare fact of effective policing of Community rules. Direct effect is a constitutional device that shapes a system within which Community law and national law are not distinct layers, but instead part of the same mixture. Community law becomes national law and is enforced through the national system. National courts become Community courts and enforce Community rules.

Direct effect also serves as a means of creating individual rights. This is vividly part of the Court's message in *Van Gend en Loos*. Its declaration that Community law is intended to confer on individuals 'rights which become part of their legal heritage' was a central part of the Court's mission to make real its own commitment, loosely based on its perception of the Treaty's commitments, to construct a legal order that went far beyond the regulation of relations between states. Mancini and Keeling comment that:

As a result of *Van Gend en Loos*, the unique feature of Community law is its ability to impinge directly on the lives of individuals, who are declared to be the 'subjects' of the new legal order, entitled as such to invoke rights 'which become part of their legal heritage'. The effect of *Van Gend en Loos* was to take Community law out of the hands of politicians and bureaucrats and to give it to the people. Of all the Court's democratising achievements none can rank so highly in practical terms.[3]

The Preconditions for Direct Effect

The conditions necessary to find a provision of Community law to be directly effective have typically been identified as resting on the character of the provision as sufficiently precise, unambiguous, and unconditional. In fact such detailed requirements seem no more than specific manifestations of an overall requirement of 'justiciability'. Advocate General van Gerven's extended Opinion of 27 October 1993 in *H. Banks & Co Ltd* v. *British Coal Corporation* preceded a very short and unambitious judgment by

---

[3] 'Democracy and the European Court of Justice' (1994) 57 *MLR* 175, 183.

the Court in the case, but there is no reason to doubt the accuracy of the Advocate General's comments about:

the eminently practical nature of the direct effect test: provided and in so far as a provision of Community law is sufficiently operational in itself to be applied by a court it has direct effect. The clarity, precision, unconditional nature, completion or perfectness of the rule and its lack of dependence on discretionary implementing measures are in that respect merely aspects of one and the same characteristic feature which that rule must exhibit, namely it must be capable of being applied by a court to a specific case.[4]

It is this core characteristic of justiciability that distinguishes direct effect from direct applicability. The latter describes how regulations become law at national level. But the issue of whether something is law and whether it confers legally enforceable rights on individuals is not the same thing at all. The notion of direct effect concerns individual rights that a national court is required to protect.

A comparison between two basic Treaty provisions, Articles 6 and 2 EC, suffices to provide a flavour of the margin between provisions that are directly effective and those that lack the characteristics necessary for enforcement by a national court. Article 6 EC is perfectly uncompromising. It forbids discrimination on grounds of nationality within the scope of application of the Treaty.[5] That rule is capable of application by a national court. It is directly effective. An individual who is the subject of such unlawful discrimination is able to resort to national court proceedings in order to secure judicial protection. By contrast, Article 2 EC's reference to the inclusion among the Community's tasks of, *inter alia*, the promotion of harmonious and balanced development of economic activities and a high level of employment are 'law' in the sense that they represent binding Treaty obligations, but they do not create legally enforceable rights capable of vindication by individuals. They are not justiciable standards. They lack direct effect and could not be deployed by an an individual before a national court to challenge state or Community practices alleged to violate these norms.

A large number of the core substantive legal provisions of the Treaty have long ago been held by the European Court to attract

---

[4] Case C–128/92 [1994] ECR I–1209.   [5] Ch. 2, 39 above.

direct effect. This has placed significant power in the hands of private parties to drive forward the processes of market integration and market regulation envisaged by the Treaty. Article 12, which applies a prohibition on customs duties to trade between Member States, is clear and unconditional and was ruled directly effective in *Van Gend en Loos* itself, a ruling arising out of a challenge at national level to obstruction of the importation of ureaformaldehyde from Germany into the Netherlands. Article 30 (free movement of goods), Articles 48 and 52 (free movement of workers), and Article 59 (free movement of services) have all been found to have direct effect. Traders have seized the opportunity to use Community law at national level to secure the demolition of obstructive trading rules. In social spheres, too, the direct effect of Community law has empowered individuals to assert rights in opposition to national practices that are incompatible with Community law.

Treaty provisions are capable of direct effect against the state, commonly referred to as 'vertical direct effect'; and some are capable of direct effect against private parties too—the notion of horizontal direct effect. In *Walrave and Koch* v. *Union Cycliste Internationale* the Court ruled that Articles 48 and 59 may control employment practices in the private sector.[6] The competition rules (Articles 85, 86) are 'horizontally' directly effective. It was plainly essential to develop a competition policy directed at the private sector lest the deregulation of markets that flowed from abolition of state impediments to trade should simply breed ever more pernicious cross-border cartels and monopolies. This is reflected in the Treaty rules on competition. These are enforced by the Commission, exercising powers conferred on it by regulations, but they are also capable of direct effect. Firms may be the subject of challenge at national level where they infringe EC competition policy.

Rather more remarkably, in *Defrenne* v. *Sabena* the Court ruled that both vertical and horizontal direct effect attaches to Article 119 EC, which provides for pay equality between the sexes. The Court observed that 'The principle of equal pay contained in Article 119 is mandatory in nature, the prohibition on discrimination between men and women applies not only to the action of

[6] Case 36/74 [1974] ECR 1405.

public authorities, but also extends to all agreements which are intended to regulate paid labour collectively, as well as to contracts between individuals'.[7] This is in tune with the coherent development of an equality policy, which ought to span both public and private sectors to avoid discrepancies resulting from haphazard variations between states in the scope of public sector employment. However, the Court's ruling was delivered in spite of the wording of Article 119 which is explicitly addressed only to Member States. The effect of the ruling is to enhance policing opportunities, and also to enhance individual rights. The finding that Article 119 is horizontally directly effective extends the equality obligation into the private sphere and simply bypasses the impediment caused by the risk that the Member States will not take seriously the Treaty obligation imposed upon them to ensure equality. Although the retrospective effect of the *Defrenne* ruling itself was limited by the Court in the interests of legal certainty, there has been ample opportunity since for actions at national level by private parties designed to root out discriminatory practices incompatible with EC law.

It will be discovered below that the Court has not pursued the logic of dynamic enforcement through horizontal direct effect to its fullest extent, because it has declined to find *directives* capable of horizontal direct effect where states have defaulted on their implementation obligation. However, under Article 119 of the Treaty, private and public employers alike are vulnerable to challenge before national courts where they pay women less than men.

SUPREMACY

Direct effect is allied to supremacy in the creation and consolidation of the practical foundations of the Community legal order. The two key notions were introduced by the Court in separate rulings, but both were delivered in the early 1960s and both plainly reflected connected perceptions of the relationship between Community and national law that the Court wished to establish.

What *Van Gend en Loos* is to direct effect, *Costa* v. *ENEL* is to supremacy.[8] The European Court took the opportunity to deduce

---

[7] Case 43/75 [1976] ECR 455.   [8] Case 6/64 [1964] ECR 585.

the existence of the vital constitutional principle of supremacy from the objectives of the Treaty, despite the absence in the Treaty of any explicit mention of the supremacy of Community law. This reflects the 'teleological' approach consistently favoured by the European Court. The Court ruled that:

The integration into the laws of each Member State of provisions which derive from the Community, and more generally the terms and spirit of the Treaty, make it impossible for the states, as a corollary, to accord precedence to a unilateral and subsequent measure over a legal system accepted by them on a basis of reciprocity. Such a measure cannot therefore be inconsistent with that legal system. The executive force of Community law cannot vary from one state to another in deference to subsequent domestic laws, without jeopardising the attainment of the objectives of the Treaty.

It follows from all these observations that the law stemming from the Treaty, an independent source of law, could not, because of its special and original nature, be overridden by domestic legal provisions, however framed, without being deprived of its character as Community law and without the legal basis of the Community itself being called into question.

Supremacy, like direct effect, finds no place in the Treaty. The Treaty fails to offer any explicit statement on the priorities that should resolve a conflict between national law and Community law. Supremacy, like direct effect, has been deduced by the Court as a necessary, albeit inexplicit, element in the practical realization of the objectives of the Treaty.

In *Simmenthal* the Court made clear its view of the implications of supremacy.[9] An Italian court questioned whether it, a lower court, was supposed to disapply national law in the light of Community law or whether it should leave such a major step to a national constitutional court. The European Court was uncompromising: 'every national court must, in a case within its jurisdiction, apply Community law in its entirety and protect rights which the latter confers on individuals and must accordingly set aside any provision of national law which may conflict with it, whether prior or subsequent to the Community rule'. This is a powerful assertion of the permeation of EC law deep into the national legal order. Community law is viewed as an integral part

[9] Case 106/77 *Amministrazione delle Finanze dello Stato* v. *Simmenthal SpA* [1978] ECR 629.

of the legal order applicable in the territory of each of the Member States. Reluctance to apply EC law in the light of domestic jurisdictional restrictions was also swept aside by the Court in *Factortame*,[10] a preliminary ruling on questions referred by the House of Lords. This was a case in which the national court had been called on to suspend the application of a domestic statute until such time as it was conclusively determined whether or not that statute was compatible with EC law. The House of Lords had found that as a matter of English law it was unable to grant such interim protection, but it made an Article 177 reference seeking interpretative assistance on its obligations under EC law. The European Court ruled that 'Community law must be interpreted as meaning that a national court which, in a case before it concerning Community law, considers that the sole obstacle which precludes it from granting interim relief is a rule of national law must set aside that rule.'

The Court has regularly confirmed its view that the EC system can retain its integrity only provided that Community law holds supremacy over conflicting national law. Without that basic hierarchy, disintegration would follow. Even one breach in the dam would be too many, for one fissure would inevitably breed others. For that reason, the Court has not shied away from deciding that Community law overrides even national constitutionally protected rights. *Internationale Handelsgesellschaft*[11] was a preliminary ruling requested by a Frankfurt court dealing with an alleged clash between Community rules and certain provisions of the German constitution. The Court repeated its view, first expressed in *Costa* v. *ENEL*, that the fundamental nature of the Community legal edifice would be undermined were it to be admitted that Community law could be overridden by domestic legal provisions. Therefore the Court ruled that 'the validity of a Community measure or its effect within a Member State cannot be affected by allegations that it runs counter to either fundamental rights as formulated by the constitution of that state or the principles of a national constitutional structure.'

---

[10] Case C–213/89 *R.* v. *Secretary of State for Transport, ex parte Factortame Ltd.* [1990] ECR I–2433.
[11] Case 11/70 *Internationale Handelsgesellschaft* v. *Einfuhr- und Vorratstelle für Getreide und Futtermittel* [1970] ECR 1125.

There is an impeccable logic to the Court's insistence that Community law would be robbed of its uniform meaning and effect were testing against national constitutional standards to be permitted. However, the sensitivity of this ruling can quickly be appreciated. Even fundamental human rights are subordinated to EC law rights which, after all, largely originate in the economic sphere. This is not comforting. It raises the policy question whether the pursuit of a uniform structure of Community law is *so* important that even national constitutional choices must be set aside. It also raises the pragmatic question whether such extremism would be likely to attract loyal support from the national courts which are asked to apply the rules of the Community legal order.

The European Court has stuck to its view that EC law must override even national constitutionally protected rights. It has, however, shown itself aware of constraints of both policy and pragmatism that condition the maintenance of the supremacy of Community law. In *Internationale Handelsgesellschaft* itself, it embarked on a course of assembling at Community level, within the fabric of Community law, the legal protection under the general principles of a constitutional nature that it had ruled capable of being overridden at national level by EC law. The Court in *Internationale Handelsgesellschaft* followed its assertion of the supremacy of Community law over national law in all circumstances by adding that 'respect for fundamental rights forms an integral part of the general principles of law protected by the Court of Justice'. It was not prepared to permit national courts to check Community law against national constitutional standards but it accepted that 'the protection of such rights, whilst inspired by the constitutional traditions common to the Member States, must be ensured within the framework of the structure and objectives of the Community'.

Part of the Court's motivation for creating a Community notion of fundamental rights protection was conceivably to encourage national courts to digest the full implications of supremacy and therefore to protect its jurisprudence from rejection at national level. That has proved largely successful. But there is more to the Court's activism. This is an aspect of the replenishment and extension of the Community legal order. The Court was responding to the Community institutions' growing capacity to affect fundamental rights to an extent unforeseen at the time the Treaty of Rome was agreed in 1957. In developing fundamental rights protection, it was treating the Community legal order as a dynamic structure capable of responding to novel problems.

These rulings testify to an unswerving determination in the European Court to maintain the principle of supremacy. *Costa* v. *ENEL* is itself a strong statement. The European Court has made it very clear that it meant what it said in its statement that the 'force of Community law cannot vary from one state to another in deference to subsequent domestic laws, without jeopardising the attainment of the objectives of the Treaty' by insisting in *Internationale Handelsgesellschaft* that there is no mixing of hierarchies. Even the most minor piece of technical Community legislation ranks above the most cherished national constitution norm. In *Simmenthal* it asserted that the disapplication of conflicting national law is a task for every court or tribunal throughout the national system.

An empirical examination of the national readiness to receive and apply these principles lies far beyond the scope of this book. Unsurprisingly, there has been some incomprehension and some resistance at national level, as judges have attempted to fit the European Court's view of the nature of the Community legal order into the constitutional frameworks with which they are familiar. In general, however, there has been a remarkable level of fidelity among national judiciaries to the practical legal implications of Community membership evolved by the European Court. Of course as a matter of Community law the obligation of national judges to do what they are told by the Luxembourg judges can be located in Article 5 EC and the jurisprudence explained above. But the fact that national judges have a largely creditable record of faithful conformity to 'foreign law' in which even today many lack formal training is one of the more remarkable aspects in the evolution of the Community system. The active support of national courts supplies a major reason why EC law has moved away from international law towards a law that, in its relationship with national law, has much in common with the internal law of a federal state.

The system operates successfully only because national courts respond actively and positively to their role as Community courts. Without that support, the system would fall apart. The European

Court, indeed the Community system generally, is dependent on the acceptance of Community method and rules by national officials. National courts will not follow the European Court come what may. In states with entrenched constitutional rights it is easy to see that there will be resistance to Community rules overriding such rights. This reached the surface in the fundamental rights case law. There, the European Court had to show at least some sensitivity towards national concerns, and it adjusted the pattern of Community law. The maintenance of the Community legal system and, *a fortiori*, its development is not feasible if the European Court chooses an ever more adventurous course without reference to its national lieutenants. The European Court has a responsibility to build the legal order in a spirit of co-operation, explicit and implied, with national courts. This does not mean that the European Court must abandon courage when faced with disquiet at national level about the course that Community law is taking, but it means that it is required—legally and pragmatically—to engage in a type of indirect dialogue with its national courts about the evolution of the system. In the final section of Chapter 6, this process is further assessed.

UNIFORMITY VIA ARTICLE 177

The function of Article 177

The European Court in *Rheinmühlen-Düsseldorf* v. *Einfuhr- und Vorratsstelle für Getreide und Futtermittel*[12] declared that 'Article 177 is essential for the preservation of the Community character of the law established by the Treaty and has the object of ensuring that in all circumstances the law is the same in all states of the Community.'

Article 177 creates a channel for co-operation between the European Court and national courts or tribunals that are called on to apply Community law. The rationale for the Article 177 preliminary reference procedure may be simply stated as the need for a common legal order for a common market. Article 177 exists to secure uniformity of interpretation of Community law. Its story is mostly one of expanding jurisdiction designed to maximize the Court's supervisory role.

[12] Case 166/73 [1974] ECR 33.

The full text of Article 177 is as follows

The Court of Justice shall have jurisdiction to give preliminary rulings concerning:

(a) the interpretation of this Treaty;
(b) the validity and interpretation of acts of the institutions of the Community;
(c) the interpretation of the statutes or bodies established by an act of the Council, where those statutes so provide.

Where such a question is raised before any court or tribunal of a Member State, that court or tribunal may, if it considers that a decision on the question is necessary to enable it to give judgment, request the Court of Justice to give a ruling thereon.

Where any such question is raised in a case pending before a court or tribunal of a Member State, against whose decisions there is no judicial remedy under national law, that court or tribunal shall bring the matter before the Court of Justice.

Article 177 allows the European Court an input into litigation at national level in which points of Community law are raised. Without a system allowing, and in some circumstances requiring, national courts to seek the European Court's view on a relevant point of Community law, Community law would have a different meaning and effect state by state. This would tend to undermine the objectives of the Treaty. Article 177 cannot guarantee absolute uniformity state by state, given background diversity between legal traditions, but it establishes a structure for getting close thereto.

The importance of Article 177 can be gauged by considering how the Community legal order would have developed without it. There would be no uniformity. And, perhaps equally important, the Court would not have been fed the rich diet of cases by national courts which has provided it with the opportunity to invigorate substantive and constitutional EC law.

Article 177 envisages a co-operative judicial relationship. It is not an appellate procedure. The European Court does not decide cases under Article 177. It rules on points of Community law referred to it by national courts. It is then for that national court to apply the duly interpreted point of Community law to the case at hand. This allows national systems to be drawn into the Community structure. It is a potentially fertile relationship that avoids the rigid separation of a hierarchical appellate structure. It displays the best aspects of subsidiarity.

One consequence of the division of judicial function under Article 177 is that referral lies in the hands of the national court before which a point of Community law has been raised. There is no enforceable right vested in an individual to take a case initiated at national level to Luxembourg. Admittedly, national courts *should* refer cases in some circumstances. This is true of highest courts within Article 177(3), subject to the *CILFIT* gloss considered at page 114 below; and it is true of courts before which the validity, rather than the interpretation, of Community acts is raised.[13] However, it seems that supervision in the event of any infraction lies in the hands of the Commission, which has never felt able to bring a Member State before the European Court under Article 169 alleging a Treaty violation attributable to that state's courts. The individual is dependent on his or her ability to persuade the national court of the need to refer.

Discretionary Referral

Paragraph 2 of Article 177 establishes a power of discretionary referral. As a matter of policy the European Court has adopted an 'open-door' approach to referrals. As early as *Van Gend en Loos* and *Costa* v. *ENEL* the European Court was confronted by submissions that it lacked jurisdiction to provide rulings on questions that it had been asked. In both cases it was complained that the Court was poised to answers questions that had no bearing on the dispute at national level. In both instances the Court rejected the objections. The Court declared itself unprepared to criticize the grounds and purpose of the request for interpretation. This, as the Court was naturally fully aware in accepting the reference, then provided it with the opportunity to deliver its own vital rulings on the nature of the Community legal order. Article 177 rulings have legal effect beyond the case in which they are delivered and the procedure has provided the Court with the opportunity to establish many of the ground rules of Community law.

In *Irish Creamery Milk Suppliers* v. *Ireland*[14] the Court

---

[13] Case 314/85 *Foto Frost* v. *Hauptzollamt Lübeck-Ost* [1987] ECR 4199, Ch. 6, n. 23 below. [14] Case 36/80 [1981] ECR 735.

commented that 'Article 177 of the Treaty establishes a framework for close co-operation between the national courts and the Court of Justice based on the assignment to each of different functions. The second paragraph of that article makes it clear that it is for the national court to decide at what stage in the proceedings it is appropriate for that court to refer a question to the Court of Justice for a preliminary ruling.'

The Court's normal approach is to regard the national court as having the job of deciding whether a reference would be useful and itself as answering questions of Community law put to it. On that division of function, the Court will not interest itself in the background to the reference nor in whether the court was wise to refer. In *Irish Creamery Milk Suppliers* v. *Ireland* the Court continued 'The national court's decision must be dictated by considerations of procedural organisation and efficency to be weighed by that court.' Accordingly, any court or tribunal may make the reference, even a court at a relatively low level in the national system and even where the proceedings are of an interlocutory nature.

In practice it is a myth to regard the division of function under Article 177 as so clear cut. The notion that in the resolution of any legal dispute 'interpretation' may be placed in a separate compartment from 'application' is jurisprudentially hard to defend. The European Court roams around the borderline. On occasion it provides preliminary rulings couched in the abstract, but rather frequently its explanation is fully informed by the fact pattern of the case and is in effect a ruling decisive to the outcome of the litigation at national level. For example, in *Walter Rau* v. *de Smedt*[15] it was asked for a ruling on the interpretation of Article 30 against the background of a dispute about the compatibility with that provision of a Belgian law requiring margarine to be packed in cubes. The Court's 'interpretation' was that 'legislation prohibiting the marketing of margarine . . . where each block or its external packaging does not have a particular shape, for example the shape of a cube, in circumstances in which the consumer may be protected and informed by means which hinder the free movement of goods to a lesser degree constitutes a measure [within the scope of Article 30].' Doubtless the referring court would not have been

[15] Case 261/81 [1982] ECR 3961.

easily persuaded that this was mere interpretation! There is a risk that there might arise constitutional sensitivity at national level where the Court trespasses on the function reserved to national courts under Article 177. It might also be that some national courts will be relieved to have the matter effectively resolved for them. The saga of the EC law-inspired challenge to English and Welsh restrictions on Sunday trading concluded with the European Court's declaration that 'Article 30 is to be interpreted as meaning that the prohibition which it lays down does not apply to national legislation prohibiting retailers from opening their premises on Sundays'. In all but form, this decided the case. But, as is discussed in Chapter 8, that conclusive resolution of the matter was a relief to both domestic courts and European Court.[16]

The strict constitutional analysis that the European Court does not formally invalidate national laws has some merit in ensuring the successful operation of the system. If a national law is to be ruled inapplicable, that is done by the national court or tribunal that originally requested the preliminary ruling. The possibility of political defiance at national level is reduced by placing the order-making power in the hands of a national court that cannot readily be resisted by a public authority. The European Court is sheltered from the risk that national political authorities may judge defiance feasible or even attractive for domestic political reasons. This in turn re-emphasizes the critical importance that the European Court must attach to maintaining the support of the national courts.

On occasion the Court has perceived itself as being lured into deciding points of Community law that were not in truth the subject of a dispute between the parties. In *Foglia* v. *Novello*[17] the open-door policy under Article 177 was suspended. The Court explained its refusal to provide a ruling on points of Community law in the following terms: 'the parties to the main action are concerned to obtain a ruling that the French tax system is invalid for liqueur wines by the expedient of proceedings before an Italian court between two private individuals who are in agreement as to the result to be attained and who have inserted a clause in their contract in order to induce the Italian court to give a ruling on the point'. The Court considered the litigants' ploy artificial; there was

---

[16] 265 below.   [17] Case 104/79 [1980] ECR 745.

no genuine dispute. The Court decided it had no jurisdiction to give a ruling on the questions asked. It repeated its refusal when the matter was re-referred to it a short time later.[18] This was, in the Court's view, a procedural device arranged by the parties to induce the Court to rule on aspects of Community law which did not correspond to an objective requirement inherent in the resolution of a dispute.

The parties may indeed have been in agreement about the intended outcome, but that did not detract from the fact that there was a point at issue which depended on an interpretation of Community law. Perhaps the Court was shy of proceedings that could lead to the courts of one Member State declaring the laws of another Member State to be incompatible with Community law. But in *Walter Rau* v. *de Smedt*, mentioned above, the Court delivered a preliminary ruling that made quite plain its view that Belgian laws were incompatible with Community law in a reference made to it by a German court. Moreover there was suspicion in *Walter Rau* that the dispute was fictitious, yet the Court commented rather grandly that 'there is nothing in the file on the case which provides grounds for doubting that the dispute is genuine'.

It is left rather unclear how hard the Court will look for doubts about the genuine nature of a dispute between the parties. The *Foglia* v. *Novello* pair of cases shows that it is at least possible that the Court might look beyond its theoretical role as interpreter of points of Community law that a national court has judged appropriate for referral. However, instances of inquiry into the 'legitimacy' of the dispute are the exception not the rule in the Court's practice.

More recently, further occasions on which the Court has let slip its normal receptivity suggest a sharper desire to concentrate on effective problem-solving in disputes of immediate relevance. In *Meilicke* v. *ADV/ORGA F. A. Meyer AG*[19] the Court was asked a range of questions that were relevant to alleged collisions between German and Community law in the company law field, but which did not seem to be germane to any dispute. The Court declined to be drawn. In *Telemarsicabruzzo* v. *Circostel*[20] the Court refused

---

[18] Case 244/80 *Foglia* v. *Novello (No 2)* [1981] ECR 3045.
[19] Case C–83/91 [1992] ECR I–4872.
[20] Cases C–320–322/90, judgment of 26 Jan. 1993.

to give a ruling in circumstances where it had been provided with inadequate background information about the litigation. Such inadequacy would formally impede the Court from giving an appropriately targeted interpretation of relevant Community law, but one may equally surmise that the Court was exasperated at the poor performance of the national court, which obstructed the European Court from playing a useful role in dispute-resolution.

These rulings should probably be taken in part as manifestations of the Court's unease about its ever increasing workload. Understandably it has no desire to decide pointless cases. It also wishes to direct a hint at national courts that they should take seriously their duties as Community courts by deciding cases themselves and, where reference is unavoidable, by formulating references with care. The Court is torn. It wants to trust national courts with the task of applying Community law. This would serve as a sign of the maturity and depth of penetration of Community law into the national legal order. But the Court must even yet fear conscious or unconscious mishandling of Community rules by national judges that will damage the integrity of the Community legal order that it has worked so hard to sustain. Moreover, the Court cannot adopt an unduly obstructive attitude to referrals at a time when the inexpert courts of the new Member States are in need of the direction provided by the preliminary reference procedure.

Obligatory Referral

Paragraph 3 of Article 177 provides for an obligatory reference. The obligation is placed on a court from the decision of which there is no appeal. The motivation for the third paragraph is that a case should not be able to run its course at national level without the possibility of a reference of relevant questions being made. In this sense, paragraph 3 is a backstop to paragraph 2, and it allows a litigant to pursue a matter at national level secure in the knowledge that an obligation to refer will eventually be triggered.

In practice the pattern of obligatory referral is rather less clear-cut. In *CILFIT* the Court refined the scope of the obligation imposed on national courts:[21]

---

[21] Case 283/81 [1982] ECR 3415.

the third paragraph of Article 177 . . . is to be interpreted as meaning that a court or tribunal against whose decisions there is no judicial remedy under national law is required, where a question of Community law is raised before it, to comply with its obligation to bring the matter before the Court of Justice, unless it has established that the question raised is irrelevant or that the Community provision in question has already been interpreted by the Court or that the correct application of Community law is so obvious as to leave no scope for any reasonable doubt.

These three qualifications leave some room for flexibility in the national court's assessment of the need for referral. The third, in particular, the *acte clair* doctrine, provides the national court with the opportunity itself to inquire into the interpretation of Community law and to keep the matter out of the hands of the European Court even where the point is new. The *CILFIT* guidelines have much to commend them as a means of adding a filter mechanism to the huge weight of cases that could be referred to Luxembourg; they also recognize and encourage the development of expertise in EC law at national level. However, caution is appropriate. If a filter system is to exist, it would be better placed at Community rather than national level, so there is one filter rather than multiple filters with different types of mesh. Moreover *acte clair* itself is close to internally contradictory as a doctrine within Article 177. The preliminary reference procedure exists to ensure European Court overview of the development of Community law and to preclude divergent approaches emerging in different states, yet *acte clair* assumes a capacity at national level to judge what is appropriate in the development of Community law. How can the intent of Article 177 be sustained if any court other than the European Court decides what is 'clear'? In *CILFIT* the European Court was clearly sensitive to the risks of loosening Article 177(3), and it counselled caution in declining to refer: 'The existence of such a possibility must be assessed in the light of the specific characteristics of Community law, the particular difficulties to which its interpretation gives rise and the risk of divergences in judicial decisions within the Community.'

Article 177 in general and the *CILFIT* criteria in particular serve as an object lesson in the problematic evolution of the Community legal order, built on both national and Community courts. A constructive relationship is essential, yet its development is awkward and requires adjustment over time. Pragmatic considerations of sheer workload may force a decreasingly frequent invocation of the Article 177 procedure even if that means that legal uniformity is to some extent compromised. National courts faced with increasing delay in receipt of rulings will doubtless make their own choices about whether to employ Article 177.[22] One possible route for managing this change lies in loosening the *CILFIT* criteria to reduce referrals even from highest courts. A distinct and more radical approach would be to limit or even to abolish the power of lower courts to make preliminary references. This proposal has found favour with the German government.

It is possible to view a reduction in the role of Article 177 in the positive light that it reflects the depth of penetration of Community law into the national legal order and the comfort felt nowadays by national courts in acting as Community courts. But it may prove damaging where national courts cannot adequately take on that task. More sinister, such initiatives may form an attempt to undermine the integration of national and Community legal orders and, especially, to rein in the European Court, by introducing a kind of local remedies rule more appropriate to international-law regimes that do not envisage the sophisticated protection of individual rights at national level that is the hallmark of the evolution of the EC system.

The contrast with international law is a suitable point to conclude examination of the key EC law constitutional principles of, first, direct effect; secondly, supremacy; and, thirdly, preliminary references. None of these principles as such attaches to the law of the Union outside the EC. The law that emerges from the two non-EC EU intergovernmental pillars may come to develop its own distinctive characteristics, but at present it would appear to be, in essence, traditional international law. In some states, it may exert an impact at national level comparable to supremacy and direct effect, depending on national constitutional attitudes to international law. But it will not be EC law.

---

[22] They may also come to make their choices based on unwillingness to provide the European Court with the opportunity to pursue an activist jurisprudence; see Ch. 6, 210 on the general shaping of a *modus vivendi* between national courts and European Court.

EFFECTIVENESS AS AN OVERARCHING PRINCIPLE

The EC law principles of direct effect and supremacy combine to ensure that the role of national authorities, including courts, is of great significance in the practical application of the Community legal order. Much Community law is applied at national level. The absence of any Community police force or army means that the support of national bodies for Community law is indispensable. Put simply, the Community legal order would be instantly deprived of its *sui generis* characteristics were support from national institutions, including, and perhaps especially, courts, to be withdrawn.

Article 5 provides a basic statement of the obligations undertaken by Member States towards the Community. It provides:

Member States shall take all appropriate measures, whether general or particular, to ensure fulfilment of the obligations arising out of this Treaty or resulting from action taken by the institutions of the Community. They shall facilitate the achievement of the Community's tasks. They shall abstain from any measure which could jeopardise the attainment of the objectives of the Treaty.

Article 5 has already been introduced in Chapter 2 as a key factor in the spread of EC competence. Member States are subject to duties of 'Community solidarity'. The obligations envisaged in Article 5 embrace all levels within the state structure. Article 5 binds central government but also local government. It covers both the political and the judicial institutions of the state.

Contrary to its explicit wording Article 5 binds Community as well as national institutions to the duty of Community solidarity. The Court's ruling in *Zwartveld*, examined in Chapter 2,[23] directed the Commission to offer support to a national official even in the absence of an explicit Treaty provision within which the envisaged Community/national relationship could be placed. This is a further aspect of the Court's determination to establish a comprehensive pattern of Community solidarity.

Article 5 has an increasingly pivotal role in the Court's process of constitutionalization. The scope of the obligation is ever wider and catches an expanding number of entities; the nature of the obligation is being made more concrete. This is especially marked

[23] Case C–2/Imm. [1990] ECR I–3365, 47 above.

in the realm of the obligations of national courts to protect Community law rights. Direct effect and supremacy lay down the constitutional framework within which individuals may rely on Community law at national level to defeat conflicting provisions of national law. Article 5 obliges national courts effectively to protect those rights. The European Court has ever more boldly pinned down precisely what this requires in the shape of specific remedies. In this way direct effect and supremacy have become part of a bolder and more ambitious notion of 'effectiveness'. Effectiveness encapsulates the notion that Community law shall confer rights plus remedies that make real the practical enjoyment of those rights.

The Court's activism in this area makes great demands on national judges. They are required to become Community judges. Practical and policy considerations dictate an urgent need to regard national courts as an adequate method of securing the decentralized enforcement of EC law, but it is questionable how much the European Court can now confidently entrust to the national courts. Is the European Court astutely moulding a legal framework within which it presides over a body of national judges acting as its loyal lieutenants; or is it asking far too much of national judges who are neither able nor willing to take on the task of applying Community law? *CILFIT* raised questions in relation to the operational scope of the obligation imposed on highest courts to make preliminary references.[24] Parallel questions arise in relation to the practical workability of the idea that Article 5 contains a notion of effectiveness enforced at national level. In assessing the remarkable sophistication of the European Court's stance, study of which follows below, it is wise to bear in mind, as far as possible, the question whether its approach is truly being carried over into the national legal order. *If not*, then the Court's stance may be worse than useless; it may be damaging, for it will present a picture of an effective, operational, and uniform legal order which does not exist.

Under the second limb of 'dual vigilance',[25] a national court is expected to apply the substantive rules of Community law buttressed by the key constitutional principles of supremacy and direct effect. It must uphold EC-derived rights, if necessary

[24] See text at n. 21 ff. above.   [25] 98 above.

refusing to apply conflicting national law. In this sense, national courts are converted into EC courts. But there is no general EC legislation on matters such as time limits or quantum of damages in national proceedings. It would therefore seem that EC law rights are vindicated through national legal procedures and the grant of remedies recognized by national law.

This notion of 'national procedural autonomy' was the Court's starting point in *Comet* v. *Produktschap voor Siergewassen*.[26] The Court ruled that:

In application of the principle of cooperation laid down in Article 5 of the Treaty, the national courts are entrusted with ensuring the legal protection conferred on individuals by the direct effect of the provisions of Community law . . . it is for the national legal order of each Member State to designate the competent courts and to lay down the procedural rules for proceedings designed to ensure the protection of the rights which individuals acquire through the direct effect of Community law.

There were qualifications. The procedures made available for the vindication of Community law rights must not be less favourable than those governing the same right of action on an internal matter; and it must not be impossible in practice to exercise rights which the national courts have a duty to protect. The second of these qualifications has been significantly extended in a manner which has steadily eroded national procedural autonomy. The requirement in *Comet* that it should not be 'impossible in practice' to vindicate EC law rights at national level has been recast in more positive terms to require that EC law rights be 'effectively protected' at national level. That obligation to provide 'effective protection' is imposed on national courts by Article 5 of the Treaty and forms an increasingly vigorous complement to the principle of direct effect. EC law exerts a growing influence over what is required of national remedies in support of EC law rights.

In *Factortame*, Spanish fishing interests alleged that they were the victims of unlawful discrimination on grounds of nationality contained in the United Kingdom's Merchant Shipping Act 1988. The applicants complained to the Commission, which was eventually persuaded to pursue the matter. The United Kingdom was subsequently found by the European Court to be in violation

---

[26] Case 45/76 [1976] ECR 2043.

of its Treaty obligations.[27] The applicants had also initiated proceedings before the English courts. The High Court sought clarification of the substantive issues by making an Article 177 preliminary reference. Eventually, the European Court replied in terms which confirmed the incompatibility of the legislation with Community law.[28]

All this took time. The key issue for Factortame was the status of the Act *pending* the eventual ruling of the European Court. It sought interim relief against its application. The House of Lords ruled that, as a matter of English law, no such order could be made. Factortame then submitted that, as a matter of Community law, the national court must have competence to award interim protection. This submission was based on the notion that Community law demanded that national systems provide effective protection and that the unavailability of interim relief fell short of this standard of effectiveness. It pointed out that if it was denied interim protection and was accordingly to be driven out of business, a final ruling in its favour would be useless.

The House of Lords referred to the European Court questions relating to the duties of national courts in such circumstances. The applicants' arguments were largely accepted by the European Court.[29] As already mentioned above,[30] the Court ruled that 'Community law must be interpreted as meaning that a national court which, in a case before it concerning Community law, considers that the sole obstacle which precludes it from granting interim relief is a rule of national law must set aside that rule.' The House of Lords responded by granting the relief sought by Factortame.[31] Lord Bridge took pains to adopt a receptive approach; 'there is nothing in any way novel in according supremacy to rules of Community law in those areas to which they apply and to insist that, in the protection of rights under Community law, national courts must not be inhibited by rules of national law from granting interim relief in appropriate cases is no more than a logical recognition of that supremacy'.

---

[27] Case 246/89R *Commission* v. *UK* [1989] ECR 3125; Case C–246/89 *Commission* v. *UK* [1991] ECR I–4585.
[28] Case C–221/89 [1991] ECR I–3905.
[29] Case C–213/89 [1990] ECR I–2433.
[30] See text at n. 10 above.
[31] [1991] 1 All ER 70, [1990] 3 CMLR 375.

These comments underplay the novelty of the decision which, although a logical consequence of decisions on supremacy such as *Costa* v. *ENEL*[32] and *Simmenthal*,[33] did represent at least a small step further by insisting on the competence of national courts to protect EC law rights even where they have not yet been shown conclusively to exist.[34] Furthermore, the European Court has attracted some criticism for treating the questions referred as if they arose from a case where national courts faced an obstruction to their jurisdiction to offer effective protection, rather than a basic want of jurisdiction to provide that effective protection.[35]

Nonetheless, the *Factortame* ruling emphasizes the Court's commitment to building the principle of effectiveness. This requires national courts to adjust, perhaps even to create, national procedures in order to secure effective protection of EC law rights. Article 5 'effectiveness' is a manifestation of the capacity of principles of Community law to intrude into what might initially appear to be areas of reserved national competence.

The principle of effectiveness is increasingly assuming concrete shape as a structure of remedies which must be offered as a Community law minimum within the national system. It is a major feature of the interpenetration of the Community and national legal orders. Factortame proceeded to claim damages before the English courts to compensate it for the loss suffered as a result of the illegal restriction of its fishing activities. Questions were referred to the European Court, where the case was joined with a reference from Germany dealing with comparable issues of state liability for violation of Community law.[36] A ruling by the Court is awaited. The possibility that a state may be liable in damages to an individual for violation of Community law has already been accepted by the European Court in 1991 in *Francovich* v. *Italian State*. The importance of this ruling justifies a separate treatment in its particular context, the non-implementation of directives. This forms the subject matter of the following section.

---

[32] Case 6/64, n. 8 above.   [33] Case 106/77, n. 9 above.

[34] An aspect tackled rather more satisfyingly in Tesauro AG's Opinion.

[35] Discussion by Barav, 'Omnipotent Courts' in D. Curtin and T. Heukels (eds.), *Institutional Dynamics of European Integration* (Dordrecht: Martinus Nijhoff, 1994).

[36] *Firma Brasseries du Pecheur* v. *Germany* and *R.* v. *Secretary of State for Transport, ex parte Factortame Ltd (Factortame 3)*, Joined Cases C–46 & 48/93 [1993] OJ C94/13.

A SPECIAL CASE—THE EFFECTIVE ENFORCEMENT
OF DIRECTIVES

The Vertical Direct Effect of Directives

The special case of directives provides a good illustration of the
obligations which are imposed on national judges to develop EC
law as a result of the effectiveness principle drawn from Article 5.
Under the terms of Article 189 of the Treaty, directives appear
plainly incapable of direct effect, for their impact is conditional on
national implementing measures.[37] In unimplemented guise they
seem inapt for judicial enforcement.

However, the system envisaged by Article 189 breaks down
where Member States fail to comply with their obligation to
implement. Such a violation wlll attract the interest of the
Commission and may lead to Article 169 proceedings against
the state. Such proceedings take time. In the interim the directive
is left dangling uselessly. The European Court has tried to find
more powerful antidotes to the poison of state infraction. Failure
to implement is, after all, a serious matter. It deprives individuals
of their intended rights—and directives in the EC structure are a
major source of social policy, broadly construed. It also allows
states to 'get away' with non-implementation, which may yield
competitive advantages and give incentives to other states to
follow suit. In that direction lies fragmentation of the Community
system. Therefore the Court has tried to draw on the apparently
unavailable second limb of dual vigilance, and it has tried to
endow directives with effect before national courts in the hands of
individuals even in the absence of the implementing legislation
envisaged and required by Article 189.

This does not simply go beyond the text of Article 189 of the
Treaty; it contradicts it. The Court's defenders might retort that its
case law on the direct effect of directives, and related concepts, is
no more than an attempt to uphold the Treaty, which declares that
directives shall be binding. After all, disgruntled states can avoid
the problems of uncertainty caused by the direct effect of
directives and related concepts simply by implementing the
directive. Judge Mancini has commented that the Court's work in
extending to directives the attribute of direct effect is 'essentially

[37] 81 above.

concerned with assuring respect for the rule of law'.[38] In this sense this area of law stands for the process of constitutionalization that flows from Articles 5 and 164, and that, where necessary, overrules the detailed wording of Article 189.

The European Court held in *Ratti* that directives are capable of invocation before national courts.[39] The individual acting in conformity with a directive left unimplemented after its deadline by Italy was able to rely on the directive to defeat a prosecution under an Italian law that should have been repealed. The process of legal reasoning in the Court's ruling in *Ratti* discloses two distinct rationales for finding directives capable of direct effect (or, at least, effects analogous thereto). At paragraph 20 the Court observed that 'It would be incompatible with the binding effect which Article 189 ascribes to directives to exclude on principle the possibility of the obligations imposed by them being relied on by persons concerned.' At paragraph 22 the Court stated that 'A Member State which has not adopted the implementing measures required by the directive in the prescribed periods may not rely, as against individuals, on its own failure to perform the obligations which the directive entails'. These are distinct rationales. The former may be summarized as effectiveness, the latter as estoppel. The former is potentially much broader, as becomes immediately apparent when one considers the scope for enforcing unimplemented directives at national level against *private* parties. The former rationale, effectiveness, would support this extension; the latter, estoppel, would not.

The ruling in favour of the direct effect of directives was not well received by some national judges. Some of the severest tests for the smooth operation of the Community system in line with the demands of the European Court have been confronted in the sphere of the direct effect of directives. In France the Conseil d'Etat in *Minister of the Interior* v. *Daniel Cohn-Bendit*[40] ruled against the ability of an individual to rely on a directive at national level. It cited Article 189 as demonstrating that national authorities retain the power to decide on the form to be given to the implementation of directives and to fix the means appropriate

---

[38] 'The Making of a Constitution for Europe' (1989) 26 *CMLRev.* 595, 602.
[39] Case 148/78 *Pubblico Ministero* v. *Ratti* [1979] ECR 1629.
[40] [1980] 1 CMLR 543.

to cause them to produce effects in national law. This meant that directives 'may not be invoked by the nationals of such states in support of an action brought against an individual administrative act'. The Conseil d'Etat ignored the European Court's explanations of why, nonetheless, Community law governing the application of directives at national level should move beyond the textual limitations of the Treaty once a state has violated the Treaty by making no choice at all on how to fulfil its obligation to implement.

The European Court cannot feasibly adopt an air of lofty disdain at such recalcitrance. It can have little confidence that the Commission will pursue Article 169 proceedings against a Member State in respect of the unlawful conduct of its courts. This is possible in theory, but its sensitivity in the light of the independence of the judiciary common to all Member States makes it barely conceivable in practice. No such action has ever reached the European Court. It is for the European Court itself to judge how best to restore the imbalance; and the task may be pressing, for national courts do not apply Community law solely with reference to their vertical relationships with the European Court but also to their horizontal relationships with other national courts. Intransigence in one Member State may spill over into other Member States. The German Federal Finance Court declared that it was not prepared to enforce unimplemented directives and commented explicitly on its awareness of the stance of the French courts.[41] Cross-fertilization of ideas between national courts offers one of the most stimulating routes for strengthening the European influence on national law, but where the ideas that are transmitted run counter to the European Court's jurisprudence, the integrity of the whole Community legal order is jeopardized.

The European Court decided in *Marshall* v. *Southampton and South West Hampshire Area Health Authority (Teaching)* to declare a significant limitation on the scope of the direct effect of an unimplemented directive.[42] Directives are capable only of vertical direct effect, that is direct effect against the state, and not of horizontal direct effect, that is, against a private individual. It opted for the estoppel rationale offered in *Ratti* in commenting

[41] [1982] 1 CMLR 527.   [42] Case 152/84 [1986] ECR 723.

that 'it is necessary to prevent the state from taking advantage of its own failure to comply with Community law'. This prompts vertical direct effect as a means of vigorous policing. But the Court quietly abandoned the effectiveness argument, which would focus on enhancing intended protection under a directive and which would have suggested direct effect consequent on non-implementation in all circumstances (subject to justiciability of the relevant terms).

The *Marshall* limitation on the scope of the direct effect of directives was purportedly based explicitly on the terms of Article 189 which binds Member States only. There are, admittedly, some good reasons for indirectly penalizing the defaulting state by opening the avenue of direct effect against it, whereas, by contrast, a private party is not at fault for non-implementation and may have a legitimate expectation of avoiding the direct application of a Community measure of which it may be wholly unaware. Yet that involves a preference for the legitimate expectations of the party against which the law drawn from the directive is supposed to be enforceable over the interests of the intended beneficiary. The fact that the Court in *Marshall* dropped the effectiveness rationale in relation to the horizontal direct effect of directives makes it difficult to avoid the suspicion that misgivings emanating from national courts affected the Court's approach.

Probably the Court was concerned to strike an indirect package deal with national courts. It showed itself prepared in *Marshall* to recognize the limits of the Treaty and of its own interpretative role; it set a boundary to the spread of direct effect. In return for such clarification and such restraint it hoped to gain from the national courts an acceptance of that more restricted notion of direct effect—against the state alone. The tactic seems largely to have worked.

The Public/Private Anomaly in the Scope of Application of Unimplemented Directives

Nevertheless *Marshall* creates a public/private anomaly. For the employee wishing to rely on an unimplemented directive conferring employment rights, success is ensured only where the employer is the state. The consumer wishing to rely on an unimplemented directive will succeed only where the supplier is the state.

The Court has interpreted the 'state' broadly in this context. The applicant in *Marshall* was able to rely on the Equal Treatment directive, wrongly left unimplemented by the United Kingdom, because she was employed by a local health authority which was for these purposes a 'state' body. The municipal authorities in Milan rebuilt their football stadium at which the opening match of the 1990 World Cup was played in breach of EC directives governing procurement by public authorities. They were open to challenge at national level in proceedings based on the direct effect of the directive.[43] The breadth of the notion of the state is even more vividly captured by the ruling in *Foster* v. *British Gas*, where the Court ruled that unimplemented directives may be enforced against entities possessing 'special powers beyond those which result from the normal rules applicable in relations between individuals.'[44] Even private firms may be caught where they hold the privileged position envisaged by the Court.

However, beyond the reach of the public sector, even broadly defined, directives are incapable of direct effect. This damages the effectiveness of Community law. Directives, properly made, lose their binding character in the private sector where a state fails to observe its implementation obligation. The Community system is left at one remove from the national legal order because of state violation. This contradicts the notion of interpenetration of the two legal orders. Control of the defaulting state via Article 169 lacks immediacy and, worse, seems symbolic of an international rather than national law flavour.

The European Court has endeavoured to sidestep the limitations on the direct effect of directives that it itself imposed in *Marshall*. It has found a means of insisting on the interpenetration of the two legal orders, by securing the enforcement of unimplemented Community directives, not as such, but via the medium of national law. It has focussed on Article 5 EC. It finds in that provision an obligation cast on national courts to achieve the objectives of a directive where the political organs of the state have failed to meet their obligation of implementation.

In *Von Colson and Kamann* v. *Land Nordrhein–Westfalen*[45] the Court insisted on:

[43] Case 103/88 *Fratelli Costazo* v. *Milano* [1989] ECR 1839.
[44] Case C–188/89 [1990] ECR I–3133.
[45] Case 14/83 [1984] ECR 1891.

the Member States' obligation arising from a directive to achieve the result envisaged by the directive and their duty under Article 5 of the Treaty to take all appropriate measures, whether general or particular, to ensure the fulfilment of that obligation, is binding on all the authorities of Member States including . . . the courts. It follows that . . . national courts are required to interpret their national law in the light of the wording and the purpose of the directive in order to achieve the result referred to in the third paragraph of Article 189.

In *Marleasing* v. *La Comercial Internacional de Alimentacion*[46] a yet firmer approach was taken in expressing the national courts' obligation to pursue 'indirect effect': 'in applying national law, whether the provisions concerned pre-date or post-date the directive, the national court asked to interpret national law is bound to do so in every way possible . . . to achieve the results envisaged by it'. If national courts act in the manner envisaged then the absence of horizontal direct effect of directives will lose its practical significance. Community directives will be absorbed into the national legal order even in the absence of implementation.

The disadvantage of this approach lies in its mediation of Community law through national law. A lot is asked of national judges. Will they do it? Should they do it? The precise scope of the 'interpretation' obligation is hazy and one would expect a resistance on the part of national judges asked simply to re-write national laws in order to do justice to the state's Community law obligations. National courts are naturally sensitive to the dividing line between their interpretative function and the process of law reform that is the province of the legislator. Fixing the precise location of that separation of powers is a notoriously imprecise science. But once it *is* reached, the limits of the unimplemented directive's influence in the national system via judicial application are reached. The probability that different judges in different states and, plausibly, within the same state will hold different levels of receptiveness to the subtle demands of interpretation contributes an additional factor to the impression that the ingenuity displayed by the Court in *Von Colson* and *Marleasing* may in practice lead to an alarming level of confusion among the national judiciary.

[46] Case C–106/89 [1990] ECR I–4135.

State Liability for Failure to Implement Directives

This morass could largely be circumvented if the states implemented directives properly. This perception suggests a need for fiercer sanctions. The European Court has responded. In *Andrea Francovich and others* v. *Italian State*[47] the Court opened up the possibility of the defaulting state being liable to an individual in *damages*.

The litigation was generated by Italy's failure to implement Directive 80/987. The directive required states to set up guarantee funds to compensate workers in the event of employer insolvency. Italian workers, of whom Francovich was one, found themselves denied the protection envisaged by the directive, but not transposed into Italian law. The question arose whether the workers could claim directly effective rights against the Italian State. They pursued the matter before the Italian courts and a preliminary reference was made to Luxembourg. The Court first examined the identifiability of intended beneficiaries of the guarantee. There was here sufficient precision and unconditionality to allow a national court to determine whether or not an individual was an intended beneficiary under the directive, even in the absence of implementing national legislation. The next element was the identifiability of the content of the guarantee. The directive envisaged payment of outstanding claims to remuneration for a period prior to a date chosen by the implementing Member States from one of three possibilities. States also have the option of fixing a ceiling for the payment and are empowered to take measures necessary to avoid abuse of the scheme. This range of options available to the Member States might seem inconsistent with the notion of unconditional individual rights that is the key to direct effect, but the European Court was not deterred. It identified the content of the guarantee as payment of outstanding claims. The availability of options did not detract from the precise and unconditional character of that intended result. Critically the Court was able to identify the minimum guarantee envisaged by the directive based on the choice that would entail the lightest burden for the guarantee institution. The fact that a range of options exists does not deprive a measure of direct effect where it

[47] Cases C–6, 9/90 [1991] ECR I–5357.

is possible to determine the minimum that the state must in any event put in place. This still left the problem of the optional ceiling and the possibility of taking action to forestall abuse. The Court was brutal. This was a situation in which the state had failed to implement a directive. That state could not rely on options that it could have but has failed to implement in order to frustrate an individual's claim to a directly effective right. Yet the Court was still forced to conclude that the directive was incapable of direct effect. The Court conceded that the wide margin of discretion granted to the Member State with regard to the structuring of the body liable for the guarantee was fatal to direct effect. Precision and unconditionality was lacking at that final point.

But the Court had still not abandoned its mission to secure the protection of individual rights. In fact its determination took it beyond direct effect as a means under Community law of protecting the individual against state interference. Even though the workers could not claim directly effective rights, the Court in *Francovich* held that Community law recognized the liability of the state to compensate them for loss suffered as a result of their being deprived of the protection it was intended they should receive under the directive. Both individual rights and effective policing in EC law were carried beyond the principle of direct effect. The Court explicitly placed its ruling in *Francovich* in the context of its previous decisions in *Simmenthal*[48] and *Factortame*.[49] This was part of the development of a constitutional structure that would ensure that Community law offered effective protection at national level. It declared that 'The full effectiveness of Community rules would be impaired and the protection of the rights which they grant would be weakened if individuals were unable to obtain redress when their rights are infringed by a breach of Community law for which a Member State can be held responsible.'[50] It added that 'the principle whereby a state must be liable for loss and damage caused to individuals as a result of breaches of Community law for which the state can be held responsible is inherent in the system of the Treaty.'

To these statements of principle in favour of state liability, the

[48] Case 106/77, n. 9 above.   [49] Case C–213/89, n. 10 above.
[50] Para. 33 of the ruling.

European Court then added specific criteria that govern the existence of liability. It identified three elements:

The first of those conditions is that the result prescribed by the directive should entail the grant of rights to individuals. The second condition is that it should be possible to identify the content of those rights on the basis of the provisions of the directive. Finally, the third condition is the existence of a causal link between the breach of the state's obligation and the loss and damage suffered by the injured parties.

This, then, is a remedy shaped in detail by the European Court, stimulated by the policy of effectiveness. Having established these three conditions, the Court then added that the state must make reparation for the consequences of the damage caused 'on the basis of the rules of national law on liability' and that 'it is for the internal legal order of each Member State to designate the competent courts and lay down the detailed procedural rules'.

The most striking aspect of the Court's dedication to the construction of a concrete right/remedy inspired by 'effectiveness' under Article 5 is that the *Francovich* ruling transcends the limitations of direct effect. Individuals obtain rights that may be enforced at national level independently of the justiciablity criterion that conditions the scope of directly effective rights. The Court will doubtless find itself asked by national courts to devote energy to clarifying the scope of the liability in damages introduced by *Francovich*. Its first opportunity found it in cautious mood. *H. Banks & Co Ltd* v. *British Coal Corporation*[51] involved a damages claim brought before the English courts arising out of practices alleged to infringe the competition rules of the European Coal and Steel Community. The Court considered that the Commission held sole jurisdiction to find infringements of the relevant provisions and that therefore an action for damages before a national court could not be pursued in the absence of a Commission finding of violation. The Court's ruling is carefully confined to the Coal and Steel Treaty. Its brevity and caution contrast with the extended and thorough Opinion on the role of national courts in providing legal protection delivered by Advocate General van Gerven. He came to quite different conclusions from the Court on the nature of the relevant ECSC provisions. Receptive to the extension of *Francovich* liability, he

[51] Case C–128/92 [1994] ECR I–1209.

130 LAW AND INTEGRATION IN THE EUROPEAN UNION

examined it as part of the general system of Community law and
favoured its application to violations by private parties. The mood
of the Court will be further tested in the two Article 177 references
from Germany and the United Kingdom, mentioned above.[52]
Both concern violation of primary Treaty Articles.[53]

A major question that requires elaboration is that of fault. The
imposition of a requirement of culpability offers the European
Court one method of circumscribing the scope of *Francovich*
liability, should it so wish. The European Court might choose to
draw a distinction between instances of genuine belief in
compliance, whether with the Treaty generally or with the
implementation of a directive in particular, and more obviously
culpable plain violations. The latter category would include a case
such as *Francovich*, where Italy had left the directive wholly
unimplemented and where that default had already been recorded
in a judgment of the European Court delivered in the context of
Article 169 proceedings.[54]

The breadth of the comments of the Court in the *Francovich*
ruling, referred to above, suggest that it was motivated to expand,
rather than restrict, its willingness to deepen the impact of the
Community system at national level. It did not attach requirements of fault. It mentioned the fact that a violation had already
been established by the European Court, but it did not choose to
emphasize the significance of this finding as a condition of liability.
Nor did the Court place any temporal restriction on the application of the ruling.[55] The Court's mood may now have changed.

*The Sustained Rejection of the Horizontal Direct Effect of
Directives*

In *Paula Faccini Dori* v. *Recreb*[56] the Court was asked to
reconsider its ruling in *Marshall* that directives were incapable
of horizontal direct effect. The Court had, since the caution of
Marshall, seemed intent on curtailing the anomalies it had created
on the public/private borderline. The state was interpreted

[52] N. 36 above.
[53] Art. 30 and Arts. 5, 7 (now 6), 52, and 221 respectively.
[54] Case 22/87 *Commission* v. *Italy* [1989] ECR 143, referred to in the ruling in
Francovich. [55] Contrast Case 43/75, n. 7 above.
[56] Case C–91/92 [1994] ECR I–3325.

broadly. National courts were called on to interpret national law in the light of unimplemented directives in *all* cases, not simply those involving the state. Would the Court accept an invitation to bring coherence to the law by holding directives capable of direct effect in all circumstances, once the deadline for implementation had passed?

In 1993 and 1994, three Advocates General had delivered Opinions in favour of overruling *Marshall* and acknowledging the horizontal direct effect of directives; van Gerven,[57] Jacobs,[58] and, in *Faccini Dori* v. *Recreb* itself, Lenz. Advocate General Lenz insisted that the Citizen of the Union was entitled to expect equality before the law and observed that, in the absence of horizontal direct effect, such equality was compromised by state failure to implement directives. Advocate General Jacobs thought that the effectiveness principle militated against drawing distinctions based on the status of a defendant. All three believed that the pursuit of coherence in the Community legal order dictated acceptance of the horizontal direct effect of directives.

Only in the third of these cases, *Faccini Dori* v. *Recreb*, was the European Court unable to avoid addressing the issue directly. It *refused* to overrule *Marshall*. It maintained that directives are incapable of horizontal direct effect.

The ruling insists that the Community is not competent to enact by directive obligations for individuals with immediate effects. This, according to Article 189 of the Treaty, is the role of the regulation. Absence of horizontal direct effect does not leave the intended beneficiary of rights under an unimplemented directive without a remedy. The Court referred both to the obligation of interpretation under *Marleasing* and to the scope for claiming compensation from the state under *Francovich*. But it ruled out the possibility of a private individual relying directly on an unimplemented directive in national proceedings against another private individual.

The Court's retreat to the text of the Treaty as a rationale for its ruling in *Dori* runs counter to the trend of thirty years of case law

---

[57] Case C–271/91 *Marshall* v. *Southampton and South-West Hampshire Area Health Authority* (*Marshall (2)*), Opinion of 26 Jan. 1993, [1993] 3 CMLR 293.
[58] Case C–316/93 *Vaneetveld* v. *SA Le Foyer*, Opinion of 27 Jan. 1994, [1994] ECR I–763.

in this area. The development of direct effect has been inspired by the desire to improve the enforcement of Community law against defaulting Member States and by the imperative of converting EC law into a system based on individual protection. In the Court's hands, these constitutional motivations, drawn from Articles 5 and 164 EC but operating at the level of general principle, have consistently trumped the literal text of the Treaty. But this did not occur in *Dori*.

Dori may have more in common with *Marshall* than its confirmation that directives are incapable of horizontal direct effect. *Marshall* was an indirect response to the unwillingness of some national courts to back up the European Court's stance on the direct effect of directives.[59] *Dori*, too, seems to be motivated by fear in the European Court about the extent to which a bold judgment would have been absorbed at national level. The 'message' to the European Court emanates not from the specific context of the direct effect of directives, but from the general area of the limits of Community competence. The German Federal Constitutional Court's approval of German ratification of the Treaty on European Union is examined more fully in Chapter 6. To anticipate some of that discussion, that court's ruling includes implicit warnings that European Court rulings that are perceived to go beyond mere Treaty interpretation into the realms of Treaty revision will not be binding. This is part of a general expression of constitutional sensitivity to the limits of Community competence. The ruling in *Dori* gives the impression of a European Court astute to the need to make explicit its own awareness of the textual limitations of the Treaty.

Maintaining a co-operative balance is not a new task for the Court. It has always been obliged to maintain an awareness that the successful and credible operation of the Community legal order depends on willing and active co-operation by national courts. The European Court has always held an appreciation of the art of the possible. Its construction of a legal system for the Community based on direct effect and supremacy, principles absent from the Treaty yet now widely accepted at national level, represents a remarkable achievement.

---

[59] 123 above.

FURTHER READING

ARNULL, A., Note on *Telemarsicabbrruzzo* (1994) 31 *CMLRev.* 377.
BARAV, A., 'Omnipotent Courts' in Curtin, D., and Heukels, T., (eds.), *Institutional Dynamics of European Integration* (Dordrecht: Martinus Nijhoff, 1994.
—— and GREEN, N., 'Damages in the National Courts for Breach of Community law' (1986) 6 *YEL* 55.
BRIDGE, J., 'Procedural Aspects of the Enforcement of EC Law through the Legal Systems of the Member States' (1984) 9 *ELRev.* 28.
BRONCKERS, M., 'Private Enforcement of 1992: Do Trade and Industry Stand a Chance against Member States? (1989) 26 *CMLRev.* 513.
CARANTA, R., 'Government Liability after Francovich' [1993] 52 *CLJ* 272.
COPPEL, J., and O'NEILL, A., 'The European Court of Justice: Taking Rights Seriously? (1992) 29 *CMLRev.* 669.
CRAIG, P., '*Francovich*, Remedies and the Scope of Damages Liability' (1993) 109 *LQR* 595.
CURTIN, D., 'The Decentralised Enforcement of Community Law Rights. Judicial Snakes and Ladders' in O'Keeffe, D., and Curtin, D., (eds.), *Constitutional Adjudication in European Community and National Law* (Dublin: Butterworths (Ireland), 1992).
—— and MORTELMANS, K., 'Application and Enforcement of Community Law by the Member States: Actors in Search of a Third Generation Script' in Curtin, D., and Heukels, T., (eds.), *Institutional Dynamics of European Integration* (Dordrecht: Martinus Nijhoff, 1994).
DE BURCA, G., 'Giving Effect to European Community directives' (1992) 55 *MLR* 215.
EMMERT, F., and PEREIRA DE AZEVEDO, C., 'L'effet horizontal des directives. La jurisprudence de la CJCE, un bateau ivre?' (1993) 29 *RTDE* 503.
GRAVELLS, N., 'Effective Protection of Community Law Rights: Temporary Disapplication of an Act of Parliament' [1991] *Pub. L* 180.
LENAERTS, K., 'Form and Substance of the Preliminary Rulings Procedure' in Curtin, D., and Heukels, T., (eds.), *Institutional Dynamics of European Integration* (Dordrecht: Martinus Nijhoff, 1994).
LEWIS, C., and MOORE, S., 'Duties, directives and Damages in European Community Law' [1993] *Pub. L* 151.
MAHER, I., 'National Courts as European Community Courts' (1994) 14 *Legal Studies* 226.
MANCINI, G. F., and KEELING, D., 'From CILFIT to ERT: The Constitutional Challenge Facing the European Court' (1991) 11 *YEL* 1.
OLIVER, P., 'Enforcing Community Rights in English Courts' (1987) 50 *MLR* 881.

PLAZA MARTIN, C., 'Furthering the Effectiveness of EC directives and the Judicial Protection of Individual Rights Thereunder' (1994) 43 *ICLQ* 26.

PRECHAL, S., 'Remedies after *Marshall*' (1990) 27 *CMLRev.* 451.

Ross, M., 'Beyond *Francovich*' (1993) 56 *MLR* 55.

SLYNN, LORD 'Looking at European Community Texts' (1993) 14/1 *Statute LRev.* 12.

SNYDER, F., 'The Effectiveness of European Community Law: Institutions, Processes, Tools and Techniques' (1993) 56 *MLR* 19.

STEINER, J., 'Coming to Terms with EEC Directives' (1990) 106 *LQR* 144.

STEINER, J., 'From Direct Effects to *Francovich*' (1993) 18 *ELRev.* 3.

SZYSZCZAK, E., 'Sovereignty: Crisis, Compliance, Confusion, Complacency?' (1990) 15 *ELRev.* 480.

TESAURO, G., 'The Effectiveness of Judicial Protection and Co-operation between the Court of Justice and the National Courts' (1993) 13 *YEL* 1.

USHER, J., *European Community Law and National Law: the Irreversible Transfer?* (London: Allen and Unwin, 1981), especially Chapter 2.

VAN GERVEN, W., 'Non-contractual Liability of Member States, Community Institutions and Individuals for Breaches of Community Law with a View to a Common Law for Europe' (1994) 1 *Maastricht J of Euro. and Comp. L* 6.

—— 'The Horizontal Effect of Directive Provisions Revisited: The Reality of Catchwords' in Curtin, D., and Heukels, T., (eds.), *Institutional Dynamics of European Integration* (Dordrecht: Martinus Nijhoff, 1994).

Voss, R., 'The National Perception of the Court of First Instance and the European Court of Justice' (1993) 30 *CMLRev.* 1119.

WEATHERILL, S., 'National Remedies and Equal Access to Public Procurement' (1990) 10 *YEL* 243.

WEILER, J., 'Journey to an Unknown Destination: A Retrospective and Prospective of the European Court of Justice in the Arena of Political Integration' (1993) 31 *JCMS* 417.

—— and LOCKHART, N., ' "Taking Rights Seriously" Seriously: The European Court and its Fundamental Rights Jurisprudence—Parts I, II' (1995) 32 *CMLRev.* 51, 579.

WINTER, J., 'Direct Applicability and Direct Effect: Two Distinct and Different Concepts in Community Law' (1972) 9 *CMLRev.* 425.

5

Pre-emption and Competence in a Wider and Deeper Union

The material that is the subject of discussion in Chapter 4 can be summarized as the legal framework within which is pursued the objective of securing a common meaning for Community law throughout the territory. Uniformity in the meaning of the law is part of the constitutional glue that holds the Community together. The subject matter of this Chapter can be summarized as an inquiry into the extent to which substantive Community law envisages uniformity. The notion of a common law for a common market has an initially appealing ring, yet it may suggest a homogeneity that is unrealistic and, perhaps, unnecessary in the modern Community of fifteen different states. The pressing issues that are examined in this Chapter focus on the extent to which a basic common framework that is undoubtedly needed for the Community to function effectively may accommodate divergence without tumbling towards disintegration.

THE EFFECT OF LEGISLATION

In Chapter 2, it was explained that the influence of the principles of Community law, both those found in the Treaty and those developed by the Court, is limited to the scope of application of the Treaty, but that in practice this limitation is treated with remarkable and occasionally erratic flexibility. It was also explained in Chapter 2 that the scope of Community legislative competence is in principle limited by the Treaty, but that it, too, has been wielded in practice in a strikingly creative fashion. However, Chapter 2 addressed only the scope of Community competence. It did not consider in any depth the consequences for national competence in areas shown to fall within the scope of Community competence.

The doctrine of the supremacy of Community law is clearly

relevant to this inquiry. In areas within Community competence, questions of conflict between Community and national rules are resolved in favour of the former. So national law within the field of application of Community law is subject to the general principles of the Community legal order. In such circumstances both Community and national rules affect the relevant subject matter. Both share competence although, in the event of conflict, Community law prevails.

In some areas, the impact of Community law runs deeper. The Community has acquired *exclusive* competence in some sectors. Where the Community's competence is of an exclusive nature, national competence is excluded. There is no question of allowing national action subject to conformity with the principles of Community law; national action is simply impermissible within the fields in which the Community is exclusively competent. Member States must keep out of such fields. In federal jargon, which is admittedly not the norm in the European Court, state powers are 'pre-empted' and the Community has 'occupied the field'. Just as Community trespass on to areas in which the Member States are exclusively competent is in principle invalid, so too state trespass on to the Community's exclusive preserve is invalid.

Nothing in the Treaty provides an explicit list of the areas in which the Community is exclusively competent. This mirrors the absence of any list of areas in which the Member States are exclusively competent. It has been for the European Court to build up a list of spheres of Community exclusivity. These are realms of dynamic development and acute sensitivity. Given the inexplicit Treaty background, the list cannot be considered closed, but the Court has in recent years been conspicuously reluctant to expand spheres of exclusive Community competence.

The Court's rulings in favour of exclusive Community competence have been especially striking in the area of the Community's external relations. The Court decided in a series of landmark cases in the 1970s that the Community enjoys an exclusive external competence in some areas. The Court has ruled that the power to implement the common commercial policy under Article 113 is held exclusively by the Community.[1] In other areas the Community may obtain exclusive external powers when it has

[1] Opinion 1/75 [1975] ECR 1355.

acted on the internal plane.[2] More remarkable still, this can occur once the deadline for agreeing a common policy has expired even though the Community has not yet actually finalized the envisaged common policy. In *Commission* v. *United Kingdom*[3] the Court determined that the expiry of the date in the Treaty by which the Council *should* have adopted fisheries conservation measures effected a transfer of the matter into the exclusive competence of the Community even though the Council had not in fact been able to reach agreement on a common policy.

Questions of competence are close to supremacy and have many of the same practical consequences for the ranking of Community law above national law. But here they are not the same thing. Pre-emption is a question of determining competence. National action is precluded not because the rules of Community law apply in the field and prevail in the event of conflict with national provisions, but instead where, even though there are no Community rules with which national rules can come into conflict, the national action is impermissible. Pre-emption in this sense logically precedes supremacy. It is more clean-cut and it is more dramatic in its exclusionary effect on national powers. But, to place this in context, Community exclusivity even where the Community has not acted is highly abnormal in the EC.

Where the Community has legislated, the Court has in a number of rulings determined that the area in respect of which legislation has been made has been transferred into the exclusive competence of the Community. In such circumstances, each legislative act bites off an area previously within national competence and pre-empts national action in the area concerned. This has been a consistent feature of the Court's interpretation of directives made under Articles 100 and 100a designed to secure the integration of the market. It has also been common in the area of the regulation by Community legislation of agricultural markets. In internal trade law, these principles of concurrent Member State/Community competence yielding, on legislative intervention, to exclusive Community competence have come to play a central role in the construction of the legal structure of the Community market. They are also a feature of the dynamic Community/State relationship,

---

[2] Case 22/70 *Commission* v. *Council* [1971] ECR 263.
[3] Case 801/79 [1981] ECR 1045.

which alters over time as the pattern of Community legislation gradually widens and deepens.

On this simplest model of exclusive Community competence consequent on harmonization, Community secondary legislation fixes common Community standards and thereby abolishes Member State competence to introduce a separate national system. This permits free trade to proceed on a uniform basis. Once Community harmonization legislation has been put in place in, for example, the sphere of the free movement of goods, a Member State's capacity to apply stricter rules by invoking the interests referred to in Article 36 is excluded. In *Oberkreisdirektor des Kreises Borken* v. *Handelsonderneming Moormann*[4] the Court observed that it had 'consistently held that where, in application of Article 100 of the Treaty, Community directives provide for the harmonization of the measures necessary to ensure *inter alia* the protection of animal and human health and establish Community procedures to check that they are observed, recourse to Article 36 is no longer justified'. In the case itself the Court considered that the system of health inspections of fresh poultry meat introduced a harmonized Community system based on full inspection of goods in the exporting state which 'replaces inspection in the state of destination and is intended to allow the free movement of the goods concerned under the same conditions as those of an internal market'. In *Karl Prantl* the Court commented that 'once rules on the common organisation of the market may be regarded as forming a complete system, the Member States no longer have competence in that field unless Community law expressly provides otherwise'.[5] In *Firma Eau de Cologne & Parfümerie-Fabrik Glockengasse* v. *Provide*[6] the Court ruled that Directive 76/768 on the approximation of laws relating to cosmetic products occupied the field which it covered. Accordingly Italian rules that required the provision of information on product packaging that went beyond that envisaged by the directive were incompatible with Community law. Such requirements had led to importers being forced to alter packaging for the Italian market, thereby impeding trade, which was precisely the economic cost that the directive was designed to eliminate.

---

[4] Case 190/87 [1988] ECR 4689.
[5] Case 16/83 [1984] ECR 1299.
[6] Case C–150/88 [1989] ECR 3891.

The case was initiated by a German producer with an obvious commercial incentive to have the Italian restrictions abolished.

If a Community measure permitted unilateral national derogation then the realization of economies of scale in the market would be thwarted. As the dicta drawn above from *Oberkreisdirektor* v. *Moormann* reveal, the principle that the Community takes over regulatory competence from the Member States is a foundation stone in the building of the internal market.

Broekmeulen v. *Huisarts Registratie Commissie* provides a parallel illustration in relation to professional qualifications.[7] The litigation related to the effect of Directive 75/632, which concerns the mutual recognition of diplomas, certificates, and other evidence of formal qualifications in medicine. Broekmeulen was a doctor of Dutch nationality who had qualified in Belgium and who found that he was refused registration in the Netherlands as a *huisarts*, a general practitioner. The Court ruled that the directive was to be interpreted as meaning that a national of a Member State who has obtained a diploma listed in the directive in another Member State and who is thereby enabled to practise general medicine in that other Member State is entitled to establish him- or herself as a general practitioner in any Member State, even, as here, in the state of which the individual is a national. The Netherlands was disallowed from raising additional training requirements against Broekmeulen.

A great deal of political effort is naturally devoted to the decision on what the content of the harmonized regime should be. Should there be rigorous Community-wide regulation of a product or a service, or should there be mild regulation only—or even a rule that there should be no rules at all, the ultimate pattern of mutual recognition without any Community regulatory requirements. All these substantive outcomes are possible. The constitutional point is that once agreement has been reached on the style of regulation or even on its absence, the mould is fixed. States may not set different rules that cut across the objectives of the Community intervention. The 'dim-dip' case, *Commission* v. *UK*,[8] provides a clear example of total harmonization, meaning that the Community has regulated the field exhaustively leaving no scope for unilateral Member State action. The United Kingdom

---

[7] Case 246/80 [1981] ECR 2311.   [8] Case 60/86 [1988] ECR 3921.

had introduced a requirement that all new vehicles should carry dim-dip lights. Such devices were not listed in a relevant directive, Directive 76/756.[9] The consequence of the rule was that the importation into the United Kingdom of vehicles made in other Member States according to the specifications set out in the directive was impeded. They did not carry the dim-dip devices and found the British market closed off to them. This was an instance of national technical rules acting as barriers to cross-border trade in goods. Under primary Community law it would fall for assessment in the light of the Treaty provisions that deal with the free movement of goods, Articles 30–36 EC. However, the fact that Community legislation was in place altered the nature of the legal assessment. The dim-dip requirement fell for assessment in the light of the provisions of the directive. The Court held that the directive was exhaustive as regards the lighting devices which might be made compulsory for motor vehicles. The United Kingdom rule unlawfully excluded cars made in other states not equipped with such lights. The United Kingdom was no longer competent to regulate the matter given the comprehensive coverage achieved under the directive.

The United Kingdom had submitted that the dim-dip mechanism allowed a reduction in the brightness of headlights and made them less likely to blind oncoming drivers. It was presented to the Court as a contribution to road safety. This may have been true; it may have been a mere ruse to protect the domestic car industry. Had the field been unregulated by the Community, the Court would have made its own judgment on the merits of these safety features weighed against their obstructive effect on trade. The United Kingdom would have remained competent to regulate the market up to the limits recognized under the Treaty rules on free movement of goods, examined in Chapters 7 and 8 of this book. However, the fact that there was in place a directive that achieved comprehensive coverage of the field completely altered the legal position. The United Kingdom was no longer competent to regulate the field. The alleged merits of the dim-dip device were simply irrelevant to the Court's examination. The case turned on the constitutional point that action by the Member State concerned was pre-empted by Community intervention. This is the core of

[9] [1976] OJ L262/1.

market-building. Such Community harmonization initiatives have as a major motivation the creation of a common economic area in which producers are able to use a single production line to service the whole Community. This permits the realization of economies of scale. In a competitive market, the fruits should be enjoyed by consumers. By ruling unlawful the United Kingdom's dim-dip rules, the European Court was applying the legal ground-rules for an integrated market.

There arise questions of defining the scope of application of the Community measure. It must be decided precisely what is the 'field' that has been occupied. The relevant legal point is that beyond a measure's field of application Member States remain free to act subject to the normal control exercised by primary Community law. So the limits of the occupied field are the limits of exclusive Community competence, beyond which states retain competence to act. But even then that competence is not exclusive national competence, for the principles of Community law, including the law of free movement, continue to apply. There is typically sufficient doubt about the intended scope of legislation for the judicial task of defining the outer limits of the occupied field to be complex. The European Court has performed this task frequently, in relation to a wide range of measures. In *Karl Prantl*, mentioned above,[10] the Court confirmed the principle that once rules on the common organization of the market form a complete system, the Member States no longer have competence in that field. However, it determined that the matter in question— protection of distinctively shaped bottles—had not been dealt with comprehensively at Community level. This left Member States free to maintain or to introduce rules in the field, subject to primary Treaty obligations. On the facts of the case the Court proceeded to examine the compatibility of German regulations with Articles 30–36, the Treaty provisions that govern the free movement of goods.

In *Commission* v. *Germany*[11] the Court was obliged to embark on a careful examination of the scope of directives relevant to the insurance industry in order to determine which aspects of German regulation of the industry fell for consideration in the light of directives and which remained outwith the occupied field and

---

[10] N. 5 above.
[11] Case 205/84 [1986] ECR 3755.

therefore subject to scrutiny under the relevant primary Treaty provisions, Articles 52 and 59. This is standard fare for the Court. Moreover these boundaries between the application of Treaty rules and legislation adopted under the Treaty are not static. The insurance industry has been the scene of intense Community legislative activity in recent years as a wave of directives has promoted liberalization of the Community market for the supply of insurance services. The expiry of the deadline for the entry into force of a directive converts the assessment of the validity of national rules within the scope of application of the directive from one undertaken against the background of the Treaty into one undertaken in the light of the directive.[12] Some of the issues at stake in *Commission* v. *Germany* in the application of Article 59 would now fall within the ambit of relevant directives. This apparently technical question of interpretation of the scope of directives is in fact a matter of central importance. It involves nothing less than the identification at a give time of the respective competences of the Member States and the Community. The Court is placed in a powerful position. It will rarely find easy answers in legislation. The legislature does not typically make explicit the intended pre-emptive scope and effect of the measure. In fact these tricky jurisdictional questions are common in federal systems.

Comparable issues of defining the margin between Community and state competence have arisen in the field of external relations. The precise scope of the external field in which the Community is competent has to be defined with care. Where an agreement contains subject matter over which the Community is competent, but also matters over which the states can claim competence, the agreement should be concluded by both the Community and its Member States. This is common practice. Some rulings handed down by the Court confirm the validity of this arrangement. In *International Rubber Agreement*[13] the Court ruled that exclusive Community competence could not be envisaged where financing of the agreement was to be provded by the Member States, even though the subject matter might fall within Community

---

[12] And this is so before national courts even where the state has failed to implement the dir. in so far as the dir. is capable of direct effect: Ch. 4.
[13] Opinion 1/78 [1979] ECR 2871.

competence. This is not in a formal sense a retreat from the earlier rulings on exclusivity;[14] each agreement depends on its particular subject matter.

In fact, even the rulings of the early 1970s, which on one level seemed to take an ambitious approach to the scope of exclusive Community competence, contained many nuances. A great deal of subsequent practice in external relations has seen use of the mixed procedure, whereby both Community and individual Member States are party to international agreements. The limited case law handed down by the Court in recent years has tended to confirm the impression of an unwillingness to extend the scope of exclusive competence and a readiness to accept the shared competence of Community and Member States. In Opinion 2/91[15] the Court was asked for an opinion pursuant to Article 228 on competence to conclude an International Labour Organization Convention concerning safety in the use of chemicals at work. The fact of internal legislative competence under Article 118a was enough for the Court to rule that the Convention, the subject matter of which coincided with several directives made under Article 118a, fell within Community competence. That competence was not judged exclusive. Conclusion of the Convention was a matter of joint competence, albeit that the Court demanded close association between Community institutions and Member States in the negotiation, conclusion, and fulfilment of obligations arising under the agreement. This proviso was a manifestation of the vigour of Article 5.[16] The 'Uruguay Round' refers to multilateral trade negotiations that culminated in 1994 in agreement on the establishment of a World Trade Organization (WTO). For the EC, there arose questions of competence, *inter alia*, to conclude the General Agreement on Trade in Services (GATS) and the Agreement on Trade-related Aspects of Intellectual Property Rights (TRIPS), annexed to the Agreement establishing the WTO. The opinion of the Court was requested.[17] The Commission had claimed that the Community was exclusively competent to conclude the agreements under Article 113; the Council, the Member States

---

[14] Nn. 1–3 above.   [15] 19 Mar. 1993.
[16] Chapter 2, 45 above.
[17] Opinion 1/94, delivered on 15 Nov. 1994.

who submitted observations, and the Parliament disagreed. After a thorough examination, the Court found that the subject matter extended beyond the areas covered by exclusive Community competence under Article 113. The Commission submitted, in the alternative, that Community competence in the field was exclusive by virtue of implication from internal powers. This was rejected. Internal powers had not been developed to a stage that would yield exclusive external powers. The subject matter fell partly within Community competence, partly within Member State competence. As in its ILO Opinion, the Court mandated the Community and the Member States to co-operate closely.

In the study of the law and practice of Community external relations, it is risky to place an over-emphasis on the Court's rulings. They are relatively few and far between and, for all the apparently strong statements in the 1970s suggesting a strong predilection in favour of Community exclusivity, this was never matched in practice, where mixed agreements were the norm. It is submitted that the Opinions on the ILO and the WTO represent a modern trend in which shared competence is more likely to be found to exist than exclusive competence. The wider the scope of Community activities, the less likely that they are to be seen as falling within its exclusive competence. This is a theme that will be traced throughout this Chapter.

PRE-EMPTION AND FLEXIBILITY— THE NEW APPROACH

Classic pre-emption has the appeal of simplicity. Once the Community has acted, its rules apply. National rules do not. This is the heartland of the basic pattern of a common set of rules for a common market. Traders can plan in accordance with the common rule. Yet pre-emption has its disadvantages. The 'dim-dip' ruling provides a helpful framework for discussion. It was not proven that dim-dip lighting really did help safety. Although this was the United Kingdom's submission, it is conceivable that the introduction of the rule may have been a protectionist ruse designed by the United Kingdom to place an awkward obstacle in the way of importers of cars. However, the constitutional decision that the directive exerted a total pre-emptive effect eliminated any discussion of the alleged merits of the dim-dip device in improving road safety.

The United Kingdom, in attempting to improve road safety, could not act unilaterally. The available method for introducing dim-dip devices into technical specifications involved the invocation of procedures for amending directives. This would require relatively extended discussion at Community level, in the relevant technical committee. It would be necessary to persuade a sufficient majority of the representatives of other Member States that the benefits of change exceeded the costs that would be imposed on traders by altering the established ground rules.

The detailed question of the merits of dim-dip lighting devices need not detain anyone with an interest in shaping policy at the general level. However, the general perception that 'classic' pre-emption is capable of impeding the implementation of innovative techniques is of concern. Setting a common Community rule, from which Member States may not unilaterally depart, may provide the basis for European market integration, but if innovation is inhibited and standards are left ossified, the quality of production is in danger of suffering. This is detrimental to Community consumers and it is likely to prejudice the competitiveness of Community producers in world markets. An important feature of current trends in Community policy-making is the attempt to retain the appealingly predictable and clear consequences of 'classic' pre-emption, while also combining with those aspects a greater sensitivity to the innovative impulse.

The pattern of standards-making itself has altered. A more flexible type of common rule is increasingly used, in place of the old-style predilection for rigid and lengthy mandatory Community technical rules. This is the new approach to technical harmonization and standards.[18] On this model, harmonization consists of establishing the 'essential safety requirements' to be satisfied by all products within the scope of a relevant New Approach directive that are to be placed on the market. These requirements are elaborated in annexes to a New Approach directive, which provide guidance on how properly to interpret the content of the essential safety requirements.

The flexible notion of essential safety requirements has replaced

[18] [1985] OJ C136.

the rigid technical specification. Characteristic of the new approach strategy of permitting flexibility in production techniques is the availability of two routes whereby producers may show conformity with the essential safety requirements. First, products may be presumed to comply with the essential requirements where they are in conformity with harmonized standards, drawn up by relevant European standards-making bodies. Secondly, there is scope for producers to seek to have a model approved by a recognized body as complying with the essential safety requirements. This is the 'type-approval' procedure. This second route is designed to encourage producers to innovate with the confidence that a new type, unrecognized by existing standards, may be submitted for approval.

The new approach has been used with increasing frequency since the late 1980s. It represents an important attempt to feed more flexibility into the Community rule-making structure. It is in part a response to the pressures of legislative overload and the Community's increasing membership. Hammering out detailed common solutions had become virtually impossible, as well as largely undesirable. However, in strict constitutional terms, the new approach as such does not abandon 'classic' total pre-emption. The Toy Safety Directive[19] is a new approach harmonization measure based on Article 100a. Its core objective is the removal of obstacles to the attainment of an internal market in which only sufficiently safe products would be sold. The directive aims to achieve this by setting common rules for the marketing and free movement of toys. All toys placed on the market shall conform to the 'essential safety requirements'. As outlined above, there is some flexibility granted to producers in achieving that standard. However, states cannot unilaterally depart from the admittedly flexible standard of safety envisaged by the directive. Toys that conform to the standard are entitled to market access; according to Article 4 of the directive, 'Member States shall not impede the placing on the market on their territory of toys which satisfy the provisions of this directive'. Competence to insist on safety standards above those established by the directive is pre-empted.

---

[19] Dir. 88/378 [1988] OJ L187/1.

THE UNFEASIBILITY OF EXCLUSIVE COMPETENCE

A major policy concern today is the extent to which pre-emption serves the Community interest. The enlargement of the Community has forced these concerns to the top of the agenda. Once a rule is introduced that transfers exclusive competence to the Community, the risk that innovation will be stifled follows. This suggests an attraction in loosening the shackles of exclusivity. The problem should also be traced back through the legislative process. Member States are naturally aware of the consequences of Community legislative action. States eye the loss of competence that agreeing to legislation entails, allied to the rules of supremacy and direct effect that lend a practical enforceable edge to their constitutional helplessness once the Community has acted. They may be tempted to vote against initiatives just in case the long-term loss of competence should prove unpalatable. The development of the Community would be impeded. This did happen. Through the 1970s and early 1980s, the legislative log-jam in the Community was notorious. The rise of qualified majority voting driven by the Single European Act, further advanced by the Treaty on European Union, was a response to this impediment. Yet the lifting of the national veto, combined with the increasing functional scope of Community activities, rendered all the more acute the fear of a regime that could pre-empt national choices.

An additional, more practical, aspect should be considered alongside these legal points. Explicit defiance of Community law is increasingly unlikely, but the nature of Community law, especially directives, is that it depends on effective national application. This is a strength where tried and tested national methods are employed to secure fulfilment of Community objectives. However, if the state is less than enthusiastic about the pattern of Community rules, and perceives no effective method for expressing its concerns within the Community structure, there may be a temptation to pursue the route of 'creative compliance'.[20] For example, the state may appear willing to conform to Community obligations and may put the law in place on paper (earning points on the Commission's implementation league table[21]) but it may

---

[20] The label is taken from P. McBarnet and D. Whelan, paper presented at the ESRC Workshop, *Compliance and the Single European Market*, IALS, London, June 1992.   [21] Ch. 3, 83.

decline adequately to resource enforcement agencies. The state may adopt a policy of criticizing Community-inspired rules with an implied invitation to national officials to police them with minimal rigour. The state may even trim away some of the more objectionable aspects of the directive when it implements it on paper. Such tactics lie close to the margin of the state's obligations of fidelity to the Community's objectives under Article 5 EC. Alleged infractions are hard to root out. The Commission may pursue the matter, but this is likely to be time-consuming. Private actions are possible. Both direct effect and *Francovich* offer routes to challenge such arguably illegal action and to deny states any advantage from unlawfully creative compliance. However, such actions require a substantial investment of time and money. *Francovich*, it should be recalled, was an 'easy' case for the litigants and for the Court, because there was a total failure to implement a directive, already recorded by the European Court.[22] This is not what is at stake in more nuanced resistance to Community rules that are perceived to be unduly inflexible. Where states are rumoured to be engaged in implementation tactics designed to minimize the domestic impact of Community rules, the atmosphere of suspicion and resentment may chip away at the credibility of the uniform legal system on which the Community is based.

This is a volatile mix. In a number of respects, directly and indirectly, the Community has retreated from the classic pre-emption model of occupation of the field involving transfer of exclusive competence into Community hands. This is a potentially creative evolution. The Member States are offered room for manœuvre. What is occurring are the inevitable adjustments to the notion of uniformity demanded by a Community structure that is supporting an ever-increasing number of Member States and an ever-increasing range of functions. Yet behind these shifts lurks the fundamental threat that what may be lost is the common legal structure within which integration is pursued.

The following discussion of these adjustments divides into two. Initially consideration is devoted to the specific issue of the extent to which the pattern of exclusive competence acquired by the

---

[22] Cases C–6, 9/90 *Andrea Francovich* v. *Italian State* [1991] ECR I–5357. See Ch. 4, text following n. 47.

Community consequent on legislative activity has been altered, directly or indirectly. This inquiry forms the subject matter of the next three topics of this Chapter. Thereafter, in the last four topics, broader issues are examined. These may be grouped around the general question of the rising willingness of the Member States to question the scope of Community competence. These are broader issues because they are not so much concerned with maintaining flexibility for states once a Community pattern has been put in place as with challenging the basic need to put in place a Community pattern.

ARTICLE 100A(4)

Under the Treaty of Rome, the main focus for harmonization activity aimed at achieving a common market under the Treaty of Rome was Article 100. It says nothing about the intended effect on national competence of Community rules made under it. The European Court has frequently stated its view that directives made under Article 100 should normally be taken to occupy the field and to deprive Member States of competence in that field.[23]

Since the entry into force of the Single European Act in 1987, the focus of harmonization activity has shifted to Article 100a. As explained in Chapter 3, the most immediately striking point of distinction between Article 100 and Article 100a is that the former requires a unanimous vote in Council, whereas the latter demands only a qualified majority vote (QMV). Article 100a eases the rigidity of a legislative process previously conducted under the shadow of the national veto. Of more immediate relevance to the present discussion is the inclusion in Article 100a of a notorious fourth paragraph that relates to the issue of pre-emptive effect. Article 100a(4) provides that:

> If, after the adoption of a harmonization measure by the Council acting by a qualified majority, a Member State deems it necessary to apply national provisions on grounds of major needs referred to in Article 36, or relating to protection of the environment or the working environment, it shall notify the Commission of these provisions.
>
> The Commission shall confirm the provisions involved after having verified that they are not a means of arbitrary discrimination or a disguised restriction on trade between Member States.

[23] See text at nn. 4–6 above.

By way of derogation from the procedure laid down in Articles 169 and 170, the Commission or any Member State may bring the matter directly before the Court of Justice if it considers that another Member State is making improper use of the powers provided for in this Article.

Fear that Community legislation could affect 'vital national interests' generated the crisis that led to the Luxembourg Compromise in 1966.[24] That 'solution' was founded on the assertion of the national veto. Thereafter tensions between national and Community interests were largely suppressed by the practice of unanimity and the ability of individual states to assert a veto over initiatives they perceived to be threatening. Once that veto power was lifted in some areas by the Single European Act as part of the process of reinvigoration and, at the same time, Community competence was enhanced so that the areas in which outvoting could occur were widened, the fear that national concerns might be subordinated to the Community interest perceived by a majority was once again revealed. Article 100a(4) reflects that persisting fear. Put simply, Member States were not prepared to move to QMV in Council, unless some incursion were made into the rigidity of total pre-emption.

Article 100a(4) recognizes that the fact of Community legislative intervention is not of itself sufficient reason to exclude the possibility of regulatory action by the Member States, where this is shown to be justified. Article 100a(4) is the price paid by established notions of pre-emption for the rise in QMV. More positively, it is a reflection of the importance of accommodating more than simply free trade on a level playing-field within the framework of Community law.

All measures adopted under Article 100a are automatically subject to the possibility that a Member State or Member States may choose to invoke the Article 100a(4) procedure. At the time of the entry into force of the Single European Act, fears were expressed that Article 100a(4) represented a damaging backward step in the pattern of a uniform Community legal order.[25] One would have hoped that it would be increasingly possible for

---

[24] 63 above.
[25] For a short and fierce criticism of the vagueness of the SEA see, Pescatore, a former judge at the Court, 'Some Critical Remarks on the Single European Act' (1987) 24 *CMLRev.* 9.

Member States to identify a congruence between their national interests and those of the Community expressed through legislative initiatives, but Article 100a(4) seemed to involve a rejection of such a *communautaire* spirit.

In fact it has infrequently been invoked. It has come before the European Court on one occasion only, when the Court anulled a Commission decision confirming German rules imposing stricter controls on pentachlorophenol (PCP), a preservative, than were laid down in the relevant directive (91/173).[26] However the Court's ruling did not go to the heart of the function of Article 100a(4) in the development of the internal market. The decision was annulled because it was inadequately reasoned within the meaning of Article 190 EC. The Commission re-issued a confirmation accompanied by fuller justification. Throughout, Germany kept in place its stricter rules on the use of PCP.

Suggestions that the step forward of QMV in Article 100a(1) was matched by the step back in Article 100a(4) have not been borne out in practice. The remarkable freeing of the legislative log-jam consequent on lifting the national veto under Article 100a(1) has not been counterbalanced by widespread use of Article 100a(4). With the advantage of hindsight it seems fair to conclude that doom-laden predictions have not been borne out by events—perhaps, of course, precisely because those predictions were made and left no state in any doubt about the damage that could have been wrought by recourse to Article 100a(4).

MINIMUM HARMONIZATION

The technique of minimum harmonization moves still further away from the pattern of total harmonization than Article 100a(4). Under this model of minimum harmonization states must certainly secure the levels of regulation set out in a directive, but they are permitted to set higher standards, provided only that those are shown to be justified under primary Community law. The Community rule sets a floor only. Stricter national rules are not pre-empted. Both Community and Member States are competent in the field.

Minimum harmonization goes further than Article 100a(4) in

---

[26] Case C–41/93 *France* v. *Commission* [1994] ECR I–1829.

providing flexibility to the Member States. Article 100a(4) defines exhaustively the available grounds for setting rules that differ from the Community standard. It specifies a management process involving the Commission. Neither restriction applies to the phenomenon of minimum harmonization. However, the motivation underlying Article 100a(4) has much in common with that which prompts minimum harmonization. Both recognize that, despite the fact of Community intervention, there remains legitimate scope for national regulatory initiatives.

Some Treaty provisions, especially those inserted by the Single European Act or the Treaty on European Union or amended thereby, state explicitly that minimum harmonization is envisaged once legislation is made under the relevant provisions. Article 118a EC, for example, envisages the adoption of directives with the objective of securing improvements as regards the health and safety of workers. These set minimum requirements only. According to the third paragraph of Article 118a, states are not prevented 'from maintaining or introducing more stringent measures for the protection of working conditions compatible with this Treaty'. Article 130s, discussed in Chapter 3, provides a legal base for legislation in the field of environmental protection. Article 130t adds that 'The protective measures adopted pursuant to Article 130s shall not prevent any Member State from maintaining or introducing more stringent protective measures. Such measures must be compatible with this Treaty. They shall be notified to the Commission.' Article 129a empowers the Council to adopt specific action which supports and supplements the policy pursued by the Member States to protect the health, safety, and economic interest of consumers and to provide adequate information to consumers. According to Article 129a(3) such action 'shall not prevent any Member State from maintaining or introducing more stringent protective measures. Such measures must be compatible with this Treaty. The Commission shall be notified of them.'

The designation of these provisions—number plus letter rather than simply number—provides a clue that these were not present in the original Treaty of Rome. In fact Articles 118a and 130r–t, the environment title, were the creations of the Single European Act. Article 129a was inserted by the Treaty on European Union. This point of history is important in achieving an appreciation of the changes that have occurred in the relationship between

Community legislative action and national rules in the field. It shows that there is a growing recognition that Community activity is capable of co-existing with national activity; that the clean-cut lines of exclusivity consequent on Community entry into a particular field are no longer the norm.

It will be noticed from the texts of these provisions that a proviso is included. Member States may set stricter rules, but must comply with primary Community law. A stricter rule that, for example, is shown to obstruct the free movement of goods within the Court's interpretation of Article 30 must be justified in accordance with the established rules in that area. Secondary Community law sets the floor for national action; primary Community law sets the ceiling.

Some individual directives include a clause that declares that the Community rule serves as a minimum standard only and that states remain free to set stricter rules. This has occurred even under directives made under Article 100 and, more recently, 100a. The existence of Article 100a(4) does not preclude the possibility that individual measures made under Article 100a may include a provision that applies the technique of minimum harmonization to the field covered by that particular measure. This is common in measures that harmonize laws relating to the protection of the economic interests of consumers. Variation between national laws in such fields causes an obstruction to the development of integrated marketing strategies. This provides a rationale for the establishment of common Community rules made under Article 100a. So, for example, the constitutional basis for the directive on Unfair Terms in Consumer Contracts[27] is Article 100a. It is a measure of market integration. Several Member States have legislation in the field, but these initiatives reveal very different techniques. This diversity distorts the development and function-ing of the internal market. The directive is designed to put in place a common Community standard for testing the fairness of terms that have not been individually negotiated that are found in consumer contracts. However, it is expressly provided that that standard is a minimum only. Article 8 of the directive provides that 'Member States may adopt or retain the most stringent provisions compatible with the Treaty in the area provided by this

---

[27] Dir. 93/13 [1993] OJ L95/29.

directive, to ensure a maximum degree of protection for the consumer'.

The inclusion of the minimum harmonization formula in individual measures pre-dates Article 100a. Directives made under Article 100 may be found which include the minimum formula. The Bathing Water Directive, mentioned at page 51 above, was an Article 100 measure, but it provided in Article 7(2) that 'Member States may at any time fix more stringent values for bathing water than those laid down in this directive'.

The value of minimum harmonization lies in its contribution to a modern Community which is more multi-functional than a mere free trade area. Total harmonization confers on the Community an exclusive competence which it is simply ill-equipped to discharge. The harmonization of laws involves the integration and regulation of markets through the establishment of a common Community rule, but it also places in the hands of the Community a responsibility for establishing a mechanism for ensuring the protection of the interests that underpinned the national rules subject to harmonization. The Community must secure the application and, where appropriate, the updating of those rules. Relying on input from national level and engaging in a dialogue with national authorities offers the Community a method for discharging that responsibility. The setting of higher standards at national level is capable of providing a prompt to the renovation of the Community's regime. The Community lacks the expertise and the institutional maturity to exclude the participatory role of national authorities. A sharing of competence is realistic and it is fruitful.

Minimum harmonization liberalizes trade without suppressing justifiable regulatory initiatives taken to deal with local problems. The objection to minimum harmonization lies primarily in the damage it may do to the process of market integration. What has happened to the notion of pre-emption as the pre-requisite for successful market integration? What are we to make of the rise of minimum harmonization in the very heartland of integration, Articles 100 and 100a? The existence of phenomena such as minimum harmonization and Article 100a(4) undermine the notion that the construction of the internal market is a matter of exclusive Community competence. Neither technique releases national authorities from the obligations of Community law, for

Article 100a(4) may be invoked only on defined grounds and measures stricter than a minimum standard must still be compatible with the Treaty, most significantly Article 30. However, within such limits, states are able to depart from the Community harmonized rule even though this may impede access to their markets by producers based in other Member States. They retain competence.

A minimalist explanation may be found in the suggestion that the areas in which minimum harmonization has achieved a high profile are areas that are not really at the core of the integrative process. Allowing diversity in environmental standards and levels of consumer protection may have some incidental effect on trade patterns. But such rules predominantly affect producers located in the regulating state. So, too, perhaps the use of the minimum formula in the Bathing Water directive reflects the fact that the measure was not *really* about market integration at all and was only located under Article 100 (and Article 235) as a result of the absence from the Treaty at the time of an explicit legal base for the adoption of environmental protection legislation.[28] And the Article 100a directives dealing with the protection of the economic interests of consumers may readily embrace the minimum approach because they touch methods of marketing rather than methods of production, and are therefore not directed at the very core of integration, the possibility of devising a single production line to serve the entire Community market.[29] By contrast, measures dealing with safety aspects of products, for example, are located in this heartland and must maintain the classic approach whereby Community rules pre-empt national rules, subject only to (the rarely invoked) Article 100a(4). This indeed occurs under the Toy Safety directive, mentioned above,[30] which does not permit states to set stricter safety rules as a precondition to market access. It envisages the Community rule as both floor and ceiling, subject only to Article 100a(4), whereas the minimum formula sets the Community rule as floor only with a ceiling set by primary Community law.

This locates the rise of minimum harmonization at the margins

[28] Ch. 2, text at n. 22.
[29] Cf from this perspective the shifting focus of Art. 30: Ch. 8.
[30] N. 19 above.

of the market-building process. However, a more positive account of minimum harmonization would place it at the heart of the process of accommodating the range of interests that combine to make up the modern heterogeneous Community. It is submitted that minimum harmonization is best seen as an inevitable and welcome response to the increasingly multi-functional nature of the Community. The substantive scope of Community activity has expanded remarkably since the days when its legislative activities could more or less accurately be packaged within the notion of a mere common market. The initial six Member States have now become fifteen, which has brought a completely new blend to the mix of aspirations of those party to the Community endeavour. In the face of such an accelerating and expanding snowball, it would be fruitless and dangerous to try to induce it to follow a single, narrow path. Minimum harmonization is one reflection of Reich's astute summary that 'the more competences the Community is acquiring, the less exclusive will be its jurisdiction'.[31]

This generalized perception of the attraction of minimum harmonization may provide a helpful framework for analysis and 'broad-brush' discussion about policy. It does not provide a precise method for identifying when minimum harmonization can be 'tolerated', notwithstanding its fragmenting effect on the uniformity of Community rules. Minimum harmonization may damage the process of market integration. There will arise disincentives to traders to put in place integrated marketing strategies. Total harmonization cannot and should not be swept away. It remains vital in supplying a valuable deregulatory impulse. The advantages of market integration accrue in many areas precisely from lifting the regulatory burden imposed by the legislative diversity between the Member States that has accumulated over centuries. However, the breadth of the Community's activities dictates an increasing role for minimum harmonization. Any reduction in the level playing field is a point of automatic criticism only if one accepts market integration as the overriding concern of the Community. But this is not the message of Articles 2 and 3 EC.

Minimum harmonization allows innovative techniques of

---

[31] 'Competition Between Legal Orders: A New Paradigm of EC Law' (1992) 29 *CMLRev.* 861, 895.

market regulation to be developed at local level. It must be conceded that there is a risk that the minimum technique may be abused by states setting stricter rules than the Community minimum for reasons of protectionism. A number of methods of tackling this problem are required, revolving fundamentally around the objective of making the administration of the market more transparent. Directive 83/189[32] requires new national technical rules to be notified to the Commission before their introduction. This allows the Commission to scrutinize the proposed measures to check conformity with Community law. If not in conformity, the Commission will seek to prevent their introduction. If in conformity, but capable of impeding trade, the Commission can require national authorities to delay implementation. It will consider whether to introduce measures at Community level to protect the interests in question in a wider framework. The Sutherland Report examined strategies necessary for the management of the internal market after the expiry of the 1992 deadline. It came out strongly in favour of administrative co-operation of a more intensive type than that foreseen by Directive 83/189. Further reflection on this institutional aspect of the process of harmonization of laws is offered in Chapter 9 of this book.

OPTIONS IN DIRECTIVES

A related phenomenon, also serving as a reflection of the demand for flexibility, is found in the pattern of options and exemptions allowed to Member States from aspects of initiatives with which they are uncomfortable. Were the Community wedded to a pattern of a single homogeneous legal order this would be anathema. In times of an enlarged, multi-functional Community, the inevitability, and to some extent the desirability, of this route, has become increasingly apparent. Part of the appeal lies in the capacity of such compromises to persuade all the Member States, or at least a number adequate for QMV purposes, to support the measure. Options may also reflect local differences that would be pointlessly damaged by a purist approach to uniformity. The risk lies in the possibility that the compromises made may fragment the

[32] [1983] OJ L109/8, as amended by Dir. 88/182 [1988] OJ L81/75.

directive to such an extent that the final text's claim to provide a source of common rules for the Community is a sham.

The Product Liability Directive

Directive 85/374, widely known as the 'Product Liability directive', provides a useful example of these tensions.[33] It is not here suggested that this directive is so flawed as to lose its value. It is, however, a measure that offers a basis for discussion of the impact of options built into directives.

The Product Liability Directive is an Article 100 measure. Its preamble refers to the need to approximate laws concerning the liability of the producer for damage caused by defectiveness of products because of the distortions in competition and the impact on the circulation of goods which are caused by divergences between the laws of the different Member States. The fight to secure adoption of this measure was fierce. The first Commission proposal in the field appeared in 1976.[34] The fact that nine years elapsed before agreement was reached reflects the depth of controversy which surrounded this initiative. Aspects of this controversy mark the text of the directive that was finally adopted. Compromise solutions were required on some points in order to secure the unanimous support in Council that is necessary under Article 100. The most notable was the so-called development risk defence.

The core harmonized liability rule is found in Article 1, which declares that 'The producer shall be liable for damage caused by a defect in his product.' The focus of the regime is on the condition of the product, rather than the conduct of the producer. It is a type of 'strict' liability, rather than the fault-based liability long preferred by English tort law.

From the simplistic perspective of market integration it does not matter what liability rule is chosen provided only that it applies uniformly Community-wide. However, the practical implications of selecting between different types of liability rule provoked such fierce debate that eventually the system that emerged in the directive did not yield uniformity.

---

[33] Dir. 85/374 on the approximation of the laws, regulations, and administrative provisions of the Member States concerning liability for defective products: [1985] OJ L210/29. [34] [1976] OJ C241/9.

A strict-liability system allocates to the producer the risk of defectiveness. This may be defended as efficient and fair in the light of the producer's capacity to buy insurance against loss and thereby to spread the costs of compensating a small number of injured consumers amongst all purchasers by reflecting insurance costs in a slightly higher price. Fault-based systems allow producers to escape some unforeseen consequences of their actions and, in effect, to impose high costs on an unlucky few consumers. The preamble to the directive justifies the choice of liability without fault with reference to 'the fair apportionment of the risks inherent in modern technological production'. In opposition to this it may be argued that, under a strict-liability system, producers have had a greatly diminished incentive to invest in new products. Potential costs of unforeseeable magnitude deter deviation from the tried and trusted. It may be that insurance cover becomes prohibitively expensive or even unavailable under a system of 'pure' strict liability. For some commentators, tying liability to fault induces technological advance, which is in the long run to the advantage of the consumer and of society generally.

Such debates are common in national systems. At Community level, even though Article 100 provided the basis for the directive, which aligns it with the process of market integration, the fixing of the substance of the harmonized regime inevitably drew in such fundamentally difficult policy issues. In the end the Member States fell back on an optional arrangement. The system of strict liability for supplying defective products on which the Directive is based is diluted by the inclusion of a so-called development-risk defence in Article 7(e). A producer of a defective product is able to escape liability by proving 'that the state of scientific and technical knowledge at the time when he put the product into circulation was not such as to enable the existence of the defect to be discovered'. Accordingly the producer of a product which is, with hindsight, certainly defective does not incur liability if able to demonstrate that the flaw is, loosely summarized, unknown and unknowable.[35] This reflects the view that 'pure' strict liability is damagingly oppressive of commercial innovation. However,

---

[35] For discussion of the precise nature of the defence, C. Newdick, 'The Development Risk Defence of the Consumer Protection Act 1987' [1988] *CLJ* 455.

Article 15(1)(b) of the directive permits Member States the option of extending liability even to defects of the type covered by the defence. They are permitted, effectively, to exclude the defence.

What price harmonization of laws in the face of this optional structure? Is the diagnosed problem of distorted competition flowing from divergent liability laws cured by the Directive? It seems feasible that commercial planning will remain fragmented. Marketing a product that has been exhaustively tested, yet which is later discovered to be defective, will attract potentially vast liability in states that have excluded the defence, but no liability at all in states that retain it. Firms that are sued will have powerful incentives to endeavour to make tactical use of the rules of private international law in order to establish that the rules under which they are properly sued are those of a state that has retained the defence. The choices may affect their decision on where to locate in the first place. Consumers in states that offer the defence are likely to be much worse off than their fellow Citizens of the Union in states that have rejected the inclusion of the defence, unless they, too, are able to exploit the rules of private international law to find the most favourable forum.

The inclusion of this option in the Directive provides an insight into the difficulty of achieving harmonization in each and every aspect of a matter which is the subject of Community intervention. The Product Liability Directive is an especially dramatic example. It is possible to view the Directive as containing at its heart a fundamental failure to agree a core liability rule. It remains contentious how far options granted in directives constitute an acceptable recognition of national peculiarities and how far they undermine the whole notion of harmonization of laws within the Community. Perhaps, broader still, the inability 'simply' to hammer out a common rule as a basis for market access is shown here to be doomed to failure because of the misperception of liability rules as mere barriers to trade. In fact, complex issues of consumer protection and commercial planning are at stake. Attempted reduction to a single, simple formula is implausible. This perception ought to put one on guard lest Community initiatives over-simplify the role of law reform. The inclusion of options in Community measures may offer scope for reflecting different interests. On the other hand, once a measure is robbed of its ostensible purpose by options it may be worse than no intitative, for it may give an entirely misleading impression of effective reform.[36]

Article 15(3) of the Product Liability Directive provides that in 1995 the Commission shall report on the operation of the development-risk defence and the optional provision that permits its exclusion. The Council shall consider whether to repeal Article 7(e), which would deprive producers of protection from liability for loss caused by unknown and unknowable defects. This review was a convenient device for avoiding final decisions on controversial issues as part of the compromise necessary to achieve the adoption of this important Directive in 1985. But the review mechanism is also a sensible reflection of the desirability of learning through experience.

The Protection of Young People at Work

Directive 94/33 on the protection of young people at work was adopted by Council in June 1994 under Article 118a EC.[37] It is explicitly presented in the light of the aspirations of the Community Charter of the Fundamental Social Rights of Workers, which was adopted at Strasbourg in December 1989 by eleven of the then twelve Member States. The United Kingdom refused to agree to the Charter. In strict legal terms the Charter laid down no new specific obligations. The test of its impact always lay in the future and in the extent to which specific directives would deepen the fabric of Community social policy in the direction broadly espoused by the majority of the Member States in agreeing to the Charter. Directive 94/33 is part of the deepening process.

Children and adolescents are considered groups which are specially sensitive to dangers at work and the Directive is presented as a response to their vulnerability. In the case of children, the minimum working age shall not be lower than the minimum age at which compulsory schooling as imposed by national law ends, or fifteen years in any event. Strict controls are

---

[36] For an argument that the Product Liability Directive's practical impact is limited and that it has forestalled more effective reform in the Member States, see Stapleton, J., *Product Liability* (London: Butterworths, 1994).

[37] [1994] OJ L216/12.

to be placed over work by adolescents. Young people are to be exposed to working conditions appropriate to their age. But derogations permeate the structure of the Directive.

Although Article 4(1) provides that 'Member States shall adopt the measures necessary to prohibit work by children', Article 4(2) permits this prohibition to be set aside in the case of children pursuing defined cultural or similar activities; children of at least 14 years of age working under a combined work/training scheme or an in-plant work-experience scheme; and children of at least 14 years of age performing light work. Light work means work that is, *inter alia*, not likely to be harmful to the safety, health, or development of children and not such as to harm attendance at school. The 'light work' exception also permits states not to prohibit such work performed by children of 13 years of age 'for a limited number of hours per week in the case of categories of work determined by national legislation'.

Subsequent provisions cover states that have chosen to make use of the option allowing children's work. Other than in respect of the exception for children pursuing defined cultural or similar activities, limits are imposed. The working time of children shall be limited to at most eight hours a day and forty hours a week, and in some circumstances to less than that. Work by children between 8 p.m. and 6 a.m. shall be prohibited. Provision is made for rest periods and annual rest. Adolescents are subject to (less extensive) protection in respect of working time, night work, and rest periods. For children, to some extent, but much more strikingly in relation to adolescents, it is provided that Member States may authorize derogations from the norms envisaged by the Directive. For example, the limitation of the working time of adolescents to eight hours a day and forty hours a week is open to derogation 'either by way of exception or where there are objective grounds for so doing'. The provisions on night work and rest periods are also subject to extended possible scope for derogation.

The recitals admit that 'the implementation of some provisions of this Directive poses particular problems for one Member State with regard to its system of protection for young people at work'. It turns out that the state in question is the United Kingdom. Implementation by 22 June 1996 is required, but the United Kingdom is permitted a further four years within which it may refrain from implementing specified provisions in the areas of working time and night work.

In its recitals the Directive claims that, although derogations appear indispensable, 'applications thereof must not prejudice the principles underlying the established protection systems'. It is hard to believe that this objective has been adhered to. The measure is, first and foremost, an appallingly unwieldy text. It lacks transparency. Once one is able to discern its intent and scope, it is seen to set up a system of protection that is so fragmented as to call into question any notion of a common Community policy. An examination of this measure reveals that it is not possible to lay the full blame for the fragmentation of EC social policy on the Maastricht 'opt-out'.[38]

Perhaps the most troubling aspect of this measure is not its lack of precision, but the fact that one Member State, explicitly and impliedly, is driving the variation in regulatory patterns. This is not an instance of building in flexibility and observing how systems develop, even though periodic review mechanisms are built into the structure. It is rather more a case of creating a minimalist Community measure and even then allowing opt-outs from it.

In the Community, there will typically be negotiation about how much leeway to allow to dissentients. Naturally there is an unavoidable need to pursue such compromises where measures require a unanimous vote in Council. But the fact that a measure is susceptible to adoption by QMV in Council (or under the social policy Protocol/Agreement) will not mean that objections by a dissenting but non-blocking minority will be overridden. Maintenance of harmony dictates an attempt to reflect the interests of all the Member States in a finalized act. Attempts are typically made to accommodate all states. It is normally a last resort to outvote objectors. But there must come a point at which the majority has to decide whether the grant of concessions deprives the measure of its core legal effect; thereupon a vote is appropriate without the grant of further concessions. Perhaps this will come sooner in future.

Direct Effect and Options in Directives
It was explained in Chapter 4 that where states fail to implement

---

[38] 174 below.

directives, the principle of direct effect and the possibility of liability under *Francovich* may place power in the hands of individuals to rely on the directive before national courts. This serves to increase the pressure to which the defaulting state is subject. However, only clear and unconditional provisions are capable of direct effect.[39] *Francovich* is broader, but it, too, requires the identification of individual rights in a directive.[40] There is a risk that the phenomenon of options and derogations in directives will preclude their justiciability before the national courts of a non-implementing state. Where Community provisions become fragmented compromises, they may be placed beyond the reach of the individual, who is then entirely dependent on national implementation.

There are signs that the Court is alert to this risk and is taking steps to adapt its case law in order to secure the effective enforcement of the option-ridden directive. This may be traced in *Francovich* itself.[41] The Court found itself confronted by a directive that allowed states to select from options in deciding the length of the period in respect of which workers who were the victim of a collective redundancy would be compensated. That directive also left it to the implementing state to choose whether or not to place a ceiling on liability. The directive dates from 1980, when the Community comprised only nine Member States, and it demonstrates that flexible directives are not new, although they are today more common. It is fair to conclude that the options granted to Member States in the Collective Redundancies directive were essentially points of detail only. They did not sacrifice the core objective of the measure to the attempt to bring all the Member States into the common framework. Nevertheless, it had seemed possible that this pattern would preclude the development of individual rights in the absence of implementation. As explained in Chapter 4, the European Court identified the content of the guarantee as payment of outstanding claims. The availability of options did not detract from the precise and unconditional character of that intended result. The Court was able to identify the minimum guarantee envisaged by the directive

---

[39] See Ch. 4.
[40] Cases C–6, 9/90, n. 22 above.
[41] See n. 22 above.

and ruled it capable of direct effect. It added that a defaulting state could not rely on options that it could have but has failed to implement as a method for depriving an individual of directly effective rights. As explained in Chapter 4, it still felt forced to conclude that absence of certainty about the identity of the guarantee institution was ultimately fatal to a finding of direct effect. However, the Court's identification of a core, minimum guarantee that was capable of direct effect is especially potent in the light of the proliferation of options in directives that attempt to accommodate the heterogeneity of the expanding Community within a common legislative framework. The Court appears concerned lest compromise settlements expressed through optional patterns in directives allow a drift away from individual rights that are intended to arise. And, most of all, in *Francovich*, the Court established that failure to implement a directive may lead to state liability to compensate an individual suffering loss caused by the state's default even where direct effect cannot be established.

All this is important for the future. It represents a potential further enhancement at national level in the impact of directives in particular and EC law in general. In *Marshall (2)* the Court dealt with a provision in the directive on equal treatment of men and women that required states to put in place a system of effective remedies.[42] The Court had in the past ruled that this provision lacked the precision necessary for direct effect.[43] But in *Marshall (2)* the Court asserted that once a state had decided to put in place a compensation scheme as its chosen implementation, it was then possible for an individual to rely on the directive to require a national court to set aside an upper limit on compensation under national law that obstructed effective enforcement. Here, too, the European Court was intent on maximizing the scope of individual protection under EC law even in the face of a measure that seemed to leave considerable discretion in the hands of the Member States.

---

[42] Case C–271/91 *Marshall* v. *Southampton and South-West Hampshire Area Health Authority* [1993] 3 CMLR 293. The relevant Dir. is Dir. 76/207.
[43] Case 14/83 *Von Colson and Kamann* v. *Land Nordrhein-Westfalen* [1984] ECR 1891.

THE JURIDIFICATION OF COMMUNITY COMPETENCE

Identification of the attributed competences to which the Community is theoretically limited matters little in practice where unanimous voting is the rule. States have a veto in Council. They have no need to test 'competence' before the Court. EC competence is in effect politically determined. Competence questions become immediately sharper where there is a rise in qualified majority voting. This, as explained, has been the firm trend since the Single European Act and is also characteristic of the Treaty on European Union. Article 100a, among the most high-profile examples, provides for the adoption by QMV of measures of harmonization.

So, whereas in the past fears among Member States of over-ambitious claims to Community competence were submerged beneath their capacity simply to block objectionable proposals, today the threat looms larger because of the absence of a veto. Article 100a(4), minimum harmonization, and the fragmented directive manifest the demands of states to an entitlement to some leeway once a Community measure is in place. But, more fundamentally, states have an incentive to complain that a measure is beyond the Community's competence; that no valid legal base truly existed.

Such a complaint may be advanced in Council. If it meets with rejection there, and the measure attracts the support necessary for adoption, the dissatisfied outvoted state is left with the option of challenging the validity of the measure before the European Court. The challenge is in principle perfectly possible. One ground for an application for annulment of Community acts under Article 173 EC is explicitly 'lack of competence'. The Community's competences are limited and it is feasible that a measure could be annulled for trespassing into an area where the Community lacks competence.

A direct challenge based on lack of Community competence (as opposed to lack of competence of individual institutions) has never been upheld by the Court. Community competence in practice has long been interpreted flexibly. As explained in Chapter 2, this has been a trend nurtured by the Council and reflected in the Court. However, the sensitivity of the issue of competence in a post-veto world of QMV may yet tempt states to seek its deeper juridification. Similarly the new demarcations, not just at the outer limits of Community activity, but also between Community and non-EC Union action, promise invigoration in tracking the limits of competence.

Germany v. *Council*[44] represents an example of what may become a growing trend of competence-related challenge. Germany objected to Article 9 of Directive 92/59 on general product-safety.[45] Article 9 confers powers on the Commission to act in defined emergency circumstances to require Member States to take specific measures. Germany submitted, *inter alia*, that the stipulated legal base of the Directive, Article 100a, governed harmonization of laws and could not be used to equip the Commission with power to apply the law in individual cases in place of national authorities. The Court rejected the German application for annulment. It stated that 'In certain fields, and particularly in that of product safety, the approximation of general laws alone may not be sufficient to ensure the unity of the market.' Article 100a therefore confers a power to 'lay down measures relating to a specific product or class of products and, if necessary, individual measures concerning those products'. The fact that the case was brought suggests a future of heightened sensitivity to the legitimate scope of Community action.[46] At least in relation to the use of Article 100a to pursue the construction of an institutional structure apt to manage the internal market, the Court, as yet, seems ready to uphold a flexible interpretative approach to the Treaty.

Analogously motivated tactics may be employed within the undisputed limits of Community competence. It is possible to envisage exploitation of the variation of the legislative procedure under different legal bases. A measure may fall plainly within the scope of Community competence, yet there may be dispute about choice of legal base. This will matter because different legal bases attract different legislative procedures.[47] The tactical point for the state outvoted under a QMV base will be that, if it is able to demonstrate that the correct legal base was one which required a unanimous vote in Council, it has protected a veto power (which it may use or it may trade off for other advantages).

[44] Case C–359/92 [1994] ECR I–3681.   [45] [1992] OJ L228/24.
[46] See further Ch. 6, 210.   [47] 85.

It is possible to track litigation of this nature. Prior to the entry into force of the Single European Act, the United Kingdom sought to persuade the Court that the correct legal base for legislation dealing with the use of certain hormones in livestock farming involved use of both Articles 43 and 100, not merely Article 43, dealing with agriculture.[48] Article 100 required unanimity, whereas Article 43 envisaged QMV. The United Kingdom (and every other Member State) would have been able to exercise a veto had Article 100 been found to be the correct choice. The Court put paid to this tactic on this particular occasion. It examined the content and objectives of the Directive. It regulated conditions for the production and marketing of meat with a view to improving its quality. This placed it within the category of measures that contribute to the achievement of the objectives of the common agricultural policy. It could therefore be adopted on the basis of Article 43 alone without the need for the Council to invoke Article 100, the more general provision dealing with the establishment of the common market.[49]

Lord Cockfield, Commissioner responsible for the development of the internal market in the second half of the 1980s, is in no doubt that the attitude of the United Kingdom Government was during this period firmly directed at maintaining the unanimity requirement for legislation, thereby preserving the brake of the national veto. He tells of attempts to add Article 235 as a legal base to proposals of which the United Kingdom disapproved in order to secure the power to vote the proposal down.[50] Such attempts to thwart the qualified majority provisions to which the United Kingdom had agreed in the Single European Act left several Member States puzzled about the intentions of the Thatcher Government towards the Community's endeavours.

The precise details of challenges to legal bases vary with each successive Treaty revision, as some institutional and constitutional differences between legal bases close while others open, offering new tactical opportunities. Generally, the drift towards QMV and

[48] Case 68/86 *UK* v. *Council* [1988] ECR 857.
[49] For other technical reasons, of little long-term value to the UK, the Court *did* annul the Dir.
[50] *The European Union: Creating the Single Market* (Chichester: Wiley Chancery Law, 1994), 64, 112.

away from unanimity in the EC Treaty reduces the scope for legal-base litigation motivated by attempts to preserve a national veto. However, another fertile field is created by the problems of distinguishing between social policy under the Treaty, which is unquestionably EC law and which binds the United Kingdom, and social policy under the Protocol, which is of a legally obscure character and which does not bind the United Kingdom.[51] Furthermore, it has been observed on several occasions in this book, especially in Chapter 3, that the Treaty on European Union hatches a fresh clutch of conundrums in the murky area of demarcation between the three pillars of the Union. A state outvoted under a QMV base in the EC pillar will be able to block action if it can instead locate the proper place for action as one of the non-EC pillars. The uncertain role of the European Court as the correct legal forum for the presentation of such an argument is yet another problem created by the oddities of the EU creature spawned by the Member States at Maastricht.[52]

SUBSIDIARITY

A related prospect is the attempted use of Article 3b EC, the principle of subsidiarity, to invalidate Community legislation for lack of competence. Article 3b provides that:

> The Community shall act within the limits of the powers conferred upon it by this Treaty and of the objectives assigned to it therein.
>
> In areas which do not fall within its exclusive competence, the Community shall take action, in accordance with the principle of subsidiarity, only if and in so far as the objectives of the proposed action cannot be sufficiently achieved by the Member States and can therefore, by reason of the scale or effects of the proposed action, be better achieved by the Community.
>
> Any action by the Community shall not go beyond what is necessary to achieve the objectives of this Treaty.

For Sir Leon Brittan, subsidiarity can be summarized as the principle that action shall be taken at the 'best level'.[53] This implies no preconception about choices between national or

---

[51] 174.   [52] 92.
[53] 'The Institutional Development of the European Community' [1992] *Pub.L* 567, 574.

Community action, excepting only that in the unlikely event of the choice being evenly balanced, the Community shall not act. Subsidiarity represents an insistence on the importance of locating the efficient level of administrative and legislative action.

In the legislative procedure, subsidiarity is likely to play its major role in Council negotiation, where it will act as a focus for arguments about the political desirability of Community action. However, it is feasible that an outvoted state might be able to submit, not that an act falls outwith the substantive limits of Community competence, but that, albeit falling *prima facie* within that area, the matter has not been shown to be more efficiently dealt with at Community rather than national level. On this analysis, Article 3b would act as an extra, distinct threshold that must be crossed before the Community is competent. The political decision in Council in favour of Community action would be open to a legal challenge.

A great deal of attention has been devoted to the extent to which Article 3b provides a justiciable test for the validity of Community legislation. Before entering this debate, it is worth recalling that there have been periodic debates throughout the Community's history about the extent to which the explicit wording of Treaty provisions may generate competence questions forming the basis for judicial review of legislation. Article 100, for example, confines harmonization to the field of state measures that directly affect the establishment or functioning of the common market. Occasional concern has been expressed about whether some adopted or proposed initiatives really did meet the 'direct' criterion. Much the same could be said of Article 235. Its scope was theoretically limited to cases of action 'necessary to attain, in the course of the operation of the common market, one of the objectives of the Community'. The test of 'necessity', *inter alia*, offered a basis for judicial supervision. The House of Lords Select Committee investigated the matter in the late 1970s, and it expressed some scepticism about the legal validity of the free hand which the Community had claimed in some areas of legislative activity under the cover of Articles 100 and 235.[54] The restrictive

---

[54] 1977/78, *22nd Report*. For an insight into comparable Danish fears, Lachmann, 'Some Danish Reflections on the Use of Article 235 of the Rome Treaty' (1981) 18 *CMLRev*. 447.

view was by no means unanimously accepted. George Close, for example, carefully explained how Community competence could properly be developed under Articles 100 and 235 into some initially surprising areas by demonstrating the broad impact of a range of national regulatory activities on competitive conditions in Europe.[55] In practical terms, the matter was never converted into a challenge before the Court. The unanimity control ensured that measures that were adopted enjoyed the support of all the states and that any opposition simply precluded adoption in Council. Judicial review was not required by a dissentient Member State.

Subsidiarity seems to apply throughout the field of Community legislative activity, save in those few areas where exclusive competence exists,[56] so its impact differs from analysis of individual legal bases. However, Article 3b has much in common with Articles 100 and 235 in the sense that phrases strictly capable of judicial application are more realistically seen as political tools. Yet the possibility that such issues will be litigated before the Court is now real in view of the widespread removal of the brake of the national veto. The Court's preparedness to inquire into political choices about the desirability of action is in doubt. In the past it would perhaps have been little deterred by the unarguable propulsion into the political arena that active interpretation and application of Article 3b would cause. Article 3b has no less potential vigour as a means of shaping and reshaping the Community structure than Article 5, that source of remarkably specific and extensive obligations.[57] However, the reason for anticipating caution lies not in the text, but in the prevailing climate within which the Court fulfils the function imposed upon it by Article 164 EC to ensure that 'in the interpretation and application of this Treaty the law is observed'. Modern sensitivity about competence suggests that today the Court is not likely to be so eager. Paradoxical though it may sound, the fact that the Member States have sufficient concern about competence questions to render subsidiarity in principle justiciable is the very reason the Court is unlikely to use it in an intrusive fashion to check the validity of adopted legislation.

---

[55] 'Harmonisation of Laws: Use or Abuse of Powers under the EEC Treaty?' (1978) 3 *ELRev.* 461. [56] 136.
[57] Ch. 2, 45 above; Ch. 4, 116 above.

The attraction of a legal challenge to legislation by an outvoted state based on alleged violation of Article 3b cannot be discounted in a Community characterized by activity in an increasingly wide range of areas. Probably the Court will demand that adequate reasons within the meaning of Article 190 EC are supplied. It showed a corresponding determination to put the institutions through this procedural hoop in its annulment of the Commission's confirmation of German rules on PCP under Article 100a(4) EC.[58] In that case it did not pursue a deep inquiry into the merits of the case and the same will probably apply to subsidiarity under Article 3b.

It is submitted that the principle of subsidiarity reflects concern about the scope of Community competence and its demarcation from national competence, but that it does little in practical terms to address that concern. It acts as an ill-defined counterweight to the expansion of Community competence agreed at Maastricht and apparent in the intense, multi-functional legislative activity since the entry into force of the Single European Act in 1987. The subsidiarity slogan provides an essentially political framework within which key issues of where power resides can be discussed. The reference to 'exclusive competence' in the second paragraph of Article 3b reveals much about the open-ended, undefined content of the subsidiarity principle. This notion is not defined in Article 3b nor, for that matter, anywhere else in the Treaty. Its scope is controversial. Subsidiarity intensifies the debate about Community competence rather than resolving it.

In conclusion, this identification of the subsidiarity principle as essentially fodder for a political talking-shop is not necessarily a point of criticism. It is not feasible that the multi-functional activities of the modern Community, characterized by close interdependence with its Member States, could be reduced to a neat set of legal rules dictating who does what. Sector by sector, close attention must be devoted to planning the respective contributions of Community and national laws and Community and national implementation and administration of law and policy. If subsidiarity, as a question rather than an answer, has stimulated a more intensive, thoughtful examination of how the evolving

---

[58] Case C–41/93, n. 26 above.

European market should be regulated, then it will have fulfilled a valuable function.

EVADING HARD LAW

The sensitivity of the Member States to the growth in Community competence now that they are largely unable to control it through the simple exercise of a veto in Council marks the Treaty on European Union in a number of areas other than Article 3b. Even where new competences have been conferred on the Community, the Member States have in some areas been very careful to limit the scope for exploitation of these competences by the Community's institutions. For example, the Treaty on European Union introduces a new Title on culture. This is Article 128, which commences with the bold statement that 'The Community shall contribute to the flowering of the cultures of the Member States'. It is, however, further provided that harmonization of laws is specifically excluded from the range of Council powers under Article 128. The desire of the Member States to keep a close check on Community activities in such a sensitive area is further emphasized by the requirement for unanimity in Council even for the type of action that is explicitly envisaged, the adoption of incentive measures. A further illustration is found in Article 129, dealing with public health, which explicitly excludes harmonization of laws.

It is worth recalling that the Court has in the past found implied powers to adopt binding acts even where this is not explicitly envisaged by the relevant Treaty base. *Germany, France, Netherlands, Denmark, and United Kingdom* v. *Commission* was discussed from this perspective in Chapter 2.[59] The Commission was found to enjoy the powers to adopt formal acts that were indispensable to fulfilment of its task under Article 118 to promote close co-operation between Member States in the social field. The fact that several states chose to challenge the Commission demonstrates the sensitivity of the issue. The lesson is that even the weakish terms of the new Titles may prove to generate a surprisingly extended legal power to act. This is a further potential

---

[59] Cases 281, 283–5, 287/85 [1987] ECR 3203.

flashpoint in fixing the scope of the Community's post-Maastricht competence.

A further problematic aspect of these new Titles arises with respect to their relationship to existing provisions. The creation of new Titles envisaging soft law might be interpreted as an effort on the part of the Member States to prevent activity in the areas covered by the new Titles leaking into the realm of hard law made under, especially, Articles 100 and 235. Probably the Court's view that Article 235 should not be used as a legal base where more specific Treaty provisions are available will suffice to prevent Article 235's use as a means of circumventing the unavailability of 'hard law' under new provisions such as Article 128 on culture.[60] Yet even this need not be conclusive, for it might be argued that, say, a directive is essential to achieve particular cultural objectives and that recourse to Article 235 is justified precisely because of the absence of sufficient power to adopt such a binding act under Article 128. Article 235's requirement of unanimity in Council may be a more practical constraint on such expansionism, but it is also plausible that Article 100a, which allows the making of both regulations and directives by QMV, will compete with the new, weaker provisions as a legal base. Demarcation of subject matter between legal bases is notoriously complex and the new, 'soft-law' provisions may simply ignite further argument about legal base.[61]

It is possible to assess the two new intergovernmental pillars from the perspective of sensitivity about competence. Member States' desire to co-operate more intensively clashed with the fear of surrendering control over the pace of development. The result was a new pattern of extra-Community co-operation within which the national veto was clearly and carefully retained and the involvement of the Parliament and the Commission was severely circumscribed.[62]

FROM OPTIONS TO OPTING OUT—SOCIAL POLICY

In the arduous negotiations at Maastricht in December 1991, the most intractable dispute about competence arose in the realm of social policy. The government of the United Kingdom was

---

[60] Case 45/86 *Commission* v. *Council*, [1987] ECR 1493.
[61] 167 above.   [62] Ch. 1, 31.

vehemently opposed to enhanced Community policy making in the social-policy field. The opposition derives from political ideology about the proper operation of the market economy. The United Kingdom's labour market policies since 1979 have been motivated by the perception that aspects of state intervention and patterns of collective labour organization have distorted the flexibility of the market. Employment-protection law, for example, diminishes individual choice. It raises costs of employment and deters employers from hiring workers. On this approach job security should be earned through the market. Where it is achieved by legal protection, damage is done to market flexibility and to job-creation. Unions, too, were suspected of bringing inflexibility to the market by asserting their collective might while enjoying a degree of statutory immunity from legal liabilities.

The hostility of the United Kingdom Government to state regulation and to collective regulation of the labour market generated a series of statutes commencing with the Employment Act 1980. These have been largely designed to lighten the regulatory burden of employment-protection law which employers were perceived to bear, and to diminish the perceived privileged position of the trade unions. This is not the place to trace the trends of this policy in any depth, nor to assess its contribution, positive or negative, to the performance of the economy.[63] For present purposes, it is important simply to appreciate that the United Kingdom was determined that its sustained domestic deregulatory programme should not be undermined by an active social-policy programme at Community level. Mrs Thatcher, in particular, openly declared herself determined to stop the regulation she felt her administrations had unravelled at national level from being reimposed at Community level. The policy was sustained under John Major, Prime Minister at the time of Maastricht. At a wider level, the United Kingdom perspective plays down the extent to which disparities between national regulations require the development of common Community rules and, instead, places an emphasis on maintaining a 'competition' between national regulatory regimes unconfined by Community

---

[63] For an examination of the development of law and policy see P. Davies and M. Freedland, *Labour Legislation and Public Policy* (Oxford: OUP, 1993).

rules.[64] It believes that the market provides a means of testing competing conceptions of the desirability of social policy. On this approach, firms should be able to choose between national regulators and locate wherever best suits them as a base for supplying the wider market. Common Community rules, it is argued, damage such competition and render the Community market inflexible, which may be especially damaging in global terms.[65]

The United Kingdom's capacity to keep Community rules at bay depended on the scope of Community competence and, at the technical level, on the relevant legal bases. After 1979, the United Kingdom was naturally unable to evade existing social-policy obligations imposed by measures adopted, in the main, through the 1970s, although it seems plain that it allowed its distaste to influence its strategy for implementation of Community obligations. A stream of rulings at national and Community level over recent years have exposed the inadequacies of British implementation of measures in the social-policy field and it is hard to escape the impression that this is part of a policy of minimalism that reflects irritation at the very existence of such legal obligations.[66] The measures in question were predominantly made under Articles 100 and 235, both of which require unanimity in Council, so once the Conservatives under Mrs Thatcher assumed power in 1979 they were in a position to veto new initiatives proposed under those bases.

Thereafter, the first major test of the Community's commitment to deepen social-policy making arose in the process of Treaty revision that yielded the Single European Act which came into force in 1987. By dint of uneasy compromise, the integrity of the Treaty social policy structure was maintained. A new legal base attracting qualified majority voting in Council was agreed. This was Article 118a, but its scope was limited to the adoption of

---

[64] For a powerful analysis of this issue, N. Reich, 'Competition Between Legal Orders: A New Paradigm of EC Law?' (1992) 29 *CMLRev.* 861.

[65] See, for an examination of the competing arguments, Deakin, S., and Wilkinson, F., 'Rights vs Efficiency? The Economic Case for Transnational Labour Standards' (1994) 23 *ILJ* 289.

[66] e.g. Cases C–382, C–383/92 *Commission* v. *UK*, [1994] ECR I–2435, 2479. At national level, e.g., *Pickstone* v. *Freemans* [1989] AC 66. See 147 above on 'creative compliance'.

directives dealing with the health and safety of workers. The United Kingdom had surrendered its veto power, but, depending on the interpretation given to health and safety matters in this context,[67] in an apparently relatively narrow field only. It will be recalled that Article 100a, allowing QMV in Council, was inserted into the Treaty by the Single European Act to stimulate the making of laws needed to complete the internal market. The possibility of using this base to invigorate social-policy legislation characterized as internal market law was foreseen by the United Kingdom which ensured that by virtue of Article 100a(2) this base was not available for provisions 'relating to the rights and interests of employed persons'. Article 100 could be used for such provisions, but it remained subject to a unanimity requirement.

In 1989 eleven of the twelve Member States agreed to the Community Social Charter of the Fundamental Social Rights of Workers. The sole dissentient was the United Kingdom. The Charter was not a formal Community act in the sense of Article 189. It did not alter the obstruction to lawmaking embedded in the Treaty's pattern of attributed powers involving the need to achieve unanimity in Council in order to develop Community laws in the social policy field, excepting only those measures subject to QMV under Article 118a. It was never suggested that the content of the Charter was radical. The United Kingdom's refusal was intensely ideological and amounted to a vivid demonstration of its absolute determination not to yield on this point. But the Charter signalled the intent of the other Member States not to allow social-policy to lie dormant.

It was therefore little surprise that when at Maastricht the majority of the Member States agreed that the time was right to deepen social policy-making, the United Kingdom was adamantly and immovably opposed. The United Kingdom knew itself to be in a minority among the Member States, although it appears not to have anticipated that it was in a minority of one. It was fully aware that to yield to an extension in Community competence would lead in practice to further legislation, at least under bases permitting qualified majority voting in Council. It could not be budged. But nor would the other states abandon their belief that the

---

[67] Dir. 94/33 (n. 37 above), made under Art. 118a, suggests a rather generous interpretation.

Community could not marginalize social-policy. They were unpersuaded by the United Kingdom's arguments in favour of labour-market flexibility and, at Community level, in favour of developing a pattern of 'competition between regulators'. A settlement was reached, but this time the gulf could not be bridged by deft footwork within the Treaty framework itself. What emerged was the social policy Protocol.

The Protocol authorizes the eleven Member States to have recourse to 'the institutions, procedures and mechanisms of the Treaty for the purposes of making and applying amongst themselves acts and decisions required to give effect to the Agreement annexed to the Protocol'. The Agreement envisages action in areas that are wider than the explicit scope of the existing Treaty provisions dealing with social-policy. Formally the structure is an 'opt-in' for the eleven Member States excepting the United Kingdom, but since the reality is that the eleven are in effect using Community institutional machinery, the popular reference to the 'UK's opt-out' is a defensible label. The United Kingdom still swims in the common stream of existing social-policy, but where the stream has been diverted through the new channel, it alone will not follow.

The Treaty on European Union declares expressly in Article B that the Union shall 'maintain in full the *acquis communautaire* and build on it'. The social policy Protocol does not contradict that statement because it does not formally touch existing commitments. The United Kingdom has not withdrawn from the provisions on social policy that have been in place since the original Treaty of Rome came into force in 1958. It has simply declined to participate in a new dimension. However, fearsome legal compexity pervades this compromise pattern. It envisages that some proposals will be covered by Treaty of Rome social policy (in which the United Kingdom participates), others by the new 'Maastricht social policy', from which the United Kingdom is insulated. This is yet another area where difficult questions of demarcation are likely to be confronted, initially in political arguments but ultimately by the Court. Charting the common stream and the new channel will be difficult. For example, it may be predicted that the Commission and, perhaps, the majority of the Member States, will be more likely to view measures as falling within the existing scope of the EC Treaty, especially the QMV-driven Article 118a EC,[68] than the United Kingdom, which will have an interest in pushing marginal cases in to the Protocol-plus-Agreement in order to insulate itself from their binding effect. Such arguments are not new; before the entry into force of the Treaty on European Union, squabbles broke out over the question where Article 118a ends and where other bases, requiring unanimity, begin. But the Protocol offers another battleground and there is a further twist. Even where there is acceptance that the text in question is properly regarded as the product of the eleven, operating under the Protocol-plus-Agreement, it is far from clear precisely what type of law will emerge. It may be a type of EC law or it may be a type of intergovernmental law.[69]

The United Kingdom Government's belief that the correct way forward was a Community-wide 'competition between regulators' did not prevail. But, in the area covered by the Protocol-plus-Agreement, there will develop a competition between two regulators—the eleven, now fourteen, versus the United Kingdom. The United Kingdom's perception is that, in so far as it can offer a more favourable regulatory environment to firms, it will succeed in attracting firms to its territory. This, the Government believes, will be an entirely deserved success, for it is the market, from which the other Member States have artificially insulated themselves, that will have rewarded it. This perception was the basis of the victory claimed by John Major in December 1991 on his return from Maastricht. Counter-arguments focus on the perceived need for a common framework of law within a common market. The equalization of competitive conditions on which the construction of an economically integrated territory is perceived to depend is shattered by such market-led competition between regulators. The pattern seems incompatible with the notion of undistorted competition in the internal market to which reference is made in Article 3(f) EC. On this view, a common European market requires a bedrock of common legal rules which is broader and deeper than the United Kingdom would regard as

---

[68] Cf Dir. 94/33, n. 67 above.

[69] Cf E. Szyszczak, 'Social Policy: A Happy Ending or a Reworking of the Fairy Tale?', ch. 20 in D. O'Keefe and P. Twomey, *Legal Issues of the Maastricht Treaty* (Chichester: Wiley Chancery Law, 1994); E. Whiteford, 'Social Policy after Maastricht' (1993) 18 ELRev. 202.

appropriate. On a connected tack, it is by no means clear that removing regulation is the best way for a state or a union to be competitive in the global economy. A low-wage, low-skill work-force may not be especially attractive to firms.

The United Kingdom approach is also attacked for its propensity to upset existing social-policy provision in other Member States where it undercuts its neighbours. That, for the United Kingdom, is the point; it is a market. Other Member States reject the application of market structures in such circumstances. The debate is close to the core issue of what the EC is *for*. The United Kingdom has been accused of subordinating individual rights and social protection to a free-market philosophy in a way which is incompatible with the basic ambitions of the EC expressed in the Preamble to the Treaty and Articles 2 and 3 EC. Competition between regulators on this perspective is simply incompatible with the EC's historical mission.

Without pressing this debate further, concluding thoughts should be directed at the legal pattern of the Protocol-plus-Agreement. It is a very visible two-speed structure for the Community. The majority of the Member States were prepared to sanction such legal and economic fragmentation rather than see the atrophy of EC social policy-making. The United Kingdom, for its part, was also prepared to opt for variable geometry rather than digest an unpalatable level of labour-market inflexibility. The post-Maastricht pattern of social policy therefore reflects a Community too heterogeneous to support a common framework. It is the most radical example of this phenomenon of all those discussed in this Chapter. It is qualitatively different from a device such as minimum harmonization, because it involves a refusal by one state to participate in the common pattern. This is not a managed compromise that reflects different perceptions about the development of Community policies. This is a rift relating to the scope of Community competence and, fundamentally, it reveals a core disagreement about the very purpose of the EC.

If the Protocol-plus-Agreement becomes a model for resolving disagreements, it points firmly in the direction of a future of widespread variable geometry. The perception that competition between national regulators is preferable to Community rule-making has a potential application in many fields beyond social policy and it is likely to loom large on the future agenda. The questions that need to be addressed revolve around the core issue of whether such developments in the Community can be regarded as creative evolution or destructive fragmentation. Such issues generally become ever more acute as the Community pursues the path of enlargement, but at present in the social policy field the real damage is wrought by one state alone distancing itself from its partners.

In 1984, Claus-Dieter Ehlermann examined the extent to which Community law accommodates diversity among its Member States.[70] He was able to pick out a number of instances in which particular states, by no means solely the United Kingdom, had been offered special treatment. He proceeded to offer the following prescription:

Economic and social differences (both terms used in the widest sense) can in principle justify differentiation; purely political phenomena cannot. For instance, the fact that the British government (or the majority in Parliament or even public opinion in the United Kingdom) is opposed to joining the European monetary system would not be a valid argument for differentiation (provided the rules governing the EMS were Community law). However, if the British pound were still in a special position compared with other currencies, a case could be made for a derogation in favor of the United Kingdom.[71]

Ehlermann added that objective differences are not in themselves enough to justify differentiation. 'The difference in treatment has to be proportionate to the differences in the factual (objective) situations.'

These remarkably prescient comments require minimal elaboration. Suffice it to say that this framework may be used to test many of the developments sketched in this Chapter and elsewhere in this book. It is submitted that Ehlermann's observations have much to commend them as a political prescription of the required conditions for the continued good health of the Community enterprise. In the social-policy field, at least, it is hard to see that Ehlermann's advice has been adhered to. It is intriguing to consider whether the type of differentiation which Ehlermann would deem unjustified could be the subject of *legal* challenge

---

[70] 'How Flexible is Community Law? An Unusual Approach to the Concept of "Two Speeds" ' (1984) 82 *Mich. LRev.* 1274.

[71] At 1289.

rather than simply serving as a basis for debate at the political level. In this vein, the next Chapter examines the role of the Court in 'constitutionalizing' the Treaty.

FURTHER READING

BARNARD, C., 'A Social Policy for Europe: Politicians 1 Lawyers 0' [1992] *Int. J of Comp. Lab. L and Ind. Rel.* 15.

BIEBER, R., 'On the Mutual Completion of Overlapping Legal Systems: The Case of the European Communities and the National Legal Orders (1988) 13 *ELRev.* 147.

CEPR, *Making Sense of Subsidiarity* (London: Centre for Economic Policy Research, 1993).

CROSS, E., 'Pre-emption of Member State Law in the European Economic Community: A Framework for Analysis' (1992) 29 *CMLRev.* 447.

CURRALL, J., 'Some Aspects of the Relation between Articles 30–36 and Article 100 of the EEC Treaty, with a Closer Look at Optional Harmonisation' (1984) 4 *YEL* 169.

CURTIN, D., 'The Constitutional Structure of the Union: A Europe of Bits and Pieces' (1993) 30 *CMLRev.* 17.

DEHOUSSE, R., 'Community Competence: Are there Limits to Growth' in Dehousse, R., (ed.), *Europe After Maastricht* (Munich: Law Books, 1994).

EIPA, *Subsidiarity: the Challenge of Change* (Maastricht: European Institute of Public Administration, 1991).

EHLERMANN, C.-D., 'The Internal Market Following the Single European Act' (1987) 24 *CMLRev.* 361.

—— 'How Flexible is Community Law? An Unusual Approach to the Concept of "Two Speeds" ' (1984) 82 *Mich. LRev.* 1274.

ERICKSON, C., and KURUVILLA, S., 'Labour Costs and the social Dumping Debate in the European Union' (1994) 48 *Ind. and Lab. Rel. Rev.* 28.

FITZPATRICK, B., 'Community Social Law after Maastricht' (1992) 21 *ILJ* 199.

HANCHER, L., 'The European Pharmaceutical Market: Problems of Partial Harmonisation' (1990) 15 *ELRev* 9.

LENAERTS, K., 'Constitutionalism and the Many Faces of Federalism' (1990) 38 *AJCL* 205.

MAJONE, G., 'The European Community between Social Policy and Social Regulation' (1993) 31 *JCMS* 153.

McGEE, A., and WEATHERILL, S., 'The Evolution of the Single Market— Harmonisation or Liberalisation' (1990) 53 *MLR* 578.

McGOWAN, F., and SEABRIGHT, P., 'Regulation in the European Community and Its Impact on the UK'. Chapter 10 in Bishop, M.,

Kay, J., and Mayer, C., (eds.) *The Regulatory Challenge* (Oxford: OUP, 1995).

MORTELMANS, K., 'Minimum Harmonization and Consumer Law' [1988] *ECLJ* 2.

REICH, N., 'Competition Between Legal Orders: A New Paradigm of EC Law' (1992) 29 *CMLRev.* 861.

—— 'Protection of Diffuse Interests in the EEC and the Perspective of "Progressively Establishing" an Internal Market' (1988) *JCP* 395.

RHODES, M., 'The Social Dimension after Maastricht: Setting a New Agenda for the Labour Market' [1993] *Int. J. of Comp. Lab L and Ind. Rel.* 297.

ROBERTS, B., 'The Impact of the Maastricht Summit on European Community social policy: A Break-through for Worker Participation or the Creation of a Two-Speed Europe?' (1993) 28 *Texas Intl. LJ* 357.

SIEDENTOPF, J., and ZILLER, J., (eds.), *Making European Policies Work: The Implementation of Community Legislation in the Member States* (London: Sage, 1988).

SHAW, J., 'Twin Track Social Europe—The Inside Track' in O'Keeffe, D., and Twomey, P., (eds.), *Legal Issues of the Maastricht Treaty* (Chichester: Wiley Chancery Law, 1994).

SZYSZCZAK, E., 'Social Policy: A Happy Ending or a Reworking of the Fairy Tale?', Chapter 20 in O'Keeffe, D., and Twomey, P., (eds.) *Legal Issues of the Maastricht Treaty* (Chichester: Wiley Chancery Law, 1994).

—— 'Future Directions in European Union social policy Law' (1995) 24 *ILJ* 19.

USHER, J., *European Community Law and National Law: The Irreversible Transfer?* (London: Allen and Unwin, 1981), especially Chapter 3.

WAELBROECK, M., 'The Emergent Doctrine of Community Pre-emption— Consent and Redelegation' in Sandalow, T., and Stein, E., *Courts and Free Markets* (Oxford: Clarendon Press, 1982).

WATSON, P., 'Social Policy after Maastricht' (1993) 30 *CMLRev.* 481.

WEILER, J., 'The Transformation of Europe' (1991) 100 *Yale LJ* 2403.

WHITEFORD, E., 'Social Policy after Maastricht' (1993) 18 *ELRev.* 202.

6

The Constitutional Court

The European Court considers that the Treaty, a creature of international law governing relations between states, has been converted in the European Community into a Constitution. In *Parti Ecologiste Les Verts* v. *European Parliament* the Court commented that 'the European Economic Community is a Community based on the rule of law, inasmuch as neither its Member States nor its institutions can avoid a review of the question whether the measures adopted by them are in conformity with the basic constitutional charter, the Treaty'.[1]

The European Court's description of the Treaty structure as a Constitution reached its zenith in its Opinion on the Draft agreement on a European Economic Area, delivered in December 1991:

the EEC Treaty, albeit concluded in the form of an international agreement, none the less constitutes the constitutional charter of a Community based on the rule of law. As the Court of Justice has consistently held, the Community treaties established a new legal order for the benefit of which the states have limited their sovereign rights, in ever wider fields, and the subjects of which comprise not only Member States but also their nationals . . . The essential characteristics of the Community legal order which has thus been established are in particular its primacy over the law of the Member States and the direct effect of a whole series of provisions which are applicable to their nationals and to the Member States themselves.[2]

Eric Stein famously described the Court as having construed the Treaties 'in a constitutional mode rather than employing the traditional international law methodology'.[3] As early as 1964 in *Costa* v. *ENEL* the Court referred to the EEC Treaty as being 'in

---

[1] Case 294/83 [1986] ECR 1339.

[2] Opinion 1/91 [1991] ECR I–6084.

[3] 'Lawyers, Judges and the Making of a Transnational Constitution' (1981) 75 *Amer. J. Intl. L* 1.

contrast with international treaties'.[4] The shift from Treaty to Constitution has taken the EC legal order into realms distinct from traditional international law to such an extent that it is likely to mislead to attempt to examine the two from the same perspective. EC law is *sui generis*.

The legal implications of this process of constitutionalization have been elaborated in the course of this book. The purpose of this Chapter is to draw together some of the strands under the general rubric of the Treaty as a constitutional order and the European Court as a constitutional court.

The core building blocks of the constitution were put in place by the Court at an early stage. The Court was concerned to establish a legal order that would permit the realization of the objectives that it discerned within the Treaty. In its pursuit of this goal it was not constrained by the absence of an explicit basis for some of its rulings in the wording of the Treaty. It regarded the Treaty as a framework, with certain points of reference in provisions such as Articles 2, 3, 4, 5, and 164, and it was its job to construct a legal system that would allow those ideals to be brought to fruition.

A survey reveals a judicial activism which the Court could justify as essential to breathe life into the Treaty. A critical current question asks whether such activism will or should be maintained today, given that the process of Treaty revision at periodic intergovernmental conferences is now close to becoming a regular feature of the Community institutional picture. A further element which places question marks alongside the legitimacy of judicial activism is provided by the renovation of the Community legislative process since the entry into force of the Single European Act in 1987. Qualified majority voting in Council is now the norm and the directly elected Parliament now plays a more prominent part. The Court can no longer justify its vigorous re-shaping of the law on the basis that, if it does not provide impetus, no other source will. This, of course, does not preclude the possibility that there may be other adequate justifications for judicial activism; nor that one new feature of the Court's task might be precisely to check the compatibility of the new creations of the Member States against the norms created under the Community constitution over its thirty years of development.

---

[4] Case 6/64 [1964] ECR 585.

The European Court's Opinion on the Draft Agreement on a European Economic Area, cited above, was much more than jurisprudential rhetoric. In accordance with Article 228 of the Treaty, the Court had been asked its Opinion on the compatibility of the draft agreement with the provisions of the Treaty. The essence of the agreement was the extension of much of the pattern of Community law beyond the Community to the territory of the states of the European Free Trade Association (EFTA) in order to create a European Economic Area (EEA). Those non-EC EEA states would form something akin to a second-tier Community and, in practice, by 1995 three of them, Austria, Finland, and Sweden, had taken the next step and become full Community members.

In December 1991, the European Court found that the planned institutional structure under the EEA agreement was *not* compatible with Community law. This forced a renegotiation of the agreement and its subsequent re-submission to the European Court's ultimately approving scrutiny.[5] The core of the Court's objection to the initial draft lay in the planned patterns for securing a homogeneous interpretation of the law throughout the EEA. Although the draft EEA agreement had used the same wording for many of its provisions as is found in the EC Treaty, this was not sufficient to satisfy the Court. It pointed out that the ambitions of the EC went deeper than the EEA and that it therefore could not be ruled out that the same words would come to be interpreted in different ways. The Court's past record confirms that identification of objectives, rather than a literal reading of the text, drives the interpretation of legal provisions. In the past the Court has placed a different, narrower interpretation on provisions in association agreements that on their face are identical to provisions of the EC Treaty.[6]

An EEA Court comprising members of the European Court and members drawn from the EFTA states was planned. But the Court considered it possible that the pattern would imperil the autonomy of the Community's legal order. As structured, that Court would not be bound to follow the European Court's rulings after the entry into force of the EEA agreement, yet its rulings would have

---

[5] Opinion 1/92 of 10 Apr. 1992 [1992] ECR I–282.
[6] e.g. Case 270/80 *Polydor* v. *Harlequin Record Shops* [1982] ECR 329.

to be taken into account by the European Court. The protection of the Community legal order could not be ensured. The changes made subsequently, of which the Court ultimately approved, involved the establishment of an EFTA Court wholly separate from the European Court with competence to deal only with matters arising in the framework of EFTA. Divergence in the interpretation of Community law and EEA law remained possible, but the Court was prepared to accept that the threat of damage to the autonomy of the Community legal order had been removed.

The Court perceives a core of Community legal values, the loss of which would jeopardize the whole system. The important message embedded within Opinion 1/91 is that the Court is determined to defend its carefully constructed constitutional edifice.

FEATURES OF A CONSTITUTIONAL COURT

The development of the supremacy of Community law is a central element in the process of constitutionalization. Supremacy establishes the relationship between Community law and national law. The development of direct effect is also constitutional in nature. Direct effect improves the methods for securing the observance of Community law, but it also ensures that Community law acts as a source of individual protection at national level. The notion of direct effect was critical to drawing Community law into the fabric of national law, and by fusing the two the Court has cut down the ability of states to pick and choose the elements of Community law that they will respect. This was explored in Chapter 4.

The pattern of supremacy and direct effect, supported by the Article 177 preliminary-reference procedure, brought to the Community legal structure much of the pattern that would normally be recognized as a federal system of law. Without a legal hierarchy that places Community law on top, the system would fragment. Once that hierarchy is established and its effective enforcement secured, the Community/state relationship has close analogies with that of Federal authority/province, state.

This is not an attempt to describe the Community simply and neatly as a federation. The use of the word federation is needlessly inflammatory in the European context and it is in any event unwise to describe the Community as *sui generis*, yet then to attempt to fit it into a well-known political pattern such as federalism. The Community is unique. Yet it is worthwhile appreciating that it has federal features. Federalism is a form of government in which power is divided between a central authority and regional authorities. The EC is based on a division of competence between Community and Member States. Its legal system is based on the need to maintain the integrity of the overall structure, which dictates the need for the supremacy of Community norms over national norms in areas in which Community law applies. By contrast with some federal systems, Community law does not permit its constitutional court explicitly to review the validity of national laws. Article 169 allows it to rule on Member State conformity with Treaty obligations; Article 171 provides that in the event of an adverse ruling the state must take the necessary steps to comply with the judgment and failure to comply may lead to the imposition of financial penalties by the Court. Article 177 allows the European Court to pronounce on the interpretation of Community law in the context of national litigation, but strictly it is not able to rule on points of national law. Neither under Article 169 nor under Article 177 does the European Court strike down national laws. Yet the practical effect should be that that result will be achieved through the response to the Court's ruling taken by national courts and/or governments. In fact, the apparently fragile structure of indirect review of national legislation by the European Court via Article 177 is one of the strengths of the system. Placing the obligation to secure conformity with Community law at national level is politically astute for it effectively removes the risk that a national government may choose to defy a ruling from Luxembourg for domestic political reasons. Such an option is effectively foreclosed where the ruling is made at national level. So the pattern reflects loyalties that are not yet as fully developed as one would expect to see in a federal state. It also depends on national judges not possessing the opportunist instincts that this analysis attributes to national politicians.

The Community's comparability to states that are constructed along federal lines is limited by the unsatisfactory nature of the allocation of competence between the Community and its Member States. The Community possesses only the powers attributed to it. Beyond that sphere the states are exclusively competent. Within that sphere, the relationship between the exercise of Community powers and Member State powers is complex and varies from sector to sector. The Treaty is obscure on many of these points, silent on others. The constitutional division of power in the Community is troublingly murky.

This is a job for a Constitutional Court. The European Court has relatively rarely been asked to fulfil a role in determining competence allocation because of the tendency of the political institutions to resolve questions of competence without the need to submit them to judicial scrutiny. In particular, the practice of unanimous voting in Council ensured that what was done was supported by all the Member States, whereas the absence of such unanimity precluded anything at all being done. Controversy did not spill over into the Court. The rise of QMV in Council has altered the political situation and provides a temptation for outvoted states to resort to litigation. Competence testing before the Court may become significant. Chapters 3 and 5 of this book have explored these realms.

JUDICIAL REVIEW—THE POSITION OF THE PARLIAMENT

The principal feature of the Court's constitutional function that is absent from this account is its role in reviewing acts of the Community institutions. Much of the remainder of this Chapter surveys some of the most prominent elements of this judicial-review function. These are important in themselves, but, of wider significance, they reveal much about the Court's perception of itself as the guardian of a constitution rather than the mere interpreter of the text of a Treaty.

The Court's construction of a coherent system of judicial review testifies to its determination to give practical effect to its commitment to constitutionalization. The dictum from *Parti Ecologiste Les Verts* v. *European Parliament* that was mentioned above can helpfully be placed in its proper context. '[T]he European Economic Community is a Community based on the rule of law, inasmuch as neither its Member States nor its institutions can avoid a review of the question whether the measures adopted by them are in conformity with the basic constitutional charter, the Treaty.' The Court, asked to review an act of the Parliament that affected the interests of the applicant political group, then considered the reference in the text of Article 173 to review of the 'legality of acts of the Council and the Commission'. No explicit reference to review of Parliamentary acts was included. The Court made concrete its concern for constitutionalization: 'An interpretation of Article 173 of the Treaty which excluded measures adopted by the European Parliament from those which could be contested would lead to a result contrary both to the spirit of the Treaty as expressed in Article 164 and to its system.'

An action for annulment was ruled admissible and the act was annulled. In effect the European Court engaged in a process of updating the Treaty. Perhaps review of acts of the Parliament went unmentioned in the original text of Article 173 in the Treaty of Rome because it was not at that time appreciated that the activities of the Parliament—then less ambitiously styled the Assembly—would come to exert significant influence over third parties. So the Court was responding to shifting patterns of power in the Community by adjusting the patterns of judicial supervision. The Court was intent on effective judicial protection within the overall scope of the Treaty and, in order to achieve this, it felt unconstrained by textual limitations in specific provisions of the Treaty. This may be described as the Court filling in the detail of the Treaty framework; it may be taken as the Court in effect rewriting the Treaty. At the time, 1986, the Member States had not made any change of substance to the original Treaty which, almost thirty years old, had an unsurprisingly threadbare appearance.

This provides a broad justification for judicial activism which may or may not satisfy a critical observer. Some would hold that the Court has overstepped its interpretative role and would judge it guilty of trespass into realms of Treaty amendment that belong with the Member States acting by common accord under Article 236 EEC, now Article N TEU. Whatever one's personal verdict, it should be plain today that assessment of the validity of the Court's activism occurs against a quite different background. The Court is no longer able to claim that it is in practical terms the sole mechanism for securing the updating of the Treaty. The process of Treaty revision through intergovernmental conferences is becoming an established feature of Community, now Union, politics. This by no means relegates the Court to a mere technical applier of rules. But the political climate in which it operates is altered.

Article 173 was amended in the Treaty on European Union, agreed at Maastricht, to allow explicitly for the review of 'acts of the European Parliament intended to produce legal effects *vis-à-vis* third parties'. This largely codified the Court's ruling in *Les Verts*. Is codification the sign for judicial restraint?

The place of the Parliament in the construction of the pattern of judicial review provides a fertile area for witnessing the depth of constitutionalization undertaken by the Court. It 'lost' the case brought against it by Les Verts, the Green Party. In fact it was rather pleased to lose. The Parliament made no real attempt in the case to deny the admissibility of the challenge to its act. This surrender was prompted by the Parliament's efforts elsewhere to establish that, notwithstanding the Treaty's textual limitations, it was entitled to bring annulment actions under Article 173 on the same terms as the other institutions. The original Article 173 imposed no standing limitations on actions brought by Member States, Council, and Commission. But the Parliament appeared to have no place. Accordingly the Parliament had an incentive to see its own acts ruled challengeable in the hope that the Court would be induced to achieve a balance by moving beyond the text of Article 173 to find the Parliament able to challenge the acts of others.

In *Parliament* v. *Council*,[7] known with reference to its subject matter as the 'Comitology' decision, the Parliament's hopes were dashed. It wished to challenge the Council's choice of legal basis for a particular measure. It hoped to persuade the Court of the appropriateness of a different legal base that would ensure it, the Parliament, an enhanced participatory role. The Court adhered to the text of the Treaty and ruled the Parliament's application inadmissible under Article 173. The Court felt able to justify this apparent refusal to ensure for the Parliament a legally protected input into the Community political process by referring, *inter alia*, to the role of the Commission in bringing annulment proceedings should the Parliament's position be prejudiced by the Council's questionable choice of legal base.

The Court assumed that where the Parliament was bullied by

---

[7] Case 302/87 [1988] ECR 5615.

the Council the Commission would stand up for it. This happens. The squabble in *Commission* v. *Council*, the 'Titanium Dioxide' case, pitted Commission and Parliament in one corner against the Council in the other.[8] However, this assumption of congruence between the perceptions of the Commission and the Parliament offered a window through which the Parliament's independent interests could subsequently be admitted into the system of judicial review. Less than two years later a conveniently adjusted fact pattern was presented to the Court. In *Parliament* v. *Council*,[9] known in turn as 'Chernobyl' and also a dispute over choice of legal base, the Commission was in agreement with the Council. The chief rationale in *Comitology* for ruling the Parliament's application inadmissible was therefore missing. The Parliament could not shelter under the Commission's wing; it had to fight alone. So, rather than depriving it of power to carry on that fight, the Court ruled that the Parliament's challenge was admissible in so far as it was aimed at the protection of its own prerogatives. Ultimately the Parliament's challenge failed, but it had at least secured a hearing into the merits of its claim.[10]

The Parliament had not managed to elevate itself to the position of the Member States, Council, or Commission which are able to initiate annulment proceedings without demonstrating any special interest. The Parliament had, however, secured for itself a distinctive means of protection commensurate with its Treaty-conferred interest in the development of Community legislation. It could bring proceedings before the Court in order to protect its prerogatives.

Ensuring protection of the Parliament's position in the legislative process was of major significance. The Single European Act had effected important improvements in the participation of the Parliament in the making of Community legislation.[11] The Court's stance in *Chernobyl* could be portrayed as no more than a response to these institutional shifts. It was ensuring that the other political institutions could not edge the Parliament out of its Treaty-conferred position without facing judicial, rather than mere political, scrutiny.

---

[8] Case C–300/89 [1991] ECR I–2867.
[9] Case C–70/88 [1990] ECR I–2041.
[10] [1991] ECR I–4561.   [11] Ch. 3, 72.

This analysis possesses an appealing fluency, but it suffers from disingenuousness. The Parliament's legislative role had indeed been enhanced by the Single European Act. But its powers under Article 173 had not been. The Court was well aware of this. In *Comitology* it referred explicitly to the Single European Act's alterations to the Parliament's position in some areas and the absence of any change to Article 173. The subsequent ruling in *Chernobyl* was an instance of judicial updating of the Treaty in an area where the Member States had decided against amendment. This seems to take the Court into realms reserved by the Treaty to the Member States under the thin cover of interpretation. Whatever one's view of the ultimate legitimacy of the Court's redistribution of institutional powers and supervisory roles within the Community though these decisions, the saga serves as a powerful statement of the Court's implicit readiness to pursue a path of constitutionalization that is divorced from, and even in opposition to, the consensus achievable among the Member States. Such activism has fed mistrust of the Court in some quarters. The implications of such tensions for the development of the Community are discussed further below.

For all these pressures, the Member States agreed at Maastricht that Article 173 would be amended in line with the Court's decision in the *Chernobyl* case. Actions brought by the Parliament for the purposes of protecting its prerogatives are brought explicitly within the Court's jurisdiction in a new third paragraph in Article 173. It is now clear that the Parliament's position is not reliant on the Commission's attitude, although its inability to challenge measures other than those that affect its prerogatives classifies it still as a second-class institution.

A final illustration of the Court's readiness to develop institutional systems that will safeguard its conception of the rule of law, whether or not those systems are explicitly foreseen by the Treaty, is provided by *Zwartveld*.[12] This arose out of Dutch investigations into allegations of fraudulent practices connected with fish quotas. It has already been discussed in Chapter 2. A Dutch judge wished to obtain Community documents concerned with fisheries and to question Community fishery inspectors. No provision in the Treaty envisages such co-operation. The Court was nevertheless

---

[12] Case C–2Imm. [1990] ECR I–3365, p. 47 above.

prepared to make an order requiring the Commission's co-operation. The absence of a specific Treaty provision seems to have been regarded as a matter of detail left inexplicit in a broad but incomplete Treaty framework dedicated to the constitutional rule of law.

The insignificance of the literal terms of the Treaty is neatly captured by the Court's reference to Article 5 as a basis for imposing obligations on the Commission. The literal terms of Article 5 are uni-directional. Article 5 refers explicitly only to obligations of Community solidarity imposed on the Member States, not on the institutions of the Community. Yet the Court was prepared to regard Article 5 as no more than a specific expression of a general principle requiring collaboration in pursuit of the success of the Community's endeavours. The Court seems prepared to treat Article 5 as the pivot of the Community constitutional order. It is questionable whether the general, imprecise terms of Article 5 are really sufficient to serve as a justification for some of the very specific obligations that the Court has drawn from it in rulings such as *Zwartveld* and *Francovich*.[13] It is possible to accuse the Court of over-ambitious lawmaking. The most visible test of whether the European Court has gone too far is the response at national level. Will national courts accept and faithfully apply rulings from Luxembourg that they perceive as lying at the margins of its competence?[14]

JUDICIAL REVIEW—INDIVIDUALS

The Court has built the pattern of judicial review inspired by the need to provide a complete system of judicial supervision. The Parliament's capacity to adopt acts affecting the legal position of third parties prompted the Court to sanction review of those acts by interested parties. In turn, the impact on the Parliament of choices of legal base induced the Court to promote the Parliament into a quasi-privileged position in seeking review of relevant acts. This account of the development of judicial review has thus far not examined the position of the individual applicant. Here, too, the Court has been seized by the spirit of establishing a coherent

---

[13] Cases C–6, 9/90 *Andrea Francovich* v. *Italian State* [1991] ECR I–5357. See also Ch. 4, text at and following n. 47.   [14] See further, 210 below.

system based on the rule of law. But its generosity towards individual applicants has been limited.

Article 173 establishes a hierarchy of applicants. The Member States, Council, and Commission belong to the top rank and are able to seek annulment of acts without having to demonstrate any special interest. In the next rank are now placed the Parliament and the European Central Bank, able to bring actions for the purpose of protecting their prerogatives. This leaves natural or legal persons. They are able to 'institute proceedings against a decision addressed to that person or against a decision which, although in the form of a regulation or a decision addressed to another person, is of direct and individual concern to the former'.

The addressee of a decision enjoys standing to challenge that decision, but beyond that obvious case the criteria appear rather forbidding. Only a decision is challengeable, albeit that form is not conclusive; and only where the requirement of direct and individual concern is satisfied. The existence of these threshold criteria reflects the desire to balance the individual's interest in access to the Court against the need to protect the legislature and the administration from challenges that will obstruct the effective discharge of functions in the public interest. Standing is limited to those with, loosely, a genuine interest in the matter. Such standing requirements are a common feature of modern systems of judicial review.

The precise meaning of these rules has been elaborated by the Court. For all their apparent strictness, it is conceivable that the Court could have softened them through a process of interpretation driven by the desire to liberalize individual access to the Court. In the main, the Court has *not* been tempted to move in this direction. Its record is rather erratic; it displays signs of recent mood changes. But the bulk of the case law reveals a Community judiciary not easily persuaded of the individual interest of applicant natural or legal persons.

The Court's long-standing approach has been to seek to identify whether or not the measure in question is of general application. Where it is of a legislative, normative nature, individual challenge is precluded. The key to individual access is the specific or individualized nature of the act. In *Plaumann* v. *Commission* the Court explained that applicants are 'individually concerned if that decision affects them by reason of certain attributes which are peculiar to them or by reason of circumstances in which they are differentiated from all other persons and by virtue of these factors distinguishes them individually'.[15] Plaumann was an importer of clementines into Germany wishing to challenge a Commission decision addressed to Germany refusing it authorization to suspend customs duties on clementines imported from third countries. Plaumann was certainly affected, but this was held insufficient to constitute an individual concern within the meaning of Article 173 because all importers, present and potential, were also affected. The measure was a response to a general problem and drafted accordingly, without specific reference to any individual trader, and could not be challenged by a trader in the regulated sector.

This decision in 1963 set the tone for the years that followed. Failure to satisfy the standing rules was far more common than success and most individual challenges to Community acts did not even reach the stage of inquiry into the merits of the case.

It seems plausible that the European Court's restrictive approach was in part based on a deliberate reluctance to improve routes that could lead to the regular calling into question of the validity of Community legislation. It was intent on striking a balance between individual access to justice and effective administration that was tipped in favour of the latter in recognition of the shallow roots put down by the Community system. If that is an accurate diagnosis, then one would not expect the Court's attitude toward standing to remain static. The activities of a stronger, more mature Community should be increasingly open to review. The standing rules applicable to natural and legal persons have not altered at all since 1958 and the entry into force of the Treaty of Rome. Since Maastricht they occupy the fourth, rather than the second, paragraph of Article 173. And today such actions by natural or legal persons are initially brought before the Court of First Instance, not the main Court. But the precise wording of the standing requirements endures. However, there are signs in the Court of recent shifts in the direction of liberalization.

Instances where the Court has moved towards a relaxation of the rules were initially regarded as exceptions to the normal restrictive rule. So the Court has shown generosity towards

[15] Case 25/62 [1963] ECR 95.

importers of products that are severely affected by the introduction of anti-dumping duties even where the measures in question seem to be generalized responses to the problems in that trade sector.[16] Complainants who provoke an investigation that leads to the adoption of a generalized Community measure have been granted standing to challenge that measure.[17] Recent developments suggest that these are only specific manifestations of a general receptiveness in the Court to the idea that measures may simultaneously be general in nature but also of sufficient interest to particular individuals to justify granting them standing under Article 173. The ruling in *Cordoniu SA* v. *Council*, a judgment of May 1994, gives every indication of landmark status in the creation of a new and wider principle of individual access to justice before the European Court.[18]

The measure in question was in the form of a regulation. That could not be decisive. It reserved the term *crémant* for particular types of sparkling wine produced in France and Luxembourg. This was severely detrimental to Cordoniu, a Spanish producer of rather fine sparkling wines which had since 1924 been marketed using the phrase *crémant*, which formed part of a trade mark held by Cordoniu. A rigid approach would categorize the measure as one of general application to the sector; and would dismiss Cordoniu as one of many producers of wine likely to be affected. However, the Court found the application admissible and annulled the measure. Cordoniu had standing because even though the act was legislative in nature, Cordoniu's historical and economic position persuaded the Court that it was individually concerned.

General legislation may affect individuals in a distinct manner that is sufficient to allow them to bring an application for annulment. This liberal attitude peeps through the Court's previous case law only in special situations, but *Cordoniu* represents a break with such incrementalism and seems to represent a general receptiveness to review of legislation that has a particular impact on a trader or traders. It is plausible that this relaxation reflects the decline of the need for a policy of protecting the Community's fledgling legislature and administration.

---

[16] Cf Case C–358/89 *Extramet* v. *Commission* [1991] ECR I–2501.
[17] Case 264/82 *Timex* v. *Commission* [1985] ECR 849.
[18] Case C–309/89 [1994] ECR I–1853.

Cordoniu may be an indirect statement of the growing maturity of the Community system.

For all the apparent recent softening of the Court's approach, the individual applicant is confronted by serious obstacles in the shape of the restrictions in Article 173 relating to time limits and standing. It may be possible to use Article 177 to circumvent these restrictions. The Court's rigidity towards individual applicants under Article 173 contrasts with its determined maximization of the use of the Article 177 preliminary-reference procedure, *inter alia* to allow challenges at national level to the validity of Community acts.

Article 177, it will be recalled,[19] allows the European Court to rule on points of Community law raised at national level. It is commonly used where points of interpretation of Community law are at stake in national proceedings, but it is equally possible for it to be employed where the validity of a Community act is in question at national level. Provided an individual is able to initiate proceedings at national level in which objection is made to the validity of a Community act, it is possible to obtain a review of that act by the European Court through the mechanism of Article 177.

The independence of the Article 177 indirect route to the European Court from the direct action under Article 173 is clearly stated in the following comment drawn from the Court's ruling in *Walter Rau* v. *Bundesanstalt für Landwirtschaftliche Marktordnung*:[20]

there is nothing in Community law to prevent an action from being brought before a national court against a measure implementing a Decision adopted by a Community institution where the conditions laid down by national law are satisfied. Where such an action is brought, if the outcome of the dispute depends on the validity of that Decision the national court may submit questions to the Court of Justice by way of a reference for a preliminary ruling, without there being any need to ascertain whether or not the plaintiff in the main proceedings has the possibility of challenging the Decision directly before the Court.

So, for example, in *Universität Hamburg* v. *Hauptzollamt Hamburg-Kehrwieder*[21] the German customs authorities based themselves on a Commission decision in making a ruling that was

---

[19] 107 above. [20] Case 133/85 [1987] ECR 2289.
[21] Case 216/82 [1983] ECR 2771.

unfavourable to the University. It was highly improbable that the University would have been able to demonstrate a sufficient interest within the meaning of Article 173 in order to bring a challenge to the decision before the European Court. It was unlikely that it would even have been aware that the decision had been made. Certainly it would have been unlikely to have become aware within the two-month time limit imposed by Article 173. Once confronted by German administrative action based on the Commission decision, the University brought an action before the German courts in which it impugned the Commission decision. An Article 177 reference was made to the European Court in which the validity of the decision was questioned, but, in addition, the referring court asked the European Court whether the University's tactics were permissible. The European Court confirmed that this was a perfectly proper use of the system of judicial remedies available under the Treaty. The University came into direct contact only with national implementation of Community law, not the Community act itself. Therefore litigation at national level was its proper means of seeking judicial protection.

An apparent drawback to the use of Article 177 lies in the absence of any individual right to referral.[22] The reference procedure is activated by the national court, not the individual, and it therefore appears to offer inferior security to the individual than the Article 173 direct action. The European Court's ruling in *Foto Frost* v. *Hauptzollamt Lübeck-Ost*[23] goes some way to removing the individual's dependence on national judicial discretion. The Court ruled that it is not open to a national court to rule a Community act invalid. Where a challenge to validity is raised at national level, the national court must make a reference to the European Court, which holds exclusive jurisdiction to declare Community acts to be void. This increases the individual's expectation of access to the European Court. But that was probably only one motivation for the Court in *Foto-Frost*. It feared the disintegration of the Community legal order that would flow from divergent rulings at national level on the validity of Community acts. It was therefore intent on taking to itself exclusive jurisdiction in questions of validity even though the

---

[22] 109 above.   [23] Case 314/85 [1987] ECR 4199.

wording of Article 177 appears to envisage that lower national courts are allowed a discretion to decide on points of validity themselves without making a reference. Article 177 is the cornerstone of the structure designed to secure a common meaning for Community law in all the Member States.

The only concession that the European Court has made in establishing its exclusive jursidiction to rule on validity lies in its acceptance that national courts may grant *interim* relief against the application of Community acts pending a definitive ruling on validity by the European Court in the context of the Article 177 preliminary-reference procedure (which the national court awarding interim relief must invoke). At the technical level, this is an important part of the scheme of judicial protection under Article 177. Of broader significance in the quest to constitutionalize the Treaty, it is striking that in its approach to interim relief, the European Court's ambitions are directed at the development of generally applicable principles. So in *Zuckerfabrik Süderdithmarschen* v. *Hauptzollamt Itzehoe* and *Zuckerfabrik Soest* v. *Hauptzollamt Paderborn*[24] the Court elaborated its *Foto-Frost* ruling by identifying the criteria to be taken into account by a national court asked to grant interim relief against the application of a Community act pending the European Court's definitive final ruling. It insisted on the importance of analogies with the principles that should apply where a national court is asked to suspend the application of a *national* measure alleged to be incompatible with Community law, pending clarification from Luxembourg on the relevant points of Community law.[25] It also drew on the principles governing its own powers to grant interim relief in cases before it.[26] The applicable rules need not be identical in all cases, but the Court's awareness of the wider picture provides further evidence of its determination to construct a coherent pattern of judicial protection out of the Treaty's patchwork.

Article 177 compensates individuals for the limits of Article 173. *Cordoniu* shows that the Court has begun to liberalize Article 173 as a means of individual access to justice. There are indications

---

[24] Cases C–143/88, 92/89 [1991] ECR I–415.
[25] Explicitly, Case C–213/89 *Factortame* [1990] ECR I–2435.
[26] Arts. 185, 186 EC.

of a contemporaneous hardening of its attitude towards use of Article 177. *TWD Textilwerke Deggendorf* v. *Germany*[27] involved a Commission decision addressed to Germany requiring repayment of sums paid to the applicant in breach of Community state aid law. The applicant, asked to repay, attacked the German authorities' demand before the German courts, alleging that the Community act was invalid. An Article 177 reference was made. The Community act was much more closely tied to the applicant, albeit not addressed to it, than the decision that prejudiced the University of Hamburg.[28] The European Court was explicitly influenced by the applicant's knowledge of the Commission decision and by the fact that it could have challenged it under Article 173 of the Treaty. Yet it had simply awaited national proceedings. The Court ruled that the applicant was not entitled in such circumstances to challenge the Community act via Article 177.

This does not rule out use of Article 177 as a means of securing review of Community acts. An applicant in the position of the University of Hamburg would be treated in the same way as before. An action at national level allied to invocation of Article 177 remains appropriate in a case where the rejection of the application by the national authority was the only measure directly addressed to the applicant of which it had been informed in good time and which it could challenge in the courts without confronting problems in showing standing. But it is plainly the view of the European Court that applicants cannot surrender available Article 173 protection in reliance on the opportunity of subsequent recourse to Article 177. Legal certainty would be compromized were a free choice between the two routes possible.

The details of this test are troublingly imprecise. It is difficult to ascertain what degree of accessibility via Article 173 leads to the Article 177 route slamming shut. It will be especially difficult for lawyers to advise clients in advance of the correct choice between Articles 173 and 177, given that standing under Article 173 is in itself such an opaque issue. Perhaps Article 173 actions will have to be started[29] just in case failure to pursue them is later found to foreclose the Article 177 route. However, the general impression

---

[27] Case C–188/92 [1994] ECR I–833.
[28] Case 216/82, n. 21 above.
[29] Within 2 months; Art. 173(5) EC.

that emerges from *Cordoniu* and *TWD Deggendorf*, decided within two months of each other, is that the long-standing perceived linkage between the Court's treatment of Articles 173 and 177 has been confirmed, but now the emphasis has shifted more towards Article 173 and away from Article 177.

The law remains in a dynamic state. It would be unwise to overstate the apparent interdependence of *Cordoniu* and *TWD Deggendorf*. It would be unwise to attempt to trace a consistent narrative linking the large amount of Court case law dealing with standing under Article 173. Remarkable though it may seem over thirty years after *Plaumann*,[30] the Court is still feeling its way and there are competing interpretations of its strategy in developing direct and indirect judicial review.[31] In future the initial forum for the refinement of this case law will be the Court of First Instance.

GROUNDS OF REVIEW

The issues of admissibility are important in themselves, but an appreciation of their development also provides an insight into the Court's policy of constructing a framework of judicial protection that harnesses national and Community procedures to a constitutional order that is largely undefined by the Treaty. An exploration of the merits of applications for annulment is equally worthwhile from the twin perspectives of their intrinsic importance and the insight provided into the Court's technique of amassing a collection of workable legal principles that extends far beyond the bare bones of the Treaty.

Article 173 provides that Community acts shall be reviewed on grounds of 'lack of competence, infringement of an essential procedural requirement, infringement of this Treaty or of any rule of law relating to its application, or misuse of powers'. Where the Court is asked to rule on the validity of a Community act in an Article 177 preliminary reference, the same grounds apply.

The open-ended reference to 'any rule of law relating to [the Treaty's] application' in particular has provided the Court with scope to develop a range of general principles of Community law

---

[30] N. 15 above.
[31] For a synthesis see P. Craig, 'Legality, Standing and Substantive Review in Community Law' (1994) 14 *Ox.JLS* 511.

against which acts adopted by the institutions may be tested. Some rules of law are found in the Treaty. Article 190 EC, for example, imposes a duty to provide reasons in support of regulations, directives and decisions. Inadequate reasoning is a basis for annulment. Particular types of discrimination are outlawed by the Treaty; failure to observe these provisions formed the basis for the annulment of the act challenged by Cordoniu.[32] Other rules of law are not the subject of explicit elaboration in the Treaty. The European Court has built a body of principles that confines the exercise of legislative and administrative power in the Community. There are places in the Treaty where the Court is offered an explicit invitation to develop general principles. Article 215, for example, envisages the shaping of principles governing the Community's non-contractual liability 'in accordance with the general principles common to the laws of the Member States'. However, as is so often the case, it would be misleading to regard explicit Treaty provision as the gateway into the field of development of general principles. The Court treats the field as a great deal more accessible. This is an aspect of the Court's commitment to constitutionalization of the Treaty transcending its explicit terms.

For example, the Court has developed notions of procedural fairness beyond the basic Article 190 duty to give reasons. In *Transocean Marine Paint* v. *Commission* it identified the grant of an opportunity to an individual to make his or her views known when his or her interests stood to be be affected by the actions of a public authority as a principle of Community law disregard of which would form the basis for annulment of the act in question.[33] In accepting that principle and giving shape to it, the Court was inspired by patterns of due process in the domestic legal systems of the Member States. It had been pushed hard down that road by the diligently researched Opinion of its Advocate-General in the case, Mr Warner.

Principles such as proportionality and the protection of legitimate expectations have been brought within the corpus of principles on which the Court will draw in reviewing the constitutionality of acts of the institutions. Neither is fully

[32] N. 18 above. The relevant (post-TEU) provisions are Arts. 6, 40 EC.
[33] Case 17/74 [1974] ECR 1063.

developed in the Treaty; both are now familiar parts of the Community legal order. These are principles that allow the Court to check the impact on the individual of legislative and administrative action. It is by no means the case that the institutions are now unable to act without finding their initiatives cut down by the Court in an individual application for annulment. Standing restrictions play a part in ensuring that the institutions are partially immunized from over-intrusive litigation, but even though the Court has developed a notion of legal protection of legitimate expectations, 'traders cannot have a legitimate expectation that an existing situation which is capable of being altered by the Community institutions in the exercise of their discretionary power will be maintained'.[34] However, the Court has ensured that the interests of the individual find expression in the pattern of judicial supervision.

The protection of fundamental rights represents the most remarkable illustration of the Court's mission to create a pattern of legal security for the individual within the framework of Community law. This evolution has already been referred to in both Chapters 2 and 4 of this book. In *Internationale Handelsgesellschaft*[35] the Court asserted that the Community legal order recognized the protection of fundamental rights and that it, the European Court, would test the compatibility of Community acts against these standards. The content of this means of individual protection is not drawn simply from national systems. In *Hoechst* v. *Commission*[36] the Court observed that it 'has consistently held that fundamental rights are an integral part of the general principles of law the observance of which the Court ensures, in accordance with constitutional traditions common to the Member States . . . The European Convention on Human Rights is of particular significance in that regard.'

European Community law feeds off national law but it is also nourished by other sources of 'European law', widely understood. All the Member States are party to the European Convention on Human Rights; so, too, are some other European states that lie

[34] Case C–350/89 *Delacre* v. *Commission* [1990] ECR I–395.
[35] Case 11/70 *Internationale Handelsgesellschaft* v. *Einfuhr- und Vorratstelle für Getreide und Futtermittel* [1970] ECR 1125.
[36] Case 46/87 [1989] ECR 2859.

outside the Union. The Community is not party to the Convention and there are doubts whether its accession is constitutionally possible.[37] But the Court has committed itself to upholding principles drawn from the Convention in reviewing Community acts. Albeit indirectly, the Community's institutions are subjected to the higher order of the Convention.

Article F(2) of the Treaty on European Union declares that 'The Union shall respect fundamental rights, as guaranteed by the European Convention for the Protection of Human Rights and Fundamental Freedoms signed in Rome on 4 November 1950 and as they result from the constitutional traditions common to the Member States, as general principles of Community law.' The choice of phrase is plainly inspired by the Court's attitude to the protection of fundamental rights under EC law and Article F(2) appears to lift this body of law on to the Union plane. However, the attraction of this commitment is tarnished by the institutional obstacles to its practical realization, examined in Chapter 1. The Union lacks legal personality. The European Court has no jurisdiction to enforce Article F TEU. The statement of Union compliance with fundamental rights law is welcome in principle, but lacks the practical support that is a feature of the developed pattern of EC law in the field.

LEGAL INFILTRATION

Community acts are subject to review to check their compliance with the general principles of Community law. But the spread of EC constitutional law ensures that these principles have a much deeper impact. National measures, too, are equally subject to review against these standards of Community law where the national authorities act within the sphere of Community law. For example, the requirements of procedural fairness that have been shaped by the European Court bind not only Community institutions. They infiltrate the national legal order and are capable of binding national authorities and should be applied by national courts. In *UNECTEF* v. *Heylens*, Mr Heylens, a football trainer of Belgian nationality, found himself prevented from

---

[37] Opinion 2/94, pending before the Court.

working in France.[38] The European Court ruled that he was seeking to exercise a Community-law right to work in another Member State. That triggered an entitlement to accompanying procedural protection drawn from Community law, to be applied at national level and binding on national authorities. Mr Heylens was entitled to, *inter alia*, a fair hearing before the relevant French authorities, just as an individual immediately affected by action taken by the European Commission would enjoy procedural rights.

Similarly, the Community law package of fundamental rights must be observed by Member States too in areas where public authorities act within the sphere of Community law. A three-link chain has been forged. The European Convention is used as a source of EC law; this then translates into the national legal order. In this sense, Member States find their courts bound to apply provisions of the European Convention in the guise of EC law. This puts a rather different perspective on the orthodox constitutional view that the European Convention on Human Rights forms no part of English law until such time as Parliament enacts its provisions in a domestic statute.[39]

The general principles of Community law control both Community institutions and national authorities when they act within the sphere of Community competence. This dictates the need to consider where lie the margins of Community intrusion into the realms of national competence beyond which national acts will not be checked for conformity with principles drawn from Community law.[40] This is one of the contexts in which the discussion of Community competence in Chapter 2 of this book should be placed.[41] The outer edge of Community competence is rather blurred. It is familiar that Community competence is not static and that the Treaty does not offer a defined list of areas in which the Member States retain exclusive authority.

---

[38] Case 222/86 *Union Nationale des Entraîneurs et Cadres Techniques Professionnels du Football* v. *Heylens* [1987] ECR 4097.

[39] Sir N. Browne-Wilkinson, 'The Infiltration of a Bill of Rights' [1992] *Pub.L* 397.

[40] e.g. J. Temple Lang, 'The Sphere in which Member States are Obliged to Comply with the General Principles of Law and Community Fundamental Rights Principles' [1991/2] *LIEI* 23.

[41] e.g. Cases 60 & 61/84, Case C–168/91, 42–5 above.

Nevertheless, in principle there are areas of national law undisturbed by Community law; areas in which litigants must seek their protection under national law alone, which may be less favourable than Community law, more favourable, or simply different. Formally, the outer margins of Community competence represent the end of the territory over which ranges the Community's constitutional order. In practice, this need not be so. The notion that there can be an enduring sharp division of a national legal system into two compartments, those infused by Community law and those that ignore it, is rather unrealistic. Such bifurcation cannot be stable. Community-law principles infiltrate areas where they have no formal role to play. Once they become part of one area of national law, they exert an influence in other areas too. They become irreversibly part of the legal currency. Community law in practice cannot be neglected by any national lawyer, for Community law is part of the influences that drive the development of his or her legal system.

This is the incoming tide of EC law to which Lord Denning memorably referred over two decades ago.[42] Beyond its formal role, EC law is causing a sea change in the nature (and outer limits) of national legal systems. EC law is in effect a new source of law; and the very style of it must spill over into domestic law. So even in areas that fall formally within national competence, EC law techniques and trends cannot be ignored. It is therefore an indispensable element of a modern legal education in any of the Member States.

Such sweeping comments tend to make some lawyers who lack an EC law training rather nervous. Others are simply sceptical. Admittedly, the speed with which this spillover will occur may be rather sluggish. Much will depend on the extent to which counsel, arguing by analogy, and the judiciary, receptive to unfamiliar concepts and sources, are sufficiently well versed in EC and comparative law to be able to look to broader legal horizons. In the United Kingdom, few lawyers over the age of 40 will have studied EC law in the formative years of their legal education. EC law has been a compulsory part of legal education in Scotland for several years, but in England the decision to take this major step came only in 1994 and will take time to influence the intellectual

---

[42] *H. P. Bulmer* v. *J. Bollinger SA* [1974]. 2 All ER 1226.

disposition of the legal profession. Doubtless some lawyers will enthusiastically participate in the legal transplant whereas others will be cautious about what may be created. Lord Slynn's overt and covert influence in the House of Lords since his return from Luxembourg will plainly be important. The current Master of the Rolls, Sir Thomas Bingham, has written of his hopes that the 1990s 'will be remembered as the time when England . . . ceased to be a legal island'.[43] However, an erratic attitude to EC law analogies as the catalyst for legal change may be expected to emerge from the pages of the Law Reports in the years to come.

The House of Lords' decision in *Woolwich Building Society* v. *IRC*[44] involved the recoverability of money from the Inland Revenue paid under a mistake of law. The House of Lords decided to remove existing obstacles to recovery under English law. There was *no* Community law aspect to the litigation, yet Lord Goff chose to draw on the European Court's ruling in *San Giorgio*[45] to the effect that Community law required repayment of charges paid by a person to a Member State in contravention of the rules of Community law. He commented that 'at a time when Community law is becoming increasingly important, it would be strange if the right of the citizen to recover overpaid charges were to be more restricted under domestic law than it is under Community law'.[46] There were several other powerful policy arguments which led Lord Goff to this conclusion. The Community-law comparison was in no way the decisive factor in this decision. Yet the fact that he nonetheless chose to make the analogy, in a situation with no direct link to EC law whatsoever, provides powerful proof of the scope for feeding Community law perspectives into 'mainstream' English law development.

EC law's role as a catalyst for legal rethinking beyond areas in which it is formally applicable will be strengthened by the growing multi-functionalism of the Community's activities. A decreasing number of areas lie so far distant from the EC-law sphere that they are immune from contagion. English contract law, for example,

---

[43] 'There is a World Elsewhere: The Changing Perspectives of English Law' (1992) 41 *ICLQ* 513.　　　　　　　　　　　　　　　　[44] [1992] 3 All ER 737.
[45] Case 199/82 *Amministrazione delle Finanze dello Stato* v. *SpA San Giorgio* [1983] ECR 3595.
[46] At 764.

could for a number of years treat EC law as of marginal interest only. Perhaps a typical law school course in contract law would mention the EC competition rules in passing in its explanation of the rules of illegality and related reasons for denying enforceability to contracts. The rise of Community legislation affecting contractual freedom could probably be confined to peripheral areas and special types of contract—those concluded with consumers away from business premises and package holidays, for instance.[47] However the adoption in 1993 of the Directive on Unfair Terms in Consumer Contracts has finally propelled EC law into the heartland of national contract law.[48] The Directive aims to control terms in consumer contracts that have not been individually negotiated with reference to a test of 'good faith'. That will be difficult for the English system to digest. Good faith is not a notion that is recognized as a general principle within the traditional framework of English contract law. In the area in which the Directive applies, some conceptual readjustment will be called for. It is submitted that it is not conceivable that the changes demanded will be capable of rigorous confinement to the area covered by the Directive alone. They will affect the broader development of the law.[49] This is not to suggest that a good-faith criterion will come to permeate the pattern of even commercial contract law. It is entirely probable that in many areas analogies with EC law will be evaluated and rejected. Tides can become floods which will do little for the fertility of the land.[50] The key point is that the influence of EC law will be felt and will demand assessment. In practice, it cannot be ignored simply because of formal questions of competence demarcation.

The stream of common development of European law widens and feeds into the dynamic process of evolution of which the common law has always been justly proud. It is fair to conclude that these processes may lead to concern among national judges

---

[47] Dir. 85/577 [1985] OJ L372/31; Dir. 90/314 [1990] OJ L158/59 respectively.

[48] Dir. 93/13 [1993] OJ L95/29. Cf Collins, H., 'Good Faith in European Contract Law' (1994) 14 *Ox.JLS* 229.

[49] Cf S. Weatherill, 'Prospects for the Development of European Private Law through "Europeanisation" in the European Court—The Case of the Directive on Unfair Terms in Consumer Contracts' [1995] *Eur. Rev. of Private L* 000.

[50] Much as metaphors can be overworked and lose their impact; an apology is offered for joining the shoals that swim with Lord Denning, n. 42 above.

that they are being asked to perform a task of legal renovation that properly lies with the legislature. This may give the impression of a matter of some constitutional weight. However, it is by no means clear that it revolves around anything more significant than the predilections of individual members of the judiciary. In *Woolwich Building Society* v. *IRC* Lord Goff was rather dismissive of the problem: 'although I am well aware of the existence of the boundary [between judicial and legislative development of the law], I am never quite sure where to find it. Its position seems to vary from case to case.'[51]

THE MODERN ROLE OF THE COURT IN CONSTITUTIONAL LAW

The European Court has a well-established track record as an innovative policy maker. Its broad justification for its invigorating contribution to the success of the Community lies in the function entrusted to it by Article 164 EC to 'ensure that in the interpretation and application of this Treaty the law is observed'. The Court has taken on the role of shaping a workable and effective legal order around the spare framework of the Treaty. The manifestations of this process of constitutionalization have been traced throughout this book.

A number of accounts have been written of the conditions which permitted the Court to develop this remarkable legal order and, critically, to secure its widespread acceptance within the legal and political systems of the Member States. Weiler famously detected a relationship between the European Court's activism and inactivism in the political institutions.[52] So, as suggested in Chapter 3, the far-reaching principles of supremacy and direct effect were developed by the European Court in a climate that was propitious to their absorption at national level, because the areas in which those principles applied were determined by all the Member States possessing a veto. The Court has involved itself in the gradual expansion of Community competence, but an even more energetic impulse towards wider competence was provided by the Member States making light of the apparent restriction of

[51] N. 44 above, at 761.
[52] J. Weiler, 'The Dual Character of Supranationalism' (1981) 1 *YEL* 267.

Community action to fields recognized by the Treaty. The states largely treated Articles 100 and 235, in particular, as authorizing the Community to act wherever the Member States in Council felt it usefully could act. Broader still, even though the Treaty has always provided explicitly for the possibility of revision by the Member States,[53] the Court's predilection for updating the Treaty did not in practice tread on Member State toes, for substantive revision of the Treaty was simply not a feature of the Community during its first thirty years.

The mix of explanations for the general acceptance at national level of the Court's ground-breaking decisions is richer than this brief summary can portray, but these factors, *inter alia*, all contribute to the adhesiveness of the Community legal order and the general, though inevitably not flawless, respect paid to the Court's rulings by political and legal institutions within the individual Member States.

Circumstances have changed. Community competence and, especially, the relationship between Community and national competence have become a much more contentious issue in the Community. This is primarily attributable to the rise in QMV voting in the Community which has stripped individual states of their veto power. Moreover, the Court's effective monopoly of the power of Treaty renovation has been broken by the readiness of the Member States to engage in the formal process of Treaty revision. This yielded first the Single European Act, coming into force in 1987, then the Treaty on European Union, agreed in 1991 and in force from 1993, and a further IGC is planned for 1996.[54] All this occurs against a background of increasing membership, which inevitably injects new shades of opinion into the structure.

Chapter 5 explored the effect of some of these trends on the quality of Community law. The question to be addressed here is whether these trends call into question the capacity or legitimacy of the innovative constitutionalizing preferences of the Court.

To take one extreme—the Court should now simply apply the law, and should abandon its law-making tendencies. It has prepared the framework and now the Member States will settle the difficult questions about its scope and effect in the future,

---

[53] Art. 236 EEC, now adjusted as Art. N TEU.
[54] Art. N(2) TEU; Ch. 1, 34 above.

while the political institutions of the Community, proceeding without the constraint of the national veto in Council and with effective Parliamentary input, will deal with the details. Or— the opposite extreme—the Member States are likely to wreck the Community endeavour if their short-term political compromises are permitted to infect the heartland of EC law. So the Court must even more now than ever before courageously defend the constitution based on individual rights which has done so much to make real the Community as a way of life for (initially) Western Europe. A middle way might cast the Court as protector of a core of Community rules, but less prepared to strike off in new directions. But what is in the core? Wherever one's views lie on this spectrum, one can readily appreciate the ferocity of the debate that is likely to break around the Court in times of regular IGCs and Treaty revision.

There is no hint of retreat in Opinion 1/91.[55] In ruling the draft EEA Agreement to be incompatible with the Community legal order, the Court provocatively referred to a transfer of powers from states to Community 'in ever wider fields', an entirely deliberate updating of the reference in *Van Gend en Loos*[56] to transfer *within limited fields*. True, the Member States themselves have played a significant part in that widening process, but the Court, too, was a major player. The Court is in many ways responsible for the multifunctional entity over which it now presides.

If it is perceived at national level that the Court is engaged in a process of Treaty revision that properly belongs to the Member States, objections are sure to be voiced. These are heard from time to time at the political level, where rumblings about the perceived lawmaking activities of the Court seem to be on the increase. The concern is not so much with the fact of lawmaking in the European Court. This has been occurring for over thirty years. The concern is that in times of QMV, in particular, the consequences of that lawmaking are felt in ever broader and deeper fields over which individual Member States are unable to exercise control. The emergence of direct or indirect attempts to confine the Court's jurisdiction may be predicted.

[55] N. 2 above.
[56] Case 26/62 *NV Algemene Transport en Expeditie Onderneming Van Gend en Loos* v. *Nederlandse Administratie der Belastingen* [1963] ECR 1.

These are also live questions among national judges. If it is perceived by national judges that the European Court has over-extended its jurisdiction, it is possible that they will resist its rulings. The Community legal order depends on willing and active co-operation between national courts and the European Court. A breach in this mutual interdependence therefore imperils the whole structure. This might suggest that a 'retreat' by the European Court to a narrower approach to competence would be a matter of pragmatic consolidation of its earlier constitution-alizing advances.

In recent years, the most potent statement of the check capable of being exercised over Community expansionism by sceptical national courts was delivered by the Bundesverfassungsgericht, the German Federal Constitutional Court, in October 1993.[57] The Court ruled that it was not incompatible with German law for Germany to ratify the Treaty on European Union. In the course of this ruling, the court offered a number of comments on the nature of the Community and its legal system which were little related to most EC lawyers' conception of the Community system. In particular, the court offered a very rigid view of Community competence, based on the text of the Treaty, and declined to recognize the dynamic process of development that has long characterized Community competence. The ruling contains much that reads as a 'warning' to both the European Court and the Community's political institutions about the dangers of undue activism. Of great significance is the message that there is a sanction. Where the Community purports to act beyond its competence, those acts will not be treated as binding within Germany;

subsequent important alterations to the integration programme set up in the Union Treaty and to the Union's powers of action are no longer covered by the [German] Act of Accession to the present Treaty [on European Union]. Thus, if European institutions or agencies were to treat or develop the Union Treaty in a way that was no longer covered by the Treaty in the form that is the basis for the Act of Accession, the resultant legislative instruments would not be legally binding within the sphere of German sovereignty. The German state organs would be prevented for

---

[57] In English, *Brunner* v. *European Union Treaty* [1994] 1 CMLR 57, from which quotations are taken here.

constitutional reasons from applying them in Germany. Accordingly the Federal Constitutional Court will review legal instruments of European institutions and agencies to see whether they remain within the limits of the sovereign rights conferred on them or transgress them.[58]

There are a number of 'red lights' in this dictum. The message to the Community legislature is that scrupulous attention should be paid to the limits of legal bases in the Treaty. Ultimately the message is that Article 235 should not be employed for legislation in novel fields when the appropriate course is to revise the Treaty, which then permits appropriate national constitutional controls to check the process. The message to the European Court is that it should not pretend to interpret the Treaty when it is really revising it. Failure to heed either 'red light' invalidates the act in the eyes of the German court, which will not apply it.

At one level there is nothing alarming in these observations. Constitutionally, it is perfectly correct to describe the EC/EU as based on a system of limited competence, defined by the Treaties. The notion of a lack of competence as a basis for the annulment of Community acts is constitutionally unobjectionable. It is explicitly recognized by Article 173 EC. However, one would assume that it is for the European Court to decide on the limits of Community competence or else the whole legal structure will be stripped of its common framework as different national courts take different views of the validity of Community laws and even Court rulings. The exclusive competence of the European Court to rule on the limits of Community competence cannot be found in explicit terms in the Treaty, although the ruling in *Foto-Frost*[59] makes plain the Court's own perception in an analogous area that to permit national courts to rule on the validity of Community acts would damage the integrity of the system. The threat of the Bundesverfassungsgericht lies less in its insistence on the existence of limits to Community competence than its intention *itself* to measure those limits. The court stated that 'the Union Treaty as a matter of principle distinguishes between the exercise of a sovereign power conferred for limited purposes and the amending of the Treaty, so that its interpretation may not have effects that are equivalent to an extension of the Treaty. Such an interpreta-

---

[58] Para. 49 of the CMLR translation, n. 57 above.
[59] N. 23 above.

tion of enabling rules would not produce any binding effects for Germany'.[60]

But where does amendment begin and interpretation start? This is not a question capable of scientifically precise resolution in any system of law. The integrity of the Community legal order depends on the European Court being equipped with the exclusive power to decide such questions. Once national courts make their own choices, the fragmentation of the Community legal order beckons.

The impact of the Bundesverfassungsgericht's ruling needs to be placed in context. For all the 'red lights', the outcome of the ruling was a 'green light' in favour of German ratification of the Treaty on European Union. This is not to suggest that the observations of the court should not be taken seriously, but it is at least a caution against overstating the depth of the objections of the Bundesverfassungsgericht to current practice.

The success of the Community system depends on the willing and active co-operation of national courts. This dictates that the sensitivity about competence which emerges from this ruling demands an assessment. For if the Bundesverfassungsgericht executes its threat to refuse to apply Community law that it regards as *ultra vires*, other national constitutional courts will doubtless follow like tumbling dominoes and the Community legal order will be placed in the severest jeopardy. The Article 177 preliminary-reference procedure is too fragile to provide an effective means of controlling a national judiciary that decides to keep the European Court at arm's length.[61] To this extent rebellion at national level is not simply a problem for the rebelling state. It is a problem for the European Court and the Community generally. This leads to the perception that the avoidance of such potential confrontations is a matter of interest to both European and national courts. So a response—doubtless indirect and inexplicit—is inevitable.

The Community system has been at this crossroads before. The development of the Community notion of fundamental-rights protection was built out of a sustained, though indirect, dialogue between the European Court and national courts, especially

---

[60] Para. 99 of the CMLR translation, n. 57 above.
[61] And Commission intervention under Art. 169 would be a last resort; 123 above.

German courts. There was understandable disquiet in Germany about the risk that Community law could undermine domestic fundamental-rights protection. There was a corresponding explicit assertion by the Bundesverfassungsgericht in 1974 that it would check Community rules against the standards of fundamental rights protection contained in the German constitution.[62] As has been explained,[63] the European Court has devoted attention to making real the protection of such standards within the framework of Community law. By 1986 the German position had altered in response to the adjustments in the pattern of Community law effected by the European Court. The Bundesverfassungsgericht declared that it no longer asserted its power to subject Community rules to constitutional review in the light of the developments at Community level with regard to fundamental rights protection and, *inter alia*, the establishment from 1979 of direct elections to the Parliament.[64]

This is not simply a question of a battle for supremacy between two constitutional orders. The relationship was remarkably fruitful. The legitimate concerns expressed at national level prompted the renovation of the Community legal order in areas that had been left out of the Treaty of Rome because of the impossibility of foreseeing in 1957 how extensive the reach of Community law would become. National courts' concerns about the trends in the development of Community law deserve to be taken seriously and not simply for the pragmatic reason that their loyal support is indispensable to the European Court's mission. National courts obtain first-hand experience of where the Community legal order may be in peril of failing to meet the demands increasingly placed on it.

So what can be drawn from the Bundesverfassungsgericht's views? The evolution of Community competence has little in common with the picture painted by it. It has evolved in a dynamic fashion in the hands of its judges and its legislators to an extent which goes far beyond any narrow, technical notion of competence-delimitation. If the message of history is that

---

[62] *Internationale Handelsgesellschaft*, often referred to as 'Solange I', English translation at [1974] CMLR 540.   [63] At 104.

[64] *Wünsche Handelsgesellschaft*, 'Solange II', English translation at [1987] 3 CMLR 225.

Community competence is not static, then what is the likely impact of the Bundesverfassungsgericht's rigid portrayal? Perhaps that the future of the Community should become more closely tied to textual limitations. There are constitutional reasons for taking seriously the fear that the evolution of the Community has created a democratic gap. Regulatory functions are drifting into the sphere of Community influence as the European market takes shape, *inter alia*, in the wake of the intense legislative activity that occurred in the run up to 1992, but the Community is not a state in any developed, structured sense. It is yet immature. It is submitted that the Bundesverfassungsgericht's general message lies in an instruction to national and to Community authorities to take care to maintain democratic accountability at a time when the Community/Union, which is not (yet) a state, is developing in a manner that affects the discharge of traditional state functions. A blurring of the allocation of competence between Community and states may lead to an absence of responsibility for actions taken. This is a message that deserves close attention in the shaping of the Union.

At a more detailed level, the Bundesverfassungsgericht's beguilingly firm assertion of the separation of powers between legislature and judiciary conceals the reality of the nuanced place of the judiciary in legal development. No one can seriously imagine judges do not 'make' law. What is really at stake is the circumstances in which judicial development is or is not justified. A simple statement that a margin exists between amendment and interpretation is theoretically undeniable and practically useless. The stability of a legal order depends to a great extent on the location of the competence to decide what is permissible interpretation and what impermissible amendment. It has always been assumed that the European Court decides on its competence authoritatively to state the scope and effect of Community law. Without any single authoritative source, the integrity of the Community legal order is in jeopardy.

It is submitted that the ruling in *Dori* in which the Court rejected the horizontal direct effect of directives provided the European Court with a chance to display its current mood and to respond to some of these admonitions.[65] The ruling in *Dori* may be

---

[65] Case C–91/92 *Faccini Dori* v. *Recreb* [1994] ECR I–3325. See 130 above.

read on several levels, but one interpretation holds that the Court was intent on preserving its credibility. The European Court must be and has been shrewdly sensitive to national reaction to the digestibility of its rulings. If the Court is considering whether to deliver a ruling that it foresees may be rejected at national level, it must weigh up whether it can justify running the risks of non-compliance and the consequent loss of credibility for itself and, perhaps, for the Community as a whole.

In *Dori*, the Court decided that it would choose restraint and a strict reading of the text of the Treaty when confronted by an opportunity to extend the constitutional reach of EC law through 'interpretation'. The powerful submissions of three Advocates General in favour of the horizontal direct effect of directives were scarcely addressed by the Court in its ruling. It contented itself with a terse insistence that '[t]he effect of extending that case-law [on vertical direct effect] to the sphere of relations between individuals would be to recognize a power in the Community to enact obligations for individuals with immediate effect, whereas it has competence to do so only where it is empowered to adopt regulations.'[66] The textual scrupulousness of this observation has little in common with the Court's attitude to direct effect over thirty years. It suggests concern in Luxembourg to quell fears about judicial lawmaking expressed, most of all, by the Bundesverfassungsgericht. The European Court seems to have concluded that, in the present state of the law, the EC legal system can survive without the horizontal direct effect of directives, but not without the support of Germany's Constitutional Court. *Dori*, like *Marshall* before it,[67] establishes a Community-law approach to the direct effect of directives that is conditioned by the climate of opinion among national judges.

This cannot mean that national courts will be permitted to dictate the content of EC law. The European Court might be damaged by reactions to perceived over-activism, but it will lose credibility still faster if it chooses to bend in the direction of the wind blown from national level. However, one may anticipate a creative and, probably, erratic period of adjustment and conciliation. The malleable principle of effectiveness, discussed in

[66] Para. 24 of the judgment.
[67] Case 152/84 *Marshall* v. *Southampton and South-West Hampshire Area Health Authority (Teaching)* [1986] ECR 723.

Chapter 4, provides a barometer. *Francovich*[68] and *Marshall 2*[69] represent its vigorous application aimed at permitting individuals to exercise control over states that default on their obligation to implement directives. *Emmott* v. *Minister for Social Welfare* may be added to this list.[70] The Court held that a state may not rely on limitation periods under national law to defeat a claim based on an unimplemented directive; time runs only from the moment of implementation. But in *Steenhorst-Neerings* the Court held that a national rule limiting recovery to a period of one year prior to a claim under an unimplemented directive could be applied in conformity with Community law.[71] *Steenhorst-Neerings* suggests a mood of judicial reluctance to extend the high-profile implications of the notion of effectiveness.

Hjalte Rasmussen's *On Law and Policy in the European Court of Justice*, published in 1986,[72] offers one of the most controversial accounts of the European Court's history of activism ever written. In the concluding chapter, Rasmussen wrote that 'it is incumb[e]nt on the Court itself to monitor closely developments in activism-related tensions along the borderline between Community and Member State competences. It has primary responsibility for taking measures which are apt to diminish tensions if they grow alarmingly.' On the final page of his book, Rasmussen added that '[a]t the end of a judicial activism running wild . . . the frightening image of court-curbing or even court-destroying initiatives emerges.' Among several points of disagreement with Rasmussen, Cappelletti has drawn very different conclusions from American constitutional history to show that courageously standing up to state defiance did *not* damage the Supreme Court's viability; quite the contrary.[73] On this view, history does not teach the European Court a lesson of prudent retreat. The pot can be stirred still further by observing that in Europe states have deeper political and economic foundations from which to unleash rebellion than

---

[68] Cases C–6, 9/90 *Andrea Francovich* v. *Italian State* [1991] ECR I–5357.

[69] Case C–271/91 [1993] 3 CMLR 293.

[70] Case C–208/90 [1991] ECR I–4269.

[71] Case C–338/91 *H. Steenhorst-Neerings* v *Bestuur van de Bedrijfsvereniging voor Detailhandel, Ambachten en Huisvrouwen*, judgment of 27 Oct. 1993.

[72] Dordrecht: Martinus Nijhoff. The extracts below are taken from 510–513.

[73] M. Cappelletti, 'Is the European Court of Justice Running Wild?' (1987) 12 *ELRev.* 3.

did states in the nascent USA, which may diminish the value of the comparison.[74] Whatever one's view, this is plainly an enduringly important debate and one that strikes today at the heart of the Court's mission.

Perhaps the major issue facing the wavering Court today is *where* to target its activism in future. It seems plain that its willingness to open up wholly new fields of Community activity is now at an end, in part in the light of the increasingly high profile of the intergovernmental conference as a means of replenishing the Community structure. Yet the Court remains a Constitutional Court. Its role lies, at least, in the defence of what has been created. Even that simplistic description offers a good deal of scope for controversy. *Francovich* is, from one standpoint, merely a means of securing the effective application of laws that have been agreed in accordance with the Community legislative procedures; from another standpoint, it is an example of the European Court inventing a right and remedy in the event of state legislative inactivity that was previously unrecognized under either national or Community law.

The first page of this Chapter picked out Opinion 1/91[75] as the zenith of the Court's commitment to constitutionalization. Opinion 1/91 is a good place to finish. The Court found the system of judicial supervision proposed under the draft EEA Agreement to be incompatible with the EEC Treaty (as it then was). It concluded its Opinion by addressing the question whether Article 238, which deals with association agreements concluded by the Community, authorizes the establishment of a system of courts as provided for in the draft agreement. The Court ruled that Article 238 did not provide any basis for setting up a system of courts 'which conflicts with Article 164 of the EEC Treaty and, more generally, with the very foundations of the Community.' The Commission had also commented that, in the event of a negative answer by the Court, Article 238 could be amended so as to permit such a system to be set up. The Court's final paragraph in Opinion 1/91 states that 'an amendment of Article 238 in the way indicated by the Commission could not cure the incompatibility with Community law of the system of courts to be set up by the

---

[74] Rasmussen, 'Between Self-Restraint and Activism: A Judicial Policy for the European Court' (1988) 13 *ELRev.* 28.   [75] See n. 2 above.

agreement'. There is here an electrifying hint that the Court will review the constitutionality of purported Treaty revision by the Member States.

FURTHER READING

ALLOTT, P., Written Evidence to the House of Lords Scrutiny of the Intergovernmental Pillars of the European Union (1992–93) HL 124.

ARNULL, A., 'Does the Court of Justice have Inherent Jurisdiction?' (1990) 27 *CMLRev.* 683.

—— 'Private Applicants and the Action for Annulment under Article *173* of the EC Treaty' (1995) 32 *CMLRev.* 7.

BENGOETXEA, J., *The Legal Reasoning of the European Court of Justice* (Oxford: OUP, 1993).

BIEBER, R., 'Les Limites Matérielles et Formelles à la Révision des Traités Établissant la Communauté Européenne' [1993] *RMC* 343.

BOYRON, S., 'Proportionality in English Administrative Law: A Faulty Transition' (1992) 12 *Ox.JLS* 237.

BRADLEY, K., 'Better Rusty than Missin'?: The Institutional Reforms of the Maastricht Treaty and the European Parliament' in O'Keeffe, D., and Twomey, D., (eds.), *Legal Issues of the Maastricht Treaty* (Chichester: Wiley Chancery Law, 1994).

BURLEY, A. M., and MATTLI, W., 'Europe before the Court: A Political Theory of Legal Integration' (1993) 47 *International Organisation* 41.

CAPPELLETTI, M., 'Is the European Court of Justice Running Wild?' (1987) 12 *ELRev.* 3.

CLAPHAM, A., 'A Human Rights Policy for the European Community' (1990) 10 *YEL* 309.

CRAIG, P., 'Legality, Standing and Substantive Review in Community Law' (1994) 14 *Ox.JLS* 511.

DE BURCA, G., 'Fundamental Human Rights and the Reach of EC Law' (1993) 13 *Ox.JLS* 283.

—— 'The Principle of Proportionality and its Application in EC Law' (1993) 13 *YEL* 105.

DE WITTE, B., 'Community Law and National Constitutional Values' [1991/2] *LIEI* 1.

DUBINSKY, PAUL R., 'The Essential Function of Federal Courts: The European Union and the United States Compared' (1994) 42 *AJCL* 295.

GAJA, G., 'The Protection of Human Rights under the Maastricht Treaty' in Curtin, D., and Heukels, T., (eds.), *Institutional Dynamics of European Integration* (Dordrecht: Martinus Nijhoff, 1994).

HARDEN, I., 'The Constitution of the European Union' [1994] *Pub.L* 609.

HARDING, C., 'The Private Interest in Challenging Community Action' (1980) 5 *ELRev.* 354.

HARLOW, C., 'Towards a Theory of Access for the European Court of Justice' (1992) 12 *YEL* 213.

HARTKAMP, A. S., HESSELINK, M. W., HONDIUS, E. H., DU PERRON, C. E., and VRANKEN, J. B. M., *Towards a European Civil Code* (Dordrecht: Martinus Nijhoff, 1994).

JACOBS, F., 'Is the Court of Justice of the European Communities a Constitutional Court?' in Curtin, D., and O'Keeffe, D., *Constitutional Adjudication in European Community and National Law* (Dublin: Butterworths (Ireland), 1992).

—— 'European Community Law and the European Convention on Human Rights' in Curtin, D., and Heukels, T. (eds.), *Institutional Dynamics of European Integration* (Dordrecht: Martinus Nijhoff, 1994).

KAPTEYN, P. J. G., 'The Court of Justice of the European Communities' in Curtin, D., and Heukels, T., (eds.), *Institutional Dynamics of European Integration* (Dordrecht: Martinus Nijhoff, 1994).

KOOPMANS, T., 'The Role of Law in the Next Stage of European Integration' (1986) 35 *ICLQ* 925.

—— 'European Public Law: Reality and Prospects' [1991] *Pub.L* 53.

—— 'The Birth of European Law at the Crossroads of Legal Tradition' (1991) 39 *AJCL* 493.

KROGSGAARD, LARS BONDO, 'Fundamental Rights in the European Community after Maastricht' [1993/1] *LIEI* 99.

LENAERTS, K., 'Constitutionalism and the Many Faces of Federalism' (1990) 38 *AJCL* 25.

—— 'Fundamental Rights to be Included in a Community Catalogue' (1991) 16 *ELRev.* 367.

—— 'Some Thoughts about the Interaction between Judges and Politicians in the European Community (1992) 12 *YEL* 1.

LEVITSKY, J. E., 'The Europeanisation of the British Legal Style' (1994) XLII *Am.Jnl. Comp. L* 347.

MARKESINIS, B. S., 'Judge, Jurist and the Study and Use of Foreign Law' (1993) 109 *LQR* 622.

—— (ed.), *The Gradual Convergence* (Oxford: OUP, 1994).

O'NEILL, A., *Decisions of the European Court of Justice and their Constitutional Implications* (London: Butterworths, 1994).

RASMUSSEN, H., 'Between Self-Restraint and Activism: A Judicial Policy for the European Court' (1988) 13 *ELRev.* 28.

—— *On Law and Policy in the European Court of Justice* (Dordrecht: Martinus Nijhoff, 1986).

—— 'Why is Article 173 Interpreted against Private Plaintiffs?' (1980) 5 *ELRev.* 112.

RINZE, J., 'The role of the European Court of Justice as a Federal Constitutional Court' [1993] *Pub. L* 426.

SCHERMERS, H., 'The European Communities bound by Fundamental Human Rights' (1990) 27 *CMLRev.* 97.

SCHWARZE, J., 'Tendencies towards a Common Administrative Law in Europe' (1991) 16 *ELRev.* 3.

SEURIN, J. L., 'Towards a European Constitution? Problems of Political Integration [1994] *Pub. L* 625.

STEIN, E., 'Lawyers, Judges and the Making of a Transnational Constitution' (1981) 75 *Amer. J Intl. L* 1.

TEMPLE LANG, J., 'The Sphere in which Member States are Obliged to Comply with the General Principles of Law and Community Fundamental Rights Principles [1991/2] *LIEI* 23.

USHER, J., 'Tide or Flood?—The Influence of Concepts of European Community Law in English Law' in Hand, G., and McBride, J., (eds.), *Droit sans Frontières* (Birmingham: Holdsworth Club, 1991).

WARD, I., 'Making Sense of Integration: A Philosophy of Law for the European Community' (1993) XVII *Journal of European Integration* 101.

WEILER, J., 'The Dual Character of Supranationalism' (1981) 1 *YEL* 267.

—— 'The Transformation of Europe' (1991) 100 *Yale LJ* 2403.

WIELAND, J., 'Germany in the European Union—The Maastricht Decision of the Bundesverfassungsgericht' (1994) 5 *EJIL* 259.

7

European Community Trade Law

An integrated European market offers to traders the opportunity to plan for the most economically rational territory, freed from the constraint of national frontiers. Sector by sector this pattern is evolving. In some areas, the commercial restructuring involves increased production combined with enlarged cross-border distribution networks. Elsewhere it may involve a policy of merger and acquisition. Whichever of the range of available methods for taking advantage of the border-free market is chosen, the underlying economic expectation is that the enlarged market will be more competitive and will allow the realization of the economies of scale that are central to economic theory's approval of common markets.

Firms drive the process of market integration. Consumers are normally seen as passive beneficiaries. Their home market for available products and services should become more competitive. Choice increases; quality improves, while prices fall. A more active consumer also comes to the fore. Consumers are able to cross borders to shop wherever most suits them and to return home with their purchases unhindered by restrictions at national frontiers.

The traditional core of substantive EC law is the set of Treaty provisions that serves to establish this pattern of economic freedom. The ground-rules for economic integration are the four freedoms, the free movement of goods, persons, services, and capital. Integration is borne along by private market decisions, but it is necessary to ensure that the process is not hampered by anti-competitive practices. Combined with the rules establishing the four freedoms are those which create a common Community policy in the area of competition. Article 85 controls cartels and restrictive practices; Article 86 prohibits the abuse of a dominant position. Together, these provisions serve to eliminate public- and private-sector obstacles to a competitive EC-wide market.

The rather innocuous description of these legal rules as contributions to efficient market structures conceals the depth of their impact. The conversion of long-standing national markets into integrated cross-border markets requires the exercise of intrusive control over functions previously assumed to be the natural preserve of the state. Where the exercise of those functions is shown to obstruct the practices of cross-border traders, there is a collision between state activities and the trends of market integration. It is here, in this collision, that some of the most sensitive aspects of application of substantive EC law have arisen. EC law, as the instrument of integration, provides a framework for resolving the clash of interests that arises where state laws, expressing national preferences, cut across the development of integrated market structures.

The trend of so-called 'negative law' provisions such as Articles 30, 48, and 59 EC, governing the free movement of goods, persons, and services respectively, is to abolish national laws that restrict the integration of the EC market. These provisions are deregulatory. A national law held incompatible with, say, Article 30 EC, may not be applied to restrict the marketing of imported goods. The result is the deregulation of the national market as part of its absorption into the wider integrated European market. The free-movement provisions of the Treaty pursue market integration through market deregulation.

The deregulatory impulse is not absolute. Substantive EC law recognizes that national interests may override the impetus towards market integration. Where a national measure is shown to obstruct the construction of a trans-frontier commercial strategy, there is scope for a state to show justification recognized by EC law. In such circumstances, deregulation does not occur; integration cannot be achieved by the simple removal of the national measure in question. The classic response of EC law to this lawful impediment to the creation of an integrated market is the introduction of harmonization legislation. This requires the identification of an appropriate legal base and use of the legislative procedure required thereunder.[1] It will also involve examination of the impact of Community intervention on national competence in the field.[2] By replacing the national rules in question with a

---

[1] Ch. 3.   [2] Ch. 5.

common Community regime, the interests that underpinned the lawful national measure remain protected, but at Community rather than national level. In this way an integrated market is opened up. This is deregulation in the sense that different national rules are replaced by a single Community rule. But it is distinct from the application of 'negative law' because the interests reflected by national obstacles to trade are not simply swept into oblivion. Instead they are reflected in Community measures. Community law deregulates national markets, but re-regulates at Community level. This is positive law.

THE LAW OF THE FREE MOVEMENT OF GOODS

Article 12 abolishes customs duties on trade in goods between Member States. Article 95 forbids national taxation systems that discriminate in favour of home produced goods and against imported goods. These two provisions combine to form the regime for controlling fiscal barriers to trade on goods.

Article 30 is the Treaty provision that governs physical and technical barriers to trade in goods. It is the provision that has attained by far the highest profile in this area of the law. This is in part attributable to its intrinsic importance as a means of opening up Community-wide markets for goods. However, on a jurisprudential level, the high profile of Article 30 is deserved because of the insight into the European Court's technique that is provided by an appreciation of its evolution.

Article 30 looks uninspiring on paper: 'Quantitative restrictions on imports and all measures having equivalent effect shall, without prejudice to the following provisions, be prohibited between Member States.' The key to its vigour lies in the Court's extraordinarily ambitious interpretation of the phrase 'all measures having equivalent effect'. Article 30 was interpreted by the Court in *Procureur du Roi* v. *Dassonville* to prohibit 'all trading rules enacted by Member States which are capable of hindering, directly or indirectly, actually or potentially, intra-Community trade'.[3] This is a broad prohibition, but above all it is an effects-based prohibition. There is no need on this test to draw up a list of the types of form in which one might expect to identify

---

[3] Case 8/74 [1974] ECR 837.

a national measure obstructive of trade. Provided a measure has this effect, its form is irrelevant. So Article 30 catches checks at borders, import licences, and technical rules that confront importers wishing to penetrate a new market, but it also catches a great deal more besides, provided only that a direct or indirect, actual or potential, obstacle to intra-Community trade be shown.

The fact that a national measure is caught by Article 30 does not automatically mean that it may not be applied. EC law does not embrace only deregulation of national markets. Under the pattern of the Treaty, exceptions are contained in Article 36: 'restrictions on imports, exports or goods in transit justified on grounds of public morality, public policy or public security; the protection of health and life of humans, animals or plants . . . Such prohibitions or restrictions shall not, however, constitute a means of arbitrary discrimination or a disguised restriction on trade between Member States.'

It is open to a state to ban pornography on grounds of public morality even where such pornography is permitted in a neighbouring Member State. An importer wishing to trade in such goods would enjoy no absolute right under Article 30, for the state is able to seek refuge in Article 36 from the damaging effects on its morality standards of unlimited free trade. Of course, it might be thought pointless to maintain stricter laws of this type in a border-free market where effective control of people and goods crossing back and forth with banned items is almost impossible. This is especially and disturbingly relevant in the light of technological advances in the area of, for example, cable and satellite television and computer graphics that render borders irrelevant and access to banned images all too straightforward. The empirical fact of market integration has done much in many areas to undermine the realistic scope of national competence to make choices about public policy, in the broad sense. The strict terms of the law in Articles 30–36, however, does not force states to abandon standards and yield to an integrated market based on the lowest common denominator of national standards.

A great many cases in the European Court Reports reveal the Court's determination to use Articles 30–36 to liberalize the market for goods. If one adopts the fundamental assumptions of market integration theory, that process is deemed to operate to the advantage of the consumer. Once the trigger of an adequate

impact on cross-border trade is identified, the Court then requires
the Member State to justify its laws. Article 36 has two sentences;
and the Court has reflected the two components in its case law.
The Member State must show an *end* recognized by Community
law which is served by the challenged measure (the first sentence);
and it must show that the *means* chosen to achieve that end are
permissible (the second sentence). Article 36 is to be interpreted
narrowly.

The Court has been rigorous in demanding that the justifying
state make a persuasive case. The Court is plainly influenced by
the fear that states may seek to rely on Article 36 to shelter their
own producers from the pain of cross-border competition. Were
that to occur, the fundamental advantages of economic integration
would be squandered, to the prejudice of the Community
generally and its consumers in particular. So, in its interpretation of Article 36, the Court has insisted that the category
of recognized *ends* goes no further than the explicit list. In
Commission v. *Ireland*[4] the Court refused to acknowledge that it
was possible to advance the protection of the economic interests of
consumers as a justification under Article 36. Even within the
Article 36 list a strict approach has been maintained. The Court
has not been tempted to use the potentially rather flexible notion
of 'public policy' as a general, 'catch-all' provision. Quite the
contrary; it has routinely dismissed appeals to public policy as
justification for obstruction of trade as unfounded.

The Court has been equally firm in its treatment of the
permissible *means* available to a Member State attempting to
defend a restrictive trading rule. The Court has insisted that this
involves a demonstration that the means chosen to achieve that
end are the least restrictive of trade necessary to achieve the end in
view. In fact, in many cases the Court has not felt it necessary to
explore at length the end alleged to be served by the national
measure once it has formed the view that, even were the end
legitimate, the measures in question go beyond what is necessary
to meet that end. Italian wines might or might not have been
sufficiently contaminated to justify French checks aimed at health
protection, but, whatever the reality of the peril, it could not

[4] Case 113/80 [1981] ECR 1625.

justify checks of up to four months' duration applied to all imports.[5]

Commission v. *United Kingdom* involved restrictions on the importation of poultry products into the United Kingdom.[6] Such restrictions plainly fell within the scope of Article 30. The dispute arose in relation to the scope for their justification under Article 36. The United Kingdom's justification for the measures lay in the threat posed by outbreaks of the highly infectious Newcastle disease in poultry. The import controls were explained to the Court as part of a scheme for ensuring effective control of the disease.

The Court felt it 'useful to set out a number of facts which may have a bearing on the way in which the problems at issue should be appreciated'. These included the steep rise in importation of turkeys from France into the United Kingdom which had, by mid-1981, led to concern among British poultry producers, prompting them to bring pressure to bear on the United Kingdom Government to take action to reduce importation from France. The measures at issue in the case had been introduced just in time to prevent importation of turkeys from France into Britain in time for Christmas 1981. This was obviously suspicious.

The European Court felt sufficiently confident about the motivation for these measures to conclude that 'the real aim of the 1981 measures was to block, for commercial and economic reasons, imports of poultry products'. The Court referred to the pressure to which the United Kingdom Government had been subjected; to the hurried introduction of the policy in such a way as to ensure that the restrictions coincided with the Christmas season; the lack of consultation with Community institutions and other Member States.

The combination of these factors would not have deprived the United Kingdom of the possibility of relying on Article 36 had there been a genuine peril that importation would deepen the threat of Newcastle disease and had the measures taken been shown to be an apt and proportionate means of tackling the problem. But there was no evidence of a systematic, scientific investigation by the British authorities into the problem and its

---

[5] Case 42/82 *Commission* v. *France* [1983] ECR 1013.
[6] Case 40/82 [1982] ECR 2793.

effective control immediately prior to the introduction of the measures in 1981. There was, moreover, evidence from practice elsewhere in the EC of the availability of adequate, less restrictive methods of control, based around vaccination programmes. The European Court concluded explicitly and damningly that 'the 1981 measures did not form part of a seriously considered health policy'.

This entertaining saga should be read with reference to the economic advantages that are supposed to flow from the free movement of goods. The British action was denying to British consumers the opportunity to choose from among a wider range of different turkeys. It was ostensibly protecting British producers, but only, at best, in the short term, for such tactics, unchecked by law, would breed retaliation denying British exporters access to the markets of other Member States. Article 30 from this perspective is one of the nuts and bolts whereby Common Market economic theory is brought to practical fruition.

The decision does not mean that free trade overrides health protection. The key point was that the alleged risk to health was a front for protectionism. The assessment would have been different had a genuine threat been shown to exist. EC law requires that national regulatory action be taken in the light of the obligations of Community membership. In fact, today, such basic matters of market-building have largely been taken within the realms of Community secondary legislation. The legislative framework replaces assessment in the light of Articles 30–36.[7] The Court made passing reference to this phenomenon in *Commission* v. *United Kingdom*. It found that existing measures did not cover the field and that therefore Article 36 remained the proper basis on which to assess the validity of the United Kingdom's measures. However, it referred to 'the beginning of a process of harmonization' initiated by a directive of 1971. This process is today much more advanced. Animal health is covered by a relatively well-developed framework of Community legislation. Action taken against perceived health risks in imports must be managed within the Community framework, invoving, typically, a process of notification and decision-making within the committee structures of the Commission.

---

[7] Chs, 3, 5.

The question of remedial action deserves to be taken as a final
point before leaving the richly illustrative tale of Newcastle
disease. The United Kingdom was ruled to have violated Article
30 EC. The sceptical lawyer bred in a tradition that values
remedies as the true test of the practical utility of a legal system
will respond: 'Yes, and?' What use is the Luxembourg Court's
finding in July 1982 that action in 1981 infringed Community law?
After all, French turkeys had been kept off the British market in
the run up to Christmas 1981. The legal obligation that flows under
EC law from a Court ruling in an Article 169 action was simply
that in Article 171 to take necessary measures to comply. There
was no specific sanction until 1993 when the entry into force of the
Treaty on European Union provided for the possibility in Article
171(2) of fines to be imposed on recalcitrant states. Rulings such as
that in *Commission* v. *United Kingdom* were doubtless politically
embarassing, but our sceptical lawyer would expect a Government
usually to be able to ride out any political pressure. Indeed, in
some circumstances an attack on the judgment of the European
Court might prove rewarding in domestic political terms. But EC
law operates at two levels. It is enforced by Commission
supervision under Article 169 leading, where necessary, to
proceedings before the European Court. This is the nature of
Commission v. *United Kingdom*. It is also enforced at national
level, by private individuals bringing actions against defaulting
states before national courts. It is the principle of direct effect of
EC law that converts it into a dynamic system of rights capable
of vindication at national level. It is here that the sceptical lawyer
must confront the fact that EC law is not simply operative at the
transnational level, but that it also creates rights that are
supported by the remedies systems of the national legal orders of
the Member States. The national courts themselves bear a
responsibility for giving practical effect to EC law; and they cannot
airily be dismissed by politicians as 'foreign'. So French turkey
importers were able to proceed before English courts to seek
compensation for their loss caused by the unlawful action of the
British authorities. Relying on the direct effect of Article 30 EC,
they were able to sue the relevant authorities. The litigation
caused the English courts some difficulty in choosing the
appropriate types of remedy, but it was never in doubt that they
were obliged to recognize and protect EC-law rights held by

individuals that were invaded by the state. Ultimately the case, *Bourgoin* v. *Ministry of Agriculture, Fisheries and Food*, was settled out of court after an inconclusive decision by the Court of Appeal with a payment to the turkey traders of £3.5 million.[8] EC law has teeth—two sets.

THE *CASSIS DE DIJON* FORMULA

The Article 30 *Dassonville* formula was examined above with reference to its application to measures that discriminate between imported goods and home-produced goods. However, it is not only discriminatory national laws that are capable of exerting a detrimental effect on cross-border trade. Apparently even-handed rules are capable of impeding trade. Imagine a rule in state X requiring that all ties be made of silk. No producer, whatever its origin, is excluded from the market for ties in state X. All that is required is that silk be used. The rule is not directly discriminatory on grounds of origin or nationality. But in practice producers in state X will use silk. Producers in other states, where the law is different, probably less rigid, will use different materials. Yet their non-silk ties will be excluded from the market of state X. The process of market integration will be impeded. Traditional products of one state may be kept out of the markets of other states because they do not conform to the technical specifications of the state of importation. Market integration is stalled because laws differ state by state.

Technical standards of this type are common in all states. In many areas such rules of market regulation were introduced with no thought of their impact on cross-border trade. The entry into force of some may have pre-dated the EC by years, even in some cases by centuries. Perhaps the use of silk in tie-making was made mandatory fifty years ago in response to consumer exasperation about the use of shoddy materials passed off as silk; perhaps the silk-producers' guild 200 years ago had been especially influential in political life as a result of the great wealth it brought to the country and had used its power then to secure the adoption of

---

[8] HC Deb. vol. 102, col. 116 (WA), 22 July 1986. Subsequent decisions of the European Court, especially *Francovich*, have elevated the profile of the damages remedy. English courts now regard *Bourgoin* as insufficiently receptive to a damages claim against the state. See Ch. 4.

the rule. But some technical rules may have been introduced as a ruse to protect the home market from competitors in other Member States. Silk-tie makers may have enjoyed a large home market share prior to their state's accession to the EC and may, when their state entered the EC, have pressed successfully for mandatory rules in order to insulate themselves from competition from state A's famous producers of ties made from other (cheap) materials.

In one sense, the background to such technical rules is irrelevant for the purposes of shaping EC law. Where such technical rules exert an impact on cross-border trade, EC law necessarily comes into play. An *effect* hostile to market integration is the trigger to the *Dassonville* interpretation of Article 30. The mandatory use of silk impedes cross-border trade in ties made in other Member States where tastes, traditions, and, fundamentally, the laws are different. The rationale behind state X's law does not affect the basic point that a trade barrier has been identified and that Article 30 comes into play. However, the reasons that underlie a rule will be relevant to the state's scope for showing a justification recognized by EC law.

This area of law represents one of the most remarkable intrusions of substantive EC law into areas that might seem to rest within the realms of exclusive national competence. It is here that the flawed notion that EC law belongs in an identifiably discrete compartment, separate from most areas of national law, has been subjected to one of its most sustained batterings. After all, technical rules of the type at stake in this area are ostensibly even-handed in their application, and, indeed, make no reference whatsoever to the phenomenon of cross-border commercial activity. The ingenious invocation of Article 30 to challenge national measures reached such a level that even the European Court felt obliged to refine its stance.[9] But even the more recent impression of caution in Luxembourg does not detract from the dynamic nature of Article 30 as an intrusive control over national market regulation.

The Court has moved a great deal beyond the text of Articles 30–36. In fact the pattern that the Court has developed for

---

[9] Cases C–267 & 268/91 *Keck and Mithouard*, judgment of 24 Nov. 1993, Ch. 8 n. 2.

controlling national technical rules that obstruct trade owes virtually nothing to the wording of Articles 30–36, but a great deal to the Court's own conception of the spirit of the Treaty. The Court has created a formula in order to balance the interest in market integration against the interest that a Member State may submit underlies the technical rule in question, be it three, thirty, or 300 years old. Although the Court's determination to control national laws that have the *effect* of restricting trade can be traced back to the *Dassonville* ruling, the starting point for the sophisticated development of Article 30's application to non-discriminatory technical standards is the '*Cassis de Dijon*' ruling; more properly and less popularly *Rewe Zentrale* v. *Bundesmonopolverwaltung für Branntwein.*[10]

Cassis de Dijon is a French blackcurrant liqueur. German law required fruit liqueurs of the category into which Cassis fell to have a minimum alcohol content of 25 per cent. This law was not discriminatory in the sense that it applied on its face to all products, irrespective of their origin. The practical result was that products made in Germany would naturally conform to the German law and would be entitled to access to the German market. Products made in other states according to different traditions and under different regulatory regimes would not follow the same pattern and would, in some cases, find that they did not meet the legal requirements for access to the German market. This was the problem encountered by the applicants in the case who wished to sell Cassis de Dijon, which was simply not strong enough under German law. Tastes differed in France.

The German law obstructed consumer choice. It limited product-availability on the German market to those products that met the tastes expressed by the German legislator. It impeded trade in the EC.

The Court declared that:

Obstacles to movement in the Community resulting from disparities between the national laws in question must be accepted in so far as those provisions may be recognized as being necessary in order to satisfy mandatory requirements relating in particular to the effectiveness of fiscal supervision, the protection of public health, the fairness of commercial transactions and the defence of the consumer.

[10] Case 120/78 [1979] ECR 649.

Under this formula, the national technical measure can be applied to exclude an unfamiliar product from the market, but only if there is a legitimate interest requiring protection which is capable of justifying such an exclusion (the 'mandatory requirement'), *and* provided that there is no way of meeting the legitimate interest by measures less restrictive of trade. This is the test of justification encompassing both ends and means that is also characteristic of the Court's approach to Article 36, but the formula used in the absence of discrimination is refined to allow a broader range of recognized ends. Disparities between national laws obstruct trade, but may be justified with reference to the flexible category of interests referred to by the Court in the above extract from the *Cassis* ruling. The Court's use of the phrase 'in particular' in introducing the types of interest it is prepared to recognize makes it clear that this is not a closed list. The Court is ready to hear justifications that are not limited to the Article 36 list, provided only that the state has shaped its law without reference to the origin of products.

The Court's formula allows it to make an assessment of the virtues of the national measure in the light of its damage to market integration. Its application of the formula in the *Cassis* ruling itself is instructive. Germany submitted, *inter alia*, that controlling the availability of weaker alcoholic drinks was part of a policy of public health protection, for 'such products may more easily induce a tolerance towards alcohol than more highly alcoholic beverages'. The Court swept aside this bizarre argument with reference, *inter alia*, to the ease with which higher strength beverages can be diluted, thereby posing an equal risk of inducing tolerance. Germany also submitted that consumers might be confused in a market offering a vast range of beverages of differing strengths. The Court made clear its view that even were there a legitimate end in view, it was 'a simple matter to ensure that suitable information is conveyed to the purchaser by requiring the display of . . . the alcohol content on the packaging of products'.

The ruling in *Walter Rau Lebensmittelwerke v. de Smedt* concerns the compatibility with Article 30 of a Belgian law requiring margarine to be marketed in cube-shaped blocks.[11] The Court's approach was to look first for an effect on inter-state

----

[11] Case 261/81 [1982] ECR 3961.

236 LAW AND INTEGRATION IN THE EUROPEAN UNION

trade. It found one. A producer in another state using different types of packaging would in theory be able to penetrate the Belgian market by adapting to the Belgian law, which was not origin-specific. In practice, such adaptation would be costly and would inhibit the development of a cross-border strategy from which economies of scale could accrue. The technical rule would have the practical effect of sheltering Belgian-based firms from competition. The Court needed no empirical economic evidence to support such a finding based on theory, but it chose to provide such evidence nonetheless: 'the protective effect of the Belgian rules is moreover demonstrated by the fact . . . that despite prices appreciably higher than those in some other Member States there is practically no margarine of foreign origin to be found on the Belgian market'. The Court turned to assessment of the justifiability of both the ends and means of the measure. It was prepared to admit that there may have been a recognised end in view: 'It cannot be reasonably denied that in principle legislation designed to prevent butter and margarine from being confused in the mind of the consumer is justified.' However, the means used to achieve this end were indefensibly intrusive: 'Consumers may in fact be protected just as effectively by other measures, for example by rules on labelling, which hinder the free movement of goods less.'

The *Cassis de Dijon* formula, employed in *Walter Rau* v. *de Smedt*, has been repeated and applied many times since by the Court. Such constant repetition does not alter the fact that this formula is not to be found anywhere in the text of the Treaty. What is the Court's justification for inventing this legal test? As in so many areas of Community law, the answer lies in the Treaty's character as a framework constructed around broad objectives. It is the Court's job to fill out the detailed pattern of law that will make sense of the wider picture. The *Cassis de Dijon* formula is merely a particularly high-profile example of that gap-filling function.

Yet it is not the Court's job alone to fill in gaps and to supply necessary detail to Community trade law. This is a task that involves the legislature too. What is the proper relationship between the Court and the legislature in this area? The original Treaty of Rome already contained a legislative means for resolving problems for the integrative process caused by disparity between national laws, the issue in the *Cassis de Dijon* litigation.

Harmonization of laws was achievable by directive made under Article 100 of the Treaty. Common rules could have been put in place by legislative action. So why did the Court enter the field by moulding Article 30—and was it justified in extending its own reach into areas apparently within the preserve of the Community legislature? That is a question that invites answers on several different levels. On a practical level, although legislative action to harmonize technical standards was indeed constitutionally possible under Article 100, for many years it was not realistic to expect progress. The requirement under Article 100 for unanimity in Council slowed the passage of legislation; the laborious technical work required to hammer out a single standard brought it to a virtual standstill. The Court, by actively moving into the field of market-partitioning technical standards, was responding to the impression that the legislature *could* not act. Additionally, there are strong policy reasons for doubting the value of harmonization in such areas. Common rules would yield 'Europroducts'; the Court's use of Article 30 keeps alive diversity and secures free trade in the traditional products of each state. In this respect the Court's reworking of Article 30 was motivated by the perception that the legislature *should* not act in this area. The majority of commentators applaud the liberalization of the market and the enhancement of consumer choice that follow from the Court's active reworking of Article 30 in *Cassis de Dijon*. To this extent, Article 30, interpreted by the Court in *Cassis de Dijon*, expresses the basic economic ideas of the Community. Nevertheless, the question of the proper relationship between the Court and the legislature in the development of the law of market integration has many nuances that have yet to be settled.

The products of the host state may still be made available in exactly the same form as before. Indeed there is no compulsion on a state to relax the application of its laws to its own producers. What changes is the insulation of home producers from cross-border competition. Consumers now have a wider choice, rather than having that choice taken on their behalf by the national regulator. The essence of the *Cassis de Dijon* formula is a transfer of power from the public regulator to the private consumer.

The *Cassis de Dijon* formula declares that national laws which obstruct trade are permissible only where shown to be necessary to satisfy a mandatory requirement. It is based on a trade-off between the advantages of market integration and the advantages of the national law which has the effect of restricting trade. Which interest prevails? It is for the Court (and national courts, because these provisions are directly effective) to make that judgment.

Cassis de Dijon accelerates the process of market-integration through law. But it does not condemn *all* obstructive national rules. Justification is possible. Whereas the rationale for imposing a technical standard is irrelevant to its effect on inter-state trade, the rationale is highly relevant to the state attempting to make out the case for justifying the measure despite its trade-restrictive effect.

Aragonesa de Publicidad Exterior SA (APESA) v. *Departamento de Sanidad y Seguridad Social de la Generalitat de Cataluna (DSSC)*[12] arose out of restrictions imposed by the Catalan authorities on the advertising of beverages having an alcoholic strength of more than twenty-three degrees. The Court was satisfied that the measures were capable of being held compatible with Article 30 where they formed part of a public health strategy.

The twenty-three-degree threshold did 'not appear to be manifestly unreasonable as part of a campaign against alcoholism'. The ruling provides a neat contrast to the Court's plain scepticism in the *Cassis de Dijon* case itself that controlling the supply of *weak* alcoholic drink could form part of a policy of public health protection.

A ruling such as that in *APESA* v. *DSSC* leaves the market regulated by national law and, in European terms, fragmented. It represents the limits of 'negative law'. Here, even the advances made in the scope of Article 30 through *Cassis de Dijon* are insufficient to produce an integrated market without the need to have recourse to legislation. The *Cassis de Dijon* formula possesses a strongly deregulatory flavour, but its acceptance of

'mandatory requirements' as legitimate grounds for maintaining even trade-restrictive technical standards sets a limit to deregulation via Article 30. Harmonization of laws is one possible next step, but, of course, the judgement may be made that it is entirely possible to envisage a common market in which some restrictions on trade arising out of local regulatory preferences are perfectly permissible. This was the theme of Chapter 5 of this book.

---

[12] Cases C–1, 176/90 [1991] ECR I–4151.

Valuable insights into the techniques favoured by the European Court may be obtained in this area. The formula envisages a choice between competing interests—those in integrating the market and the range of interests that may over the years have prompted regulation of national markets. The Court has taken to itself the job of weighing these competing interests. Two areas in particular are picked out in the following discussion. First, the compatibility with Article 30 of national laws that impede trade but which are designed to protect the environment; and then the compatibility with Article 30 of national laws that impede trade but which are designed to protect the economic interests of consumers. In both instances, the *Cassis* formula is readily applicable. In both instances, the formula involves a calculation of the benefits served by abolishing the law and thereby promoting market integration weighed against the costs incurred by abandoning national protection of the environment/economic interests of consumers.

The special jurisprudential interest in reviewing the Court's work in these two areas lies in the fact that neither of the interests in question is reflected in the original Treaty of Rome, the background to the *Cassis* ruling in 1979. More specifically, both environmental protection and the protection of the economic interests of consumers are missing from Article 36 EC. They have been drawn within the framework for assessing the reach of the law of free movement by the Court's own activism. And as part of that process the Court has been forced to develop its own notions of what national programmes to protect the environment and to defend the economic interests of consumers may permissibly include.

ENVIRONMENTAL PROTECTION AND THE FREE MOVEMENT OF GOODS

Denmark is a Member State with a reputation for sensitivity towards the demands of environmental protection. It is therefore perhaps appropriate that Danish environmental policy provided the first major opportunity for the Court to examine the tension between national initiatives in the field and the process of the liberalization of the market for goods. *Commission* v. *Denmark*[13]

---

[13] Case 302/86 [1988] ECR 4607.

manifests the Court's awareness that a deregulatory policy, favouring market integration, must be tempered by respect for national concern to protect the environment from the degradation that may flow from trade.

The acceptance of the importance of placing environmental policy within the activities of the Community has accelerated in recent years.[14] The entry into force of the Single European Act in 1987 conferred competence on the Community to legislate in the environmental sphere. Today a web of Community rules governs many important areas of environmental protection. However, although at the time that the Court decided *Commission* v. *Denmark* the greening of Community policy was well under way, the Court was forced to decide the case in the light of Articles 30–36, which are completely bare of reference to the interests of environmental protection in an assessment of the validity of national measures shown to be obstructive of trade in goods. Nor even did the *Cassis de Dijon* formula offer any explicit recognition of the place of environmental-protection measures put in place by Member States. The case was therefore a perfect opportunity for the Court to demonstrate its capacity for responding to novel policy inputs by renovating the law of the free movement of goods without having to wait for Treaty amendment or for explicit guidance in Community secondary legislation.

Denmark had introduced a system designed to address the growing menace of litter caused by discarded drinks containers. The scheme required that beer and soft drinks be marketed only in containers that were capable of being reused. It was necessary to secure approval of containers by the Danish National Agency for the Protection of the Environment, which for these purposes checked the suitability of containers for return and reuse. Although the scheme did not completely exclude non-approved containers, the exceptions made were limited and embraced only containers not made from metal and only containers for which a deposit-and-return system had been set up.

It is not difficult to identify that the scheme was likely to make a contribution to environmental protection. Fewer containers would be thrown away. Recycling would protect scarce resources. Equally, it is not difficult to identify that this system was likely to

[14] Ch. 2, 50.

have the effect of impeding the importation of goods from outside Denmark, even though the scheme was in principle open to all traders irrespective of their origin. Danish firms would follow the Danish system. Importers would be accustomed to home-state control and would find themselves forced to adapt in order to penetrate the Danish market. It was a classic *Cassis de Dijon* case of disparity between national laws leading to market fragmentation. The integration of the market would be blocked and this impediment to trade demanded an assessment of the Danish rules in the light of Article 30.

Before explaining how the Court resolved the case, it is worth pausing to assess the implications, for they illustrate the wider issues at stake. If the scheme were ruled incompatible with Article 30, free trade would prevail, but at a cost to environmental protection. If unable to exclude disposable containers, Denmark would find itself undermined in its strategy by the lower standards prevailing in other states. Worse, it might find its own producers choosing to move to states with laxer regimes in order to find the cheapest location from which to supply the whole market. And it might find other states cutting their regulatory standards precisely to attract such mobile firms. Such is the breadth of the potential fall-out from the use of Community trade law to deregulate national markets in the absence of any safety-net to permit legitimate national regulation of important concerns in the public interest. The safety net is, in the Court's terminology, the mandatory requirements. Yet, on the other hand, were the scheme to be upheld, the result would be market fragmentation; the Danish market would be insulated from competition. Permitting national rules to cut across free trade carries its own dangers of disintegration in the case under scrutiny. It may also breed spiralling disintegration in the future once the door of concealed protectionism is seen by Member States to be ajar. The neatest response lies in accommodation of these competing interests in a Community legislative intervention that occupies the field. As discussed in Chapter 5, such clean-cut solutions are extremely difficult to obtain, and this had not occurred in *Commission* v. *Denmark*. Indeed, by definition, it can never have occurred in Article 30 cases, which assume the absence of total harmonization.

The Court accepted that the deposit-and-return system for

empty containers could lawfully be implemented in accordance with Community law. In this respect the Court placed the interest in protection of the environment at national level above the interest in securing the free movement of goods. It placed a limit on market deregulation. In the result, a certain insulation of the Danish market was conceded.

In terms of explicit legal technique, the Court felt able to add environmental protection to the list of mandatory requirements that it had recognized in *Cassis de Dijon* as capable of limiting the scope of the Article 30 prohibition. It referred to its own categorization of the protection of the environment as 'one of the Community's essential objectives'[15] and added that this view had been confirmed by the Single European Act. The end was therefore recognized as capable of justifying a limitation placed on the free circulation of goods. The Court also considered that the deposit-and-return system was a means of achieving that end which did not exert a trade-restrictive effect beyond that necessary. In fact the Court viewed the deposit-and-return system as an indispensable element in ensuring re-use. By contrast, it found that the approval system organized through the Agency exerted an unduly restrictive effect on trade and ruled it incompatible with Article 30.

The flexibility of the Court's approach to the scope of the mandatory requirements is not difficult to justify. The Court drew up the list itself and, moreover, in the *Cassis de Dijon* ruling, it gave fair warning that its list of mandatory requirements was non-exhaustive by prefixing it with the phrase 'in particular'. So additions to the list, such as environmental protection, were always on the cards. The Court has placed itself in a remarkable position of being able to weigh the balance between national regulatory choices and the process of market integration; but, more fundamentally still, it in the first place chooses which national regulatory choices are capable of being invoked at all. In this respect it acts as a high-profile policy-maker, able to review national measures against the trade-law provisions of the Community constitution.

---

[15] Case 240/83 *Procureur de la République* v. *Association de Défense des Brûleurs d'Huiles Usagées* [1985] ECR 531, Ch. 2, n. 24.

The Court returned to the collision between national environmental protection strategies and the development of the
border-free market in its ruling in *Commission* v. *Belgium*.[16] By
the time this case came before the Court in July 1992, the
evolution of the Community's own environmental-protection
legislative programme had reached a much more substantial level.
This is reflected in the explicit terms of the ruling, for some of the
practices that the Commission challenged fell to be assessed in
the light of relevant directives. Other aspects remained subject to
examination in the light of Articles 30–36; but here, too, the rising
tide of legislation may have conditioned the Court's approach,
albeit, as explained below, in an unstated fashion.

The case concerned the activities of the regional administration
in Wallonia, a region of Belgium. For Community-law purposes,
the Belgian state is responsible for the activites of the regional
authorities. As part of an environmental-protection strategy, the
Walloon authorities prohibited the storage, tipping, or dumping of
waste from other Member States or from elsewhere in Belgium.
The purpose of the measure was the protection of Wallonia from
imports of waste from areas with stricter regulatory regimes. It
stopped so-called 'waste tourism'. However, waste is a product
that may be the subject of commercial transactions and the effect
of the rule was plainly to restrict patterns of trade in waste. The
law governing the free movement of goods was at stake.

In so far as hazardous waste was concerned, the matter fell to be
considered in the light of Directive 84/631, which governed the
transfrontier shipment of hazardous waste. Here there was a
violation of Community law, for the Directive did not permit an
absolute ban. The restriction on non-hazardous waste escaped the
scope of existing Community legislation and therefore fell to be
considered in the light of Article 30 EC.

The Court found the measure justified as a measure of
environmental protection. Although the Walloon initiative
exerted a restrictive effect on trade, it made a sufficient contribution to environmental protection to satisfy the Court, which
commented that '[t]he accumulation of waste . . . constitutes a
threat to the environment because of the limited capacity of each
region or locality for receiving it.' The Walloon policy of dealing

---

[16] Case C–2/90 [1992] ECR I–4431.

with its waste and no one else's was therefore firmly in line with proper waste-management policy. For the Court, this outweighed the restrictive effect on cross-border trade.

The *Walloon Waste* ruling causes a lurch in the Court's Article 30 case law, although this is something that the Court itself refused to admit in the judgment. The Walloon measure kept out imported waste (whether from other parts of Belgium or beyond Belgian borders); but it envisaged treating Walloon-produced waste in Wallonia. Advocate General Jacobs had, unusually, presented two Opinions in this tricky case, but in both he maintained that this was a measure that discriminated on the basis of the origin of the goods. Yet the consistent line in the post-*Cassis de Dijon* case law has been that a finding of discrimination is fatal to a regulating state's reliance on the *Cassis de Dijon* mandatory requirements. The taint of discrimination confines available justifications to those in Article 36. Environmental protection is not among that collection.

The Court's ruling did not ignore the point. Indeed, it declared explicitly that an absence of discrimination is essential before the mandatory requirements may be taken into account. However, the Court referred to Article 130r(2) of the Treaty's policy statement that 'environmental damage should as a priority be rectified at source'. Transport of waste should therefore be minimized. Accordingly the Court ruled, contrary to its Advocate General, that it 'follows that, having regard to the differences between waste produced in one place and that in another and its connection with the place where it is produced, the contested measures cannot be considered to be discriminatory'. And they were compatible with Article 30.

The Court's reference to the desirability of rectification of waste at source is perfectly well-founded. At the general level, it may be a good policy reason for upholding the Walloon practices. But it is submitted that it does not make the rules non-discriminatory. Walloon waste was subject to a formally different regime from any other kind of waste. This is discrimination.

The decision is not satisfyingly reasoned on a strict analysis. It is submitted that the true reading of the judgment is as follows. The Court did not want to overthrow its resistance to the expansion of the mandatory requirements into the field of discriminatory measures. The loss of that principle might give incentives to devious protectionism. Therefore it chose to insist that it was not dealing with discriminatory measures at all. It hoped to have avoided destroying the principle that a state's measures must be origin-neutral before the flexibility of the *Cassis de Dijon* formula is capable of invocation. Indeed it explicitly reasserted that principle. But, on the facts of the particular case, the Court recognized the damage that could be done by a rigid approach to its own jurisprudential creation. It therefore allowed itself some dexterity in order to ensure the primacy of the environmentally sound objective that waste should be treated at source. That principle is recognized elsewhere in the Treaty and in the body of relevant directives, and the Court was bent on feeding it into its application of Articles 30–36. After all, the *Cassis de Dijon* principle was developed partly as a result of the inadequacy of solutions under Community secondary legislation.[17] It would be wilfully foolish to stick rigidly to the framework at a time when solutions are being developed in legislation.

It is therefore entirely possible that the growing wealth of multi-functional Community market-regulation will come to cause adjustments in the Court's approach to the role of Article 30. True, the result of this in *Commission* v. *Belgium* was rather illogical. Hazardous waste could not be controlled in the strict way planned by Wallonia, for Directive 84/631 precluded such steps; but non-hazardous waste, presumably less dangerous, could be so controlled. This is symptomatic of the lack of coherence from which the Community suffers while a harmonization programme is gradually taking shape.

THE ECONOMIC INTERESTS OF CONSUMERS

Where the national rule that obstructs trade is labelled a measure of consumer protection, the application of Article 30 involves a trade-off between two distinct conceptions of the consumer interest. Elimination of the rule would serve the consumer interest in the wider availability of products and services in an integrated market, but would override the consumer interest in maintaining legal protection at national level. The *Cassis de Dijon* ruling itself fits this model. In fact that was an uncontroversial decision, for the

---

[17] 237 above.

German regulation was thoroughly unconvincing in its claim to offer the consumer any real protection. It was relatively easy to find advantages to the consumer in increased choice and difficult to find real benefit in keeping weaker liqueurs off the German market. One would expect to see the intensity of national regulation reduced in an integrating market and the *Cassis* ruling reflects that pattern. Hence the incompatibility of the rule with Article 30; and the preference for decision-making by private parties in the market in place of state regulators. But elsewhere the choice is much more evenly balanced.

Where the Court finds itself choosing between more realistic instruments of national consumer protection and the consumer interest in the market liberalization that would follow from abolition of those instruments, the Court is forced to elaborate its own notion of the consumer interest. It finds itself involved in examination of the question of how it perceives the functioning of the market as a means of maximizing consumer welfare; and what type of consumer, feeble or self-reliant, it believes the market serves.

Drei Glocken GmbH and Kritzinger v. *USL Centro-Süd and Provincia Autonoma di Bolzano*[18] is one of the most powerful illustrations available in the Court's case law of the tensions that exist between different conceptions of the capacity of the consumer to cope with the deregulated and integrated market. Lack of confidence in the ability of the consumer properly to inform him- or herself about products that would be newly available were national technical standards swept away as incompatible with Article 30 will yield the response that a good justification has been made out for maintaining those rules. But the perception that the consumer is robust and able to take care of him- or herself by finding out about and choosing between new products yields the contrary response that there is no justification for maintaining obstructive national technical rules; that the consumer interest lies in deregulation, integration, and enhanced choice.

So the 'consumer' is the lever to the application of the law, but there is no homogeneous consumer, and Community law therefore requires the identification of what type of consumer is envisaged.

[18] Case 407/85 [1988] ECR 4233.

The ruling in *Drei Glocken* v. *USL Centro-Süd* is especially appealing because the Advocate General and the Court in the case possess quite different images of the consumer and, equipped with those divergent views, they come to opposite conclusions on the compatibility of the challenged national law with Article 30.

At issue were Italian rules that required the use of durum wheat alone in the manufacture of pasta products. The effect of the rules was to exclude pasta made in other Member States according to different recipes using different types of wheat. The litigation was driven by a German producer of pasta made from different types of wheat, perfectly lawful and popular in Germany. This was at heart a 'classic' *Cassis de Dijon* instance of market fragmentation flowing from the fact of disparity between national laws. The rule denied Italian consumers a wider choice. But Italy explained that its consumers would not associate pasta with anything other than the traditional Italian recipe. Its rule had the objective of protecting the consumer from being misled. Wider choice would, for lack of experience, not be a choice at all. The resolution of the case turned on an assessment of the capabilities of the Italian pasta consumer.

Advocate General Mancini supported the Italian state's perception of the cultural inability of the Italian consumer to make an informed choice between different types of pasta. Italians, one learns from the Advocate General's Opinion, like their pasta *al dente, glissant des deux côtés de la fourchette*.[19] The use of durum wheat is the only method of achieving this happy result. This led him to conclude that the restrictive effect of the technical rule served a legitimate purpose. He would have ruled Italy's requirement compatible with Article 30.

Could Italy not have required pasta products to be clearly labelled to reveal their composition in order to permit consumer choice while ensuring it was informed? The Advocate General inquired into this aspect thoroughly. He went shopping. He produced four packets of pasta, Italian, Belgian, German, and Swiss, purchased in a Luxembourg supermarket. All bore the word 'spaghetti'. All displayed a range of further information about their differing composition, some 'in microscopic letters'. He concluded that an Italian consumer could *not* be adequately

[19] Mr Mancini draws here on the Journal of André Gide, 22 June 1942.

informed by labels about production of differently constituted pasta in other states, given the depth of cultural expectation in Italy about pasta, its many forms of presentation, and the exclusive use of durum wheat.

The Advocate General considered that market liberalization would lead to an unacceptable level of consumer confusion. He believed that the matter of pasta recipe laws should be left untouched by the deregulatory influence of Article 30 and should instead be resolved through the introduction of 'positive' common Community rules. For Mr Mancini, the removal of the law would liberalize the market, but this process would wreck the market as if hit by 'a sudden and devastating earthquake'. This is an important statement of the perceived limits of the judicial role and the start of the role of the legislature.

In sharp contrast, the Court placed the matter within the scope of the deregulatory application of Article 30. There was no need to await legislative intervention. The market for pasta was to be opened up, and consumer choice enhanced, by holding the Italian rule incompatible with Article 30. Traditional products from other Member States could therefore be sold in Italy, where they were definitely not traditional.

The Court was presumably unconvinced that the Italian consumer was incapable of picking up new habits. The ruling lacks any extended discussion of Mr Mancini's fears about the incomprehension of an Italian consumer when confronted with the idea that pasta need not be made from durum wheat alone. The Court observed that it remained open to the Italian authorities to restrict the description 'pasta made from durum wheatmeal' to pasta products made exclusively from durum wheat. The Court assumes that consumer expectations can be shifted and then fulfilled by the operation of the market, once the legal mould into which that product market has been forced to fit has been broken. The Court feels able to leave decisions about how to react to unfamiliar products to the potential buyer.

Deceptive marketing practices are the subject of legal control in all Member States. At stake is the potential harm that such practices may inflict on consumers' economic interests. Yet the legal rules may impede trade where they differ state by state. The impediment arises where the use of a technique employed in state A is forbidden in state B, which forces the trader to pursue a different strategy when planning to penetrate the market of state B. The integration of markets is thwarted; economies of scale are lost. This is a reworking of the question of how to reconcile two different types of consumer interest; that in national protection, expressed through the maintenance of the national rule, and that in an integrated market in which consumer choice is maximized, expressed through the abolition of the restrictive national measure.

In fact the whole field of controlling 'deceptive' marketing practices demands an image of the consumer who, after all, is the party subject to the deception. National law has to fix a borderline between clever commercial tactics and unfair commercial tactics. National law has to decide whether it is 'deceptive' to use a campaign that fools some consumers most of the time; or most consumers some of the time. It is necessary to decide when 'hard sell' shades into 'unfair sell'. Different states have adopted different views about the extent to which they will protect gullibility. EC law is forced to choose its own notion of deception when it comes to balancing the interest in protection against deception (however defined) against the impetus towards integrated marketing strategies. Cases in which national laws have been held incompatible with Article 30 have revealed a perception in the European Court that the consumer is rather more self-reliant than some national laws admit.

In *GB-INNO* v. *Confédération du Commerce Luxembourgeois*[20] Luxembourg rules restricted the provision by a trader of information about prices of goods. Such practices were permitted as part of an advertising strategy in Belgium. So there was a disparity between national laws that cut across GB-INNO's ability to construct an integrated cross-border marketing strategy in support of its goods. Luxembourg was unable to persuade the Court that there was an adequate justification for the rules. The Court was unpersuaded by the notion that the consumer might benefit from suppression of information. The Court drew on a soft-law source, the 1981 Resolution adopting a Consumer Protection and Information Policy, in asserting a close connection between consumer protection and consumer information. Had Luxembourg been seeking to suppress inaccurate information,

---

[20] Case C-362/88 [1990] ECR I-667.

then doubtless the result of the case would have been different. But simply to block the supply of information by a trader could not be justified.

A similar approach to market deregulation emerges from *Schutzverband gegen Unwesen in der Wirtschaft* v. *Y. Rocher GmbH.*[21] At stake was a law that formed part of the pattern of German law controlling unfair competition, a category of market regulation closely related to consumer protection. It was a law that will strike most non-German lawyers as highly peculiar. For that reason, it offers an intriguing insight into the distinctive perceptions of German trade practices law. German law prohibited advertisements in which individual prices were compared, except where the comparison was not eyecatching. Rocher was able to show that the rule interfered with its ability to construct an integrated marketing strategy, because it could not use in Germany techniques that it was able to use in states with different, more liberal regimes. The European Court ruled that the German law was incompatible with Article 30. Its judgment makes great play of the fact that the German law controlled eyecatching advertisements *irrespective* of their truth. Had the focus been on untrue claims, the result would have been different, but the Court could not accept a law that suppressed the supply of accurate information to the consumer.

German law had developed from the perception that some consumers, at least, were capable of being misled by such practices. Perhaps such regulation pays unusually little regard for the capacity of consumers to take care of themselves. The European Court certainly thought so. But the German law was not pointless. It was a law based on a different perception of deception from the European Court's norm and it had to yield to the imperatives of Community trade law.

The perceived over-protective tendencies of German law also fell foul of Article 30 in *Verband Sozialer Wettbewerb eV* v. *Clinique Laboratories SNC.*[22] German law prohibited the use of the name 'Clinique' for cosmetics. The rationale lay in the alleged risk that consumers would be misled into believing the products possessed medicinal properties. This rule impeded trade in goods

---

[21] Case C–126/91, judgment of 18 May 1993.
[22] Case C–315/92 [1994] ECR I–317.

that were lawfully marketed in other Member States where the 'Clinique' name was permitted. Germany was unable to show justification for the rule. The Court was not persuaded that there was sufficient likelihood of consumer confusion for a barrier to trade to be justified. Here, too, German law had an image of a consumer more gullible than the European Court was prepared to acknowledge. The European Court seems to envisage a self-reliant consumer in the market who is able to enjoy the fruits of integration.

There is, however a limit to the Court's perception of the consumer's ability to fend for him- or herself. Other cases have seen the Court uphold the lawfulness of national measures of market regulation even where an obstructive effect on cross-border trade is shown to follow.

Dutch law controlled the offer of free gifts as an inducement to purchase encyclopedias. Traders who favoured this marketing technique in other Member States, where it was permitted, were prevented from putting together a cross-border strategy. However in *Oosthoek's Uitgeversmaatschappij*[23] the Court ruled that the Dutch law was compatible with consumer protection in the light of its contribution to the protection of the consumer. 'It is undeniable that the offering of free gifts as a means of sales promotion may mislead consumers as to the real prices of certain products and distort the conditions on which genuine competition is based. Legislation which restricts or even prohibits such commercial practices for that reason is therefore capable of contributing to consumer protection and fair trading.' It is important that the Court here admits that the consumer may in some circumstances be unable properly to process information. This may constitute a justification for action by Member States to offer protection even where that impedes the process of market integration.

In *Buet* v. *Ministère Public*[24] the Court held that a French law which prohibited 'doorstep selling' of educational material was not incompatible with Article 30 in view of its contribution to the protection of the consumer from pressure-selling tactics. This was a case that straddled the judicial and legislative contributions to market integration. A Directive on 'Doorstep Selling'[25] touched

[23] Case 286/81 [1982] ECR 4575.   [24] Case 328/87 [1989] ECR 1235.
[25] Dir. 85/577 [1985] OJ L372/31.

the area in which France had legislated, but the existence of the Directive did not pre-empt French action in the field, for that Directive, although made under Article 100, is 'minimum' in character.[26]

Strikingly, the laws at issue in *Oosthoek* and in *Buet* controlled 'hard-sell' techniques which need not be deceptive to an alert consumer, but which might admittedly have led to a consumer unfamiliar with the technique being misled. The cases display a rather more paternalistic approach to the consumer than that which emerges from *GB-INNO*, *Rocher*, and *Clinique*.

PARALLEL PRINCIPLES IN THE LAW GOVERNING THE FREE MOVEMENT OF SERVICES

The cases above concern Article 30 and the free movement of *goods*. That sensitive and delicate balance between free trade and national market regulation also arises in connection with Article 59 and the free movement of *services*. Here, too, national laws which obstruct trade may require justification under Community law. This may require resolution of a collision between national laws protecting social/moral values and Community laws governing economic integration.

The infiltration of the deregulatory influence of the *Cassis* principle into the field of the free movement of services seemed to be precluded by the Treaty. Article 60(3) permits the supply of services to be regulated by the host state on 'the same conditions as are imposed by the state on its own nationals'. This seems to envisage that each state may apply its own professional qualification rules, for example, to all those wishing to operate on its territory even where this will have the effect of obstructing market access by those professionally qualified under different sets of rules in other Member States. A qualified professional would in practice be excluded from competing in the market for the supply of professional services in another Member State simply because he or she possesses *different* qualifications, irrespective of any inquiry into whether they are *inadequate* qualifications. Divergence in technical rules state by state tends to isolate national markets from each other. Companies, too, face obstacles

[26] Ch. 5, 151.

arising out of different regulatory regimes state by state. But the Court has denied states the possibility of simply relying on Article 60(3) without showing further justification for market-partitioning rules. Where rules impede market access by suppliers based in other Member States they must be objectively justified. That the Court has not been deterred from developing this principle despite Article 60(3) testifies to its determination to construct a core set of principles of Community trade law, drawing together the separate Treaty provisions, most of all Articles 30 and 59.

Dennemeyer, a company registered in the United Kingdom, specialized in providing patent renewal services. It provided those services to clients throughout the EC, especially in Germany. It advised clients when fees for renewing patents fell due and it paid the fees on their behalf. Naturally it charged a commission, but this was rather lower than that levied by German patent agents performing similar services. Säger was a Munich patent agent whose business was under threat from this competition. He brought proceedings before the Munich courts on the basis of a German law on legal advice of 1935 which required parties involved in this business to hold a permit.

Dennemeyer, established in the United Kingdom, did not hold the required permit, although it was acting lawfully as far as British law was concerned. A reference was made to the European Court asking its view on the compatibility of the German law with Article 59. This was *Säger* v. *Dennemeyer*.[27] Dennemeyer was being asked to conform to German domestic regulatory standards as a precondition to gaining access to the German market. Its capacity to plan an integrated cross-border strategy was impeded, albeit by a non-discriminatory national law. This was the *Cassis* problem of disparity between national systems causing trade barriers, arising here in the field of service rather product market-integration. The Court responded to the parallel fact patterns by employing a parallel legal approach.

It observed that the permit system, although non-discriminatory on grounds of nationality, operated in practice to exclude non-national service providers. This led to a restriction in the choice of those wishing to employ agents in the field. Such limitations required justification based on the demonstration of 'imperative

[27] Case C–76/90 [1991] ECR I–4221.

reasons relating to the public interest'. It must also be shown that the concern underlying the rules is not adequately addressed by the regulatory system of the state in which the service provider is established. Moreover, and familiarly, the restrictive effect of the rules must not go beyond that which is strictly necessary to attain the objective in view.

The objective of the German law was accepted by the European Court as a potential justification. Such regulatory intervention was designed to protect consumers against harm that they could suffer were they to be advised by inadequately qualified persons. However the German permit system went beyond what was necessary to achieve this objective. Dennemeyer provided services 'essentially of a straightforward nature'. It alerted clients to renewal and helped them carry through their wishes. It did not offer expert legal advice on the substance of patent law. And even if Dennemeyer let its clients down, the German system did not cast the patent holder adrift. A reminder was sent by the German patent office to the holder two months after the due date for renewal, and even then the patent would not expire for a further four months. An extra 10 per cent was payable on the fee in the event of late renewal, but this could not be thought disastrous. The barrier to entry to the market for supplying such services caused by the German permit system was disproportionate. It was incompatible with Article 59.

National market-regulation must take account of the integrating market. Here the restriction in consumer choice could not be justified. Part of the ruling is based on the perception that Dennemeyer was not actually providing a particularly important service. The graver the consequences for the consumer of the supplier mishandling the task, the stronger the state's justification for exercising regulatory control over the supplier.

In developing the *Cassis* principle in the services sector, the Court has prevented states converting the Article 59 right into a mere Article 52 right. Were states able to insist on the application of non-discriminatory national technical rules such as that at issue in *Säger* v. *Dennemeyer* then the practical realization of a right to provide to services across borders would be emptied of content; there would in practice be no more than a right to establish oneself in another Member State. This would be economically damaging. It would block the realization of economies of scale in the services sector. Temporary establishment (or no establishment at all) is distinct from permanent establishment and the application of national regulation must respect that distinction. In practice this will frequently dictate a lighter regulatory control exercised over an out-of-state supplier involving respect for controls exercised in that supplier's home state.

The use of Article 59 to challenge national technical standards is especially vital for the expanding range of services that is capable of being provided cross-border without any movement of people as a consequence of technological advance. This was at stake in *Säger* v. *Dennemeyer* itself. Here especially it would be irrational were this area of law not developed hand-in-hand with the law on the free movement of goods. This point seems to be implicitly accepted by the European Court. It is explicitly and thoroughly examined in the Opinion of Advocate General Jacobs. He refers to the wide spectrum of activities that may fall within the notion of provision of services. Some aspects shade into Article 30—sending a set of educational books or videos. Such a transaction is close to the border between Article 59 and Article 30. Provided the law operates in parallel, any oddity arising out of precise choice of categorization is avoided. But at the other end of the spectrum Article 59 rubs shoulders with Article 52. Advocate General Jacobs cites the architect supervising a large project in another Member State. Here a state might be able to impose some or all of its own domestic regulatory standards in full even if this tends to place the migrant in or close to the same position as a person wishing to establish him- or herself permanently in the host state. The public interest might warrant such thorough supervision.

Commission v. *France, Italy, Greece* involved national rules that made the provision of services by tourist guides accompanying groups of tourists from another Member State subject to the possession of a licence, itself dependent on possession of a particular qualification.[28] The Court found the rules to be in violation of Article 59. In the ruling against France it pointed out that the rule 'prevents both tour companies from providing that service with their own staff and self-employed tourist guides from offering their services to those companies for organized tours. It also prevents tourists taking part in such organized tours from

---

[28] Cases C–154/89, 180/89, and 198/89 [1991] ECR I–659, 709, 727.

availing themselves at will of the services in question.' The European Court did not deny that states were entitled to take steps to secure proper dissemination of knowledge about artistic and cultural heritage even where those steps might lead to a restriction on the freedom to provide services. The national licensing system went far beyond what was necessary to achieve that objective. Indeed the Court was able to point to the damage done to the flexibility of the market by such rules. They would tend to force tour parties to use local guides, who would in practice be the only people holding the required licence. 'That consequence may have the drawback that tourists who are the recipients of the services in question do not have a guide who is familiar with their language, their interests and their specific expectations.' The Court commented that in a competitive market for organized tours one would expect firms to seek quality in the guides they employed, including, where demanded by consumers, proper cultural and artistic knowledge of the host state. So the Court was firmly in favour of the maintenance of standards through the operation of a liberalized, competitive market rather than through the regulatory choices of public authorities. This led to the finding of violation of Article 59.

Market deregulation is not inevitable. The Court's approach to restrictive technical rules under Article 59 shares with Article 30 an acceptance that in some circumstances the public interest underlying the national rule in question may be shown to carry more weight than the interests of integration and enhanced choice. The market will remain segmented pending Community legislative intervention. The Court assumes a power to make choices. In *Säger* v. *Dennemeyer* no adequate interest was shown, although the Court appears to have left open the probability that in cases of provision of more expert, technical advice, a state could permissibly have decided that the market could not simply be left to operate unregulated. In the tourist guide cases, the Court was plainly perfectly content to allow the unregulated market to serve the consumer. But in *Customs and Excise Commissioners* v. *Schindler and Schindler*[29] the Court ruled that national restrictions on cross-border trade were justified.

The Schindlers acted as agents for a German lottery promoter.

---

[29] Case C–275/92 [1994] ECR I–1039.

They had dispatched advertisements and application forms from the Netherlands to the United Kingdom as part of an attempt to drum up business for the lottery. Acting under statutory powers the Commissioners seized the letters. The United Kingdom's controls were designed to suppress large-scale lotteries irrespective of the nationality of the organizer or the Member State where they originated. There was no discrimination. However, the Schindlers considered that their rights to trade under EC law had been unlawfully blocked. A reference was made by the English High Court to Luxembourg.

The Court considered that the Schindlers were involved in the organization of a service allowing buyers of a ticket a chance to participate in a lottery. This brought the matter within the scope of Article 59. The Court agreed that lotteries were restricted in different ways and to different extents in different Member States, but they were not capable of being equated to a trade in illegal services. The Court found the conclusion unavoidable that the Schindlers' economic activity had been impeded. The question arose whether the United Kingdom could justify its restriction on the freedom to provide services.

The objectives of the legal controls over lotteries were several, according to information supplied by the referring court, the High Court in London. The restrictions contributed to the prevention of crime and they served to ensure the honest treatment of gamblers. They were aimed at avoiding stimulating demand for gambling, an activity that is socially damaging where pursued to excess. They existed to ensure that the operation of lotteries pursued charitable, sporting and cultural purposes, rather than personal and commercial profit.

The European Court took a rather surprisingly benevolent view of the restrictive national rules. It found controls capable of justification 'in the light of the specific social and cultural features of each Member State, to maintain order in society'. Concerns of social policy and the prevention of fraud justified the United Kingdom's system. The ruling demonstrates the Court's sensitivity to the impact that the law of market integration may have on national social and cultural choices. It decides to offer latitude to the regulating Member State. The ruling is noticeably cautious.

A question that anyone reading the *Schindler* judgment must immediately ask is: what now, after the creation of the United

Kingdom's national lottery in late 1994? The European Court's ruling in *Schindler* was explicitly directed at a situation in which a state prohibits the operation of large-scale lotteries and where this has the effect of impeding actors such as the Schindlers who are trying to encourage nationals to participate in such lotteries organized in other Member States. The ruling mentions explicitly that it is dealing with the non-discriminatory situation prior to the 1993 Act that authorized the establishment of the national lottery. Is the United Kingdom entitled to act against large-scale lotteries organized from other states, as it did in *Schindler*, now that it has started its own large-scale lottery?

In so far as this would yield discrimination, one might suppose not; at least, not on the grounds advanced in *Schindler*. In any event the establishment of a national lottery seems to undermine the submission that the United Kingdom has coherent laws that are aimed at avoiding stimulating demand for gambling; or that it is concerned to ensure that the operation of lotteries pursues charitable, sporting, and cultural purposes, rather than personal and commercial profit, given the relatively high percentage taken as profit by the private lottery organizer, Camelot. Nevertheless Advocate General Gulmann commented briefly on the effect of the national lottery. He felt that this need not be incompatible with continued restrictions. He suggested that this might be an instance where the state could permissibly require all operators of large-scale lotteries to be established within the United Kingdom. This would prevent the use of Article 59 by agents of lotteries in other Member States to liberalise the cross-border market. Perhaps submissions drawn from the role of the lottery in structuring a coherent state tax system could assist in this difficult argument; were free trade to prevail a small state would have great difficulty in running a cost-effective lottery for fear of being overwhelmed by a much larger and more attractive lottery run from a big neighbouring state. On the other hand, the idea that lotteries are fair methods of raising tax hardly withstands scrutiny when one takes into account the disproportionately heavy participation in lotteries of lower income groups. This will remain a moot point until such time as agents for lotteries outside the United Kingdom decide to test the potential of EC law as a means of forcing the United Kingdom's national lottery to take its chances in the wider Community market. When that occurs, the

Court will once again be driven into a difficult area of balancing different types of public interest.

Society for the Protection of Unborn Children v. *Grogan*[30] is a remarkable decision. The litigation arose against a background of the right to life of the unborn enshrined in the Irish Constitution. The unavailability of abortion in Ireland causes thousands of Irish women annually to travel to London to secure termination of their pregnancies. In recognition of this demand, a student association in Dublin provided information about abortion services available in the United Kingdom. It provided the information free of charge. Legal proceedings were initiated before the Irish courts by the Society for the Protection of Unborn Children (SPUC) against the union. The question of EC law that arose was whether the suppression of such information that reflected the Irish Constitutional position was contrary to EC trade law. Ireland's Constitution reflected social and moral choices about the nature of the rights of people—even, most fundamental of all, about when a person comes into being. Yet it collided with an economic activity. Abortion is a service provided for payment. The provision of information in Dublin about a service available in London was part of the process of developing the cross-border market for services. This is the province of Article 59. So could the students rely on EC law to defeat the application of Irish law?

The prospect for the European Court was rather alarming. How could it balance moral choices and economic motives? How could it resolve a clash between two different constitutional legal orders? Yet the obligation to make that choice seemed to be the inevitable consequence of the European Court's drive to use EC trade law to open up 'the market', in its widest sense. The European Court was, however, able to exploit a fortuitous element in the fact pattern to wriggle free of the need to make the choice. It decided there was here one missing element that prevented the dispute being sufficiently 'economic' for the purposes of EC trade law. The students' association was providing the information completely free of charge. It did not receive any direct payment from students seeking an abortion. It did not receive any payment from British abortion clinics in return for providing what were, in effect, free advertisements. There was a market for

---

[30] Case C-159/90 [1991] ECR I-4685.

abortion services, but on a strict contractual reading the students' association was not part of its commercial structure. So the students' association was not able to show the 'economic' aspect that is a prerequisite to the invocation of EC trade law.

Relief is not difficult to identify lurking beneath the judgment in *Grogan*. Had the Court had to balance the competing interests, it would have faced an unenviable choice. At a more fundamental level, it would have been open to criticism for having placed itself in the position of establishing hierarchies between differently motivated constitutional values. On its own facts, the case may be capable of rationalization as the identification by the European Court of the limits of an economic constitution for the EC, beyond which national constitutional values in moral and cultural matters can be left undisturbed. But that neat demarcation is an illusion. Were a London clinic to pay for an advertisement in an Irish publication, the required economic nexus would be established and the European Court's reason for excluding the application of Article 59 would vanish. The separation of economic activity from moral and cultural values would vanish with it. National constitutionally protected interests would be testable against the standards of EC trade law.

It was therefore obvious that the approach taken in *Grogan* allowed a temporary evasion of highly sensitive areas. The temperature in Ireland was raised still further by action taken by the public authorities to prevent a rape victim leaving the country to obtain a termination of her unwanted pregancy. Litigation involving claimed EC-law rights to travel to receive a service was initiated, although the Luxembourg court was not involved. On this occasion, the Irish courts felt able to resolve that matter under Irish law alone.[31] The complexity was deepened by a ruling of the European Court of Human Rights. Aspects of Irish law which the European Court had avoided reviewing in *Grogan* were found incompatible with Article 10 of the European Convention in *Open Door and Dublin Well Woman* v. *Ireland*.[32] Ireland had imposed a disproportionate interference on rights of freedom of information. This led to domestic law reform. Some restrictions on travel and information-provision were eased in Ireland.

[31] *A.G.* v. *X* [1992] 1 CMLR 277 (Irish Sup. Ct.).
[32] (1992) Series A, no 246 (1993) 15 EHRR 244.

The European Court's ruling in *Grogan* suggests that institutions affected by potentially sensitive clashes between the law of the EC and that of the European Convention have incentives to keep such clashes in the realm of theory rather than practice. The Treaty on European Union expresses a Union commitment to observe fundamental rights, but this is not justiciable before the European Court.[33] Community accession to the Convention would encourage the planning of a clearer hierarchical arrangement.[34] However, in the meantime, the general message of this Chapter is that EC trade law cannot readily be confined to narrow limits. In effect, the European Court has acquired a wide-ranging power to review national laws against the standards of Community trade law. That requires the Court to develop its own conception of the importance of trade liberalization judged against the relative weight of competing interests such as consumer protection, environmental standards, and maintenance of public morality that are expressed through national laws.

FURTHER READING

DEMIRAY, D., 'The Movement of Goods in a Green Market' [1994/1] *LIEI* 73.

GERADIN, D., 'Trade and Environmental Protection: Community Harmonization and National Environmental Standards' (1993) 13 *YEL* 151.

HANCHER, L., and SEVENSTER, H., Case Note on Case C–2/90 *Commission* v. *Belgium* (1993) 30 *CMLRev.* 351.

KRAMER, L., 'Environmental Protection and Article 30 EEC Treaty' (1993) 30 *CMLRev.* 111.

McGEE, A., and WEATHERILL, S., 'The Evolution of the Single Market— Harmonisation or Liberalisation?' (1990) 53 *MLR* 578.

O'LEARY, S., 'The Court of Justice as a Reluctant Constitutional Adjudicator' (1992) 17 *ELRev.* 138.

PEARCE, R., 'Abortion and the Right to Life under the Irish Constitution' [1993] *JSWFL* 386.

SLYNN, LORD, 'The European Community and the Environment' (1993) 5 *Jo. En.L* 261.

---

[33] 205 above.

[34] The European Court is considering the constitutionality under EC law of accession: Opinion 2/94.

SPALIN, E., 'Abortion, Speech and the European Community' [1992] *Jo. Social Welfare and Family L* 17.

VAN EMPEL, M., 'The 1992 Programme: Interaction between Legislator and Judiciary' [1992/2] *LIEI* 1.

VON WILMOWSKY, P., 'Waste Disposal in the Internal Market: The State of Play after the ECJ's Ruling on the Walloon Import Ban' (1993) 30 *CMLRev.* 541.

VON HEYDEBRAND U.D. LASA, H.-G., 'Free Movement of Foodstuffs, Consumer Protection and Food Standards in the European Community: Has the Court of Justice got it wrong?' (1991) 16 *ELRev.* 391.

WILKINSON, B., 'Abortion, the Irish Constitution and the EEC' [1992] *Pub.L* 20.

8

The Future of Internal Market Law

Chapter 7 surveyed the depth of the potential intrusion of EC trade law into national choices about not simply market regulation, but also other apparently non-economic types of legislation. The alarmingly wide scope of the review power so acquired has begun to breed a new caution on the part of the European Court. Several aspects of the material examined in the preceding chapter may be assessed from this standpoint. *Grogan*[1] is a manifestation. The Court there found a method of holding EC trade law inapplicable on the facts of the case. But the rationale was impermanent. It could not operate as a general method for protecting national choices from scrutiny in the light of EC trade law. Cases such as *Commission* v. *Belgium*,[2] concerning Wallonia's regulation of waste, and *Customs and Excise Commissioners* v. *Schindler and Schindler*[3] also testify to caution in the European Court. But in these cases the Court tested national rules against Community standards and held them lawful, notwithstanding their restrictive effect on cross-border trade. It did not place them beyond the reach of Community law.

There is evidence of a desire in the European Court to find a firmer jurisdictional basis for fixing the outer limits of EC trade law. It frees itself of a controversial job of arbitration and of allegations of over-ambition where it is able to rule a national law untouched by, rather than justified under, EC trade law. If the Court is able to establish a clearer jurisdictional limit to EC trade law, it will in consequence give a clearer shape to national competence existing beyond the reach of primary Treaty provisions such as Articles 30 and 59.

In so far as there is a perceived problem in the reach of EC trade

---

[1] Case C–159/90 *Society for the Protection of Unborn Children* v. *Grogan* [1991] ECR I–4685.   [2] Case C–2/90 [1992] ECR I–4431.

[3] Case C–275/92 [1994] ECR I–1039.

law, it arises from the remarkable scope of the *Dassonville* formula.[4] The application of EC trade law is triggered by a finding that the national rule obstructs the process of market integration. The crossing of that threshold has long been seen to be remarkably easy. The *Dassonville* formula's flexible reference to trading rules that 'are capable of hindering, directly or indirectly, actually or potentially, intra-Community trade' ensures a large haul of national measures. Once the required impact on trade is shown, it then falls to the regulating state to demonstrate that its rules are justified.

The Court has shifted its approach. It is now slower to find the required impact on trade. The threshold is less readily crossed. This reduces the depth of intrusion of EC trade law. In *Keck and Mithouard*[5] the Court decided, in its own words, to 're-examine and clarify' its case law in this area. It ruled that there is no actual or potential, direct or indirect, barrier to inter-state trade where national laws limit or prohibit certain methods of sale, provided those laws apply to all traders active on the national territory and provided that they affect in the same way in law and in fact the marketing of national products and those originating in other Member States.

The impetus for this ruling lies in earlier ingenious resort to Article 30 in cases that seemed to lie rather a long way from the true purpose of EC trade law. Article 30 catches discriminatory national rules that impede the free movement of goods. The *Cassis de Dijon* principle takes Article 30 into the realms of national rules that are not discriminatory, but which protect national markets. On its terms, the *Dassonville* formula does not stop there. It is capable of taking Article 30 into the sphere of any national rule that restricts commerce, even where it is even-handed in its application. That stretching of Article 30 occurred in several remarkable cases in the late 1980s and early 1990s, and those cases prompted the reorientation in *Keck.*

Perhaps the most notorious pre-*Keck* example is provided by the 'Sunday trading' saga. This involved litigation to challenge the Shops Act 1950, which imposed a range of odd restrictions on the ability of English and Welsh shops to trade on Sundays. The

---

[4] Case 8/74 *Procurer du Roi* v. *Dassonville* [1974] ECR 837.
[5] Cases C–267 & 268/91, judgment of 24 Nov. 1993.

laws had grown by accretion over the years and looked quite bizarre. Fresh milk could be sold, but not tinned. Traders had been endeavouring to have them abolished or, at least, changed, but law reform had been blocked by Parliamentary disagreements. But what did EC law, specifically Article 30, have to do with the matter? This was a national choice—odd, admittedly—about the structure of society.

The tactical success of the traders lay in their persuasion of the magistrates in South Wales that shutting on Sundays restricted the volume of sales of imported goods; and that, once that effect on trade had been shown, the *Dassonville* formula was satisfied and Article 30 came into play. Preliminary references were then made to the European Court. It approached the Sunday trading cases on the basis that the threshold of demonstrating an effect on inter-state trade had been crossed, and that therefore all that remained was for the United Kingdom to justify its laws. It took several years for justification to be shown. Two European Court rulings were needed to define precisely what was required of the justifying state. The first ruling, in *Torfaen Borough Council* v. *B & Q plc*,[6] offered very little clear guidance. The Court ruled that Article 30 does not apply to 'national rules prohibiting retailers from opening their premises on Sunday where the restrictive effects on Community trade which may result therefrom do not exceed the effects intrinsic to rules of that kind.' This obscure formula largely left the matter in the hands of the national courts. Perhaps one could forgive the European Court for wishing to avoid becoming embroiled in a mess of the United Kingdom's own making, but it failed to provide a clear rationale as to how and why EC law did not provide a solution to the matter. Shops were able to take advantage of the legal uncertainty to open on Sundays in many parts of the country.[7] This emphasizes the tactical advantage which a trader enjoys once he or she is able to demonstrate a trade-restrictive effect sufficient to allow the invocation of the *Dassonville* formula.

A second reference was made. This was *Stoke-on-Trent and Norwich City Councils* v. *B & Q*[8] The European Court, doubtless

---

[6] Case 145/88 [1989] ECR 765.
[7] See R. Rawlings 'The Eurolaw Game: Some Deductions from a Saga' (1993) 20 *Jo. of L and Soc.* 309.   [8] Case C–169/91 [1993] 1 CMLR 481.

disturbed by the reign of complete confusion at national level, chose to move to the opposite extreme from the abdication of decision-making that had characterized its first ruling. It effectively decided that the Shops Act was compatible with EC law: 'Article 30 is to be interpreted as meaning that the prohibition which it lays down does not apply to national legislation prohibiting retailers from opening their premises on Sundays.'

A key point about the nature of the challenged laws was obscured in the Sunday trading cases, to the enormous advantage of the traders. The rules did not put imported goods at a disadvantage in comparison with domestic goods. There was no discrimination; nor was there even a *Cassis*-style protective effect. Volumes of sales were probably reduced by the suppression of the 'Sunday Pound', but all goods, irrespective of origin, suffered. Goods imported from other Member States were not hindered in their attempt to gain access to the British market. It was only once on the British market that irritation arose. So should Article 30 have been in issue at all?

Keck and Mithouard[9] afforded the Court the opportunity to rule that Article 30 had been pushed too far. The Court delivered a very important judgment which curtails the scope of Article 30. Keck and Mithouard had resold goods at a loss. This violated a French law forbidding such practices. They submitted that the law restricted the volume of sales of imported goods and that it was therefore incompatible with Article 30. Any restrictive effect on trade plainly affected *all* goods, not just imports. This placed the fact pattern alongside the Sunday trading cases. However, the European Court took a different tack. The Court referred explicitly to the increasing tendency of commercial parties to invoke Article 30 to challenge rules which limit their commercial freedom, even where those rules are not directed at imported products. It then declared it necessary to re-examine and clarify its case law. The Court stated that:

the application to products from other Member States of national provisions restricting or prohibiting certain selling arrangements is not such as to hinder, directly or indirectly, actually or potentially, trade between Member States, provided that the provisions apply to all affected traders operating within the national territory and provided that they

---

[9] N. 2 above.

affect in the same manner, in law and in fact, the marketing of domestic products and those from other Member States.

Rules of this nature fall outside the scope of application of Article 30.

The ruling is obscure on a number of levels. It is thoroughly regrettable that, although the European Court's use in the judgment of the phrase 'contrary to what has previously been decided' makes it plain that it has it in mind to overrule some earlier decisions, it failed to name names. The ruling is brief. It fails to draw on the outstanding preparatory work of its Advocates General in this case and in the two Sunday trading cases. Perhaps most remarkable of all, the Court's peevish reproof for the increasing tendency of commercial parties to invoke Article 30 to challenge rules which limit their commercial freedom is hard to take at face value. Of course lawyers representing traders have come up with some apparently far-fetched arguments based on Article 30, but that is what they are (handsomely) paid for! Litigation such as that in the Sunday trading cases was pursued only because the European Court's dithering case law had provided such a tempting target for traders. The *Keck* ruling and its precursors make a strong case for requiring the European Court to provide reasons when it departs from its Advocate General's Opinion; and for permitting dissenting judgments to emerge from behind the traditional insistence on a single, collegiate judgment.

However, for all these criticisms of the detail and tone of the *Keck* ruling, it is submitted that it is a move in the right direction. The interpretation and application of the test of legal and factual equality will not be simple. However, for all the obscurity about its detailed application, it seems now that Article 30 is being refocussed by the Court on the objective of market integration. Its use to challenge measures which affect trade patterns but which do not partition markets is to be blocked. States are allowed to make their own distinctive choices about the regulation of markets free of the need to fit a justification within the categories recognized by Community law, providing only that the test of equality in factual and legal impact is met. The Court is attempting to ensure that Article 30 is in future to be used only in application to:

(i) national rules which discriminate against imported goods; and
(ii) national rules which exert a protectionist effect in favour of home production

but not to

(iii) national rules which restrict trade, but where the restrictive
effect is felt equally by all products irrespective of origin.

On this reading, *Keck* would not challenge the *Cassis de Dijon* line
of case law. In those cases, trade barriers arise because of diversity
between national rules. There is protectionism, and category (ii)
applies. *Keck* does, however, challenge the control of Sunday-
trading-type rules under Article 30. Such rules have no impact on
specifically cross-border aspects of trade. They are within category
(iii) above. After *Keck*, the type of trade restriction shown in the
Sunday trading litigation would no longer suffice to trigger Article
30. That being so, the state falls under no obligation to justify its
rules under Community law.

This interpretation of *Keck* accordingly holds that in future
traders will find it more difficult to employ Article 30 to require
Member States to justify rules which inhibit commercial freedom.
They will have to show that the rule in question falls into category
(i) or (ii) above before the onus shifts to the state to show
justification. Where they show that the rule is restrictive only in
the category (iii) sense, the Article 30 argument is of no avail. The
state is not called on to justify its rules.

The *Keck* ruling effectively redistributes the respective
competences of the Community and of the Member States in the
sphere of economic regulation in favour of the Member States.
The potential of Article 30 to act as an element in the construction
of a general principle guiding the place of state intervention in the
market economy is cut short.

Anti-competitive State Practices

The ruling in *Keck*, as a concession to national competence,
should be read with that in *Meng*, delivered by the European
Court precisely one week earlier.[10] Wolf Meng was a financial
adviser in Germany. He had special interests in insurance. Several
of his clients had concluded contracts with insurance companies.
He had received commission from the insurance companies and he
then paid that commission to his clients. This was part of his
strategy for attracting custom. However, the payment of

---

[10] Case C–2/91, judgment of 17 Nov. 1993.

commission to the clients infringed German law and Meng was fined. He complained that, broadly, this inhibition on his commercial freedom was incompatible with EC law. He was unable to employ free movement law because there was no inter-state element to the case. He complained instead that the German rules distorted competition between private parties contrary to the basic objectives of the Community. Competition on price was effectively impeded by the German rules. Articles 3(f) EEC, now Article 3(g) EC, and 85(1) envisage free competition as the guarantor of consumer welfare. Article 5 obliges Germany to facil-itate the achievement of the Community tasks, which include the establishment and maintenance of a competitive market, and there-fore Meng argued that the combination of Articles 3(f)/3(g), 5 and 85(1) precluded the application to him of the German restrictions.

He was unsuccessful. The Court referred to an established line of decisions in which it had accepted that Articles 5 and 85 prohibit Member States from introducing or maintaining measures which might render ineffective the competition rules. Encouragement or support for anti-competitive cartels or the delegation to private traders of responsibility for decisions affecting the economic sphere would count as violations of this Community-law obliga-tion. However, the rules at issue in *Meng* were 'simple' state regulation of conduct in the insurance sector. They neither encouraged nor supported private restrictive practices. They did not delegate decision-making responsibility to the private sector. They were compatible with Community law.

It is submitted that Article 5, that industrious prompt to the development of the Community legal order and its relationship with national law,[11] could have played a major role in *Meng*. The Court has been prepared to read Article 5 with other provisions of the Treaty to prevent Member States from arranging their economies in a way that the Court judges incompatible with the objectives of the Community. In *Höfner and Elsner* v. *Macrotron*[12] for example, Höfner and Elsner had provided Macrotron with a candidate for a post as a sales director. Macrotron did not appoint him despite his suitability and refused to pay Höfner and Elsner. German law granted exclusive rights relating to employee-recruitment to a public agency. Therefore the contract on which

[11] Ch. 2, 45.   [12] Case C–41/90 [1991] ECR I–1979.

Höfner and Elsner sued Macrotron was void. Höfner and Elsner relied on Community law to challenge the German law which excluded them from the market for supplying staff. As in *Meng*, absence of a cross-border element precluded the deployment of Article 59, but the European Court used Articles 5 and 86 as the basis of an obligation imposed on the state not to sustain a market which was uncompetitive. The German law's creation of monopoly powers prevented the match of supply to demand in private economic relations, and this fell foul of EC law. The assertion of control over state regulatory choices that affected the pattern of the market without forestalling integration in *Höfner and Elsner* v. *Macrotron* contrasts starkly with the reticence to intrude in *Meng*.

On past evidence, it would not have been over-ambitious to anticipate that the Court in *Meng* might have considered that Article 5 was capable of controlling the type of regulation adopted by Germany and that it lies with Germany to show justification for such rules, based on, for example, consumer protection. Article 5 could have been used to develop a general notion of law applicable to the economy based on free and fair competition. From the German perspective the search was on for the EC's Wirtschaftsverfassung—its Economic Constitution.[13] But the ruling in *Meng* displays a much more cautious approach to the scope of the Treaty. The Court picks its way delicately through the individual provisions of the Treaty. It conspicuously fails to make any attempt to draw on overall principles. It drew a distinction between national rules that give force to a pre-existing cartel, which are subject to control via Articles 5 and 85, and rules that are introduced independently by the state, which escape control under Articles 5 and 85.

Vereniging van Vlaamse Reisbureaus v. *Sociale Dienst*[14] concerned a price-fixing cartel among Belgian travel agents that was maintained by the ability of members of the trade association to obtain court orders against price-cutters. The cartel was in breach of Article 85 and the European Court found that the state acted in violation of its Treaty obligation, drawn from Articles 5

---

[13] Essential reading for the non-German lawyer: D. Gerber, 'Constitutionalizing the Economy: German Neo-Liberalism, Competition Law and the "New" Europe' (1994) 42 *AJCL* 25.   [14] Case 311/85 [1987] ECR 3801.

and 85, by providing for judicial enforcement of the arrangement. The state is not permitted to support private anti-competitive practices and thereby to deprive Article 85 of its effectiveness. The situation in the Belgian travel agents' case is distinct from that in *Meng* in that a pre-existing private arrangement operated in Belgium, on which state protection had been conferred. However, the impact of the state intervention was in essence the same in both cases. Both interventions had the effect of suppressing price competition. There seems no rational reason based on economic effect for drawing a significant legal distinction between the two situations. However, the Court in *Meng* stuck closely and cautiously to the text of the Treaty. It clearly felt that Article 5 was in the current climate no basis for it to construct a general theory of economic law that transcends the law of free movement and that controlling anti-competitive practices. It declined to intrude on national competence. It declined to fill gaps in the Treaty.

A further suggestion of judicial reticence when offered the opportunity to extend review of national regulations against the standards of Community trade law is provided in the area of state aids, covered in the Treaty by Articles 92–94. The Court has taken a consistently broad view of what constitutes a state aid. The notion naturally catches direct payments to a firm, but also embraces indirect conferral of advantages, for example through tax rebates or provision of facilities at a cost below the true market rate. Effect on the market, not the form in which provision is made, is critical. This broad interpretation is motivated by the need to ensure that Member States do not use cunning subterfuges to confer benefits on domestic firms in violation of the rules. However a shift of emphasis is apparent in *P. Kirsammer-Hack* v. *Hurhan Sidal*,[15] a judgment of November 1993, the same month in which both *Keck* and *Meng* were decided. The Court ruled that the exemption of small businesses from laws against unfair dismissal did not constitute a state aid. It considered that such a measure did not amount to an advantage afforded directly or indirectly from state resources and that it fell outwith Article 92. However, it is hard to deny that such laws confer competitive advantages on those able to benefit from them. It is submitted that the Court in

[15] Case C–189/91, judgment of 30 Nov. 1993.

gap-filling mood, ready to pursue a general theory of economic law for the Community, would have been capable of interpreting Article 92 in such a way as to draw such national rules within its scope, as potential market distortions. This would then require the state to show justification (based, for example, on the imposition of a lighter regulatory burden on small firms commensurate with their small size and limited resources). In general policy terms, this would have allowed the Court to travel down a road towards the identification of Community-law criteria for judging the legitimacy of regulatory competition between states in standards of labour laws and, more generally, perhaps even social welfare laws.

The Court's decision in *Kirsammer-Hack* to avoid developing any such wide-ranging review power is not in direct conflict with earlier case law under the state aids provision. But it marks a cautious attitude to extending the scope of those provisions towards a general theory of economic law for the Community.

Perhaps *Keck*, *Meng*, and *Kirsammer-Hack*, taken as a trio of contemporaneous rulings, represent a sensible and sensitive readjustment of the scope of the relevant Treaty provisions. Community law lays the ground-rules for the integrated market without overworking itself by exercising control over local regulatory choices that do not harm the realization of economies of scale or the enhancement of consumer choice. If this *is* the basis of the rulings, then it is regrettable that the Court's explicit reasoning in the judgments is so thin. The absence of full explanations of how the rulings in these cases fit within the pattern of typically more ambitious law previously developed by the Court breeds scepticism about whether the Court's lighter touch in the application of Community trade law to national regulatory choices is truly motivated by anything other than sensitivity to the political pressures to curtail the reach of Community law to which it now finds itself increasingly subject.[16]

DEFINING THE MARGIN BETWEEN THE JUDICIAL AND THE LEGISLATIVE ROLES

A further feature of the shifting patterns of Community trade law lies in the relationship between primary Community law and

---

[16] See Ch. 6, 210 above.

secondary Community law. The Court is widely perceived to have decided *Cassis de Dijon* as a means of propelling forward the process of market integration in the full awareness that Community legislative activity had at the time reached an impasse.[17] The blockage was caused by the national veto in Council and by the tendency to draft Community harmonization proposals in laborious and time-consuming detail. The Court could not simply await legislative harmonization. A reworking of Article 30 invigorated market integration.

In recent years, the growth in legislative activity, especially in connection with the internal market project, has presented the Court with a critical question. Should it adopt a less active approach to the development of primary Community trade law as a response to the greater legislative involvement? The capacity of the Community to adopt legislation more readily since the rise of QMV in Council is one element in this suggestion of a call for judicial restraint. A further aspect lies in the increased input of the Parliament which has enhanced the democratic credentials of Community legislation. Moreover, the style of Community harmonization has changed for the better, through the new approach and through the shift away from rigid rules of pre-emption.[18] If part of the rationale for the *Cassis de Dijon* ruling was that in the face of legislative inertia the Court alone could deregulate the market, that basis for judicial activism is now eliminated. It is tempting to suppose that the Court can and should slow down now that the torch of market integration and market regulation has been taken up by an active legislature.

Perhaps the rulings in *Keck*, *Meng*, and *Kirsammer-Hack* contain elements of this perception. The Court made explicit reference to the role of legislation in its 1994 ruling in *IHT Internationale Heiztechnik GmbH* v. *Ideal Standard GmbH*.[19] The American Standard group held the trade mark 'Ideal Standard' through subsidiaries in France and in Germany. In 1984 the French subsidiary sold the trade mark to an independent third party buyer. IHT, a German subsidiary of the buyer, began to sell French-made goods in Germany that bore the (French) Ideal Standard trade mark. It found itself sued before German courts by

---

[17] 237 above.   [18] Ch. 5.
[19] Case C–9/93 [1994] ECR I–2789.

Ideal Standard for infringement of the German Ideal Standard trade mark.

The European Court ruled that reliance on the German trade mark to exclude French-made goods impeded trade (Article 30), but that it was nevertheless justified (Article 36). The Ideal Standard trade marks had a common origin, but had fallen into separate hands as a result of voluntary assignment by the owner. Short-term integration would have been served by a ruling that the assignment for part of the Community territory could not justify reliance on the right to preclude importation of goods bearing the trade mark from other parts of the Community. The pattern of Articles 30–36 is sufficiently flexible for that to have been a plausible outcome. That result was proposed by the Commission in its submissions in the case. However, the European Court preferred a result that allowed persisting market segregation dictated by national territorial protection of the right.

On policy grounds the ruling in *Ideal Standard* can be supported. For example, to have ruled against reliance on the right might have destroyed the market for the sale of trade marks. It might have led to consumer confusion about the origin of goods. However, for present purposes that policy debate is an interesting side issue. The main point is that the Court felt the need to respect legislative diversity between the Member States despite the unfavourable consequences for integration. The Court made explicit its perception of a margin between its own role and that of the Community legislature. In ruling the protection of the German market compatible with Article 36 despite the effect on inter-state trade, the Court declared explicitly that it could not introduce through case law a solution that would render void assignments of trade marks which are confined to certain states only. It stated that the Community legislature must act by directive or regulation made under Article 100a in order to eliminate obstacles arising from the territoriality of national trade marks.

This seems far from the previous chapter's account of the spirit of the Court's integrationist activism under Article 30 when confronted by trade-restrictive national laws. Yet the approach conformed to the Court's caution in 1990 in the *HAG 2*[20] case when the Court went so far as to overrule its 1974 ruling in *HAG*

---

[20] Case C–10/89 *SA CNL-Sucal NV* v. *HAG GF AG* [1990] ECR I–3711.

I[21] to the effect that where trade marks have a common origin a holder in one state cannot rely on the mark to exclude goods made by an independent holder of the mark in a third country where the marks had been separated by governmental action. After *HAG 2* the right-holder is able to rely on the trade mark in such circumstances. *Ideal Standard* adds that a right holder is able to rely on the trade mark against goods bearing a mark with a common origin where ownership has been split by voluntary assignment, as well as where the split is the result of governmental action, as in *HAG 2*. In combination, *HAG 2* and *Ideal Standard* focus on the value to the consumer of using the trade mark as a guarantee of the identity of the producer who has exercised control over the goods bearing the trade mark. The interest of the consumer in market integration is subordinate to the maintenance of the integrity of national territorial protection which offers that guarantee. The rulings envisage persisting market segregation.

This examination of *Ideal Standard* is not intended to overstate the insights into the Court's attitude that may be gleaned from the area of trade mark law. It must be conceded that intellectual property is an area where there has been intense attention paid in recent years to the potential for Community legislative activity. The Regulation on the Community Trade Mark was made in December 1993,[22] although it does not resolve the issue of different national trade marks, which continue to exist alongside the additional Community system. In the area of intellectual property, where national territorial protection is at the heart of the existing legal pattern, the collision between national territorial rights and market integration is peculiarly acute and in need of legislative activity. Judicial restraint in deference to the legislative role is especially tempting and, probably, appropriate in the field in which *Ideal Standard* arose. Nevertheless, the Court's record in the 1970s, in particular, displayed a much greater readiness to subordinate national protection to market integration. One could observe a distinct unwillingness passively to await legislative solutions. For example, in *Musik-Vertrieb Membran* v. *GEMA*[23]

---

[21] Case 192/73 *Van Zuylen Frères* v. *Hag AG* [1974] ECR 731.

[22] Reg. 40/94 [1994] OJ L11/1.

[23] Cases 55 & 57/80 [1981] ECR 147.

the relevant exclusive right arose under the German Urheber-rechtsgesetz, which creates rights comparable in function to the English copyright. M-V M took advantage of the lower prices applicable in the United Kingdom in comparison with Germany and bought up goods marketed in the United Kingdom by the right-holder and imported them into Germany, where it was able to undercut the market price. GEMA, as right-holder, sought to rely on the right to claim exclusivity within Germany. The Court's existing approach to the development of Articles 30–36 made it plain that once products had been marketed in the United Kingdom with the consent of the German right-holder, the power to restrain their importation into Germany was lost. But here the price differentials were attributable to disparity between national laws, for higher royalty rates were payable under German law than under English law. GEMA submitted that, pending harmonization of laws, it should not be exposed to cross-border competition stimulated by the absence of common Community rules. However, the Court ruled in favour of M-V M's strategy. Reliance on the German right was lost once the right-holder had consented to marketing the goods in the United Kingdom. This promotes the impetus of market integration even where, in truth, the market is *not* common because of the existence of different state systems. The Court commented in its judgment that 'the existence of a disparity between national laws which is capable of distorting competition between Member States cannot justify a Member State's giving legal protection to practices of a private body which are incompatible with the rules concerning free movement of goods'.

Musik-Vertrieb Membran v. *GEMA* is not on all fours with *Ideal Standard*. In *Ideal Standard*, in contrast to *Musik-Vertrieb Membran* v. *GEMA*, consensual marketing of goods by the right-holder outside the state in which the right was subsequently relied on had not occurred. However, it is submitted that the two decisions, read together, are symptomatic of the Court's reluctance to drive forward market integration through an extension in the application of Articles 30–36. The climate has changed: The Court is more willing today to await action at legislative level and to reject appeals to deepen integration through application of primary Community law, in part because it now knows that legislation is a practical possibility.

How significant is this hint of a sea change? *Commission* v. *Italy*[24] concerned Italian rules restricting the marketing of certain types of vinegar. Italy submitted that the Commission should have attempted to achieve harmonization of rules in the sector by submitting proposals based on Article 100 before resorting to Article 169 proceedings alleging infringement of Article 30. The Court emphatically rejected this argument. The principle of free movement of goods is not subject to a precondition of attempted or actual harmonization. Were it otherwise 'the principle would be reduced to a mere cipher'. Articles 30 and 100 have quite different purposes. This determination has motivated the Court in many other areas in which it has developed the scope of primary Community law. In *Reyners* v. *Belgian State*, for example, the Court dramatically insisted that it would not await the adoption of directives to liberalize the market for professional services.[25] The principle of non-discrimination on grounds of nationality applied even in the absence of relevant Directives. Article 119 was also used to secure equality rights between the sexes in advance of legislative elaboration;[26] so much so that much of the substance of amplifying Directive 75/117 was rapidly seen to be superfluous, having been overtaken by the Court's expansion of Article 119.[27]

Ideal Standard in no way overrules any of this insistence that primary Treaty law applies notwithstanding the possibility of subsequent legislative amplification. It remains fundamental that breaches of Article 30 cannot be excused by an anticipation of legislation. But *Ideal Standard* suggests the possibility of a Court that is likely to prove less eager to identify a breach of Article 30 in 'grey areas' where national laws impede integration. The ruling suggests a greater awareness of the role of legislation as reason for declining invitations to widen the prohibitive impact of primary Treaty law.

It is not in the nature of the Court's case law that a theme will emerge that fits every case. *Commission* v. *Belgium*, the *Walloon Waste* case examined in the previous chapter,[28] fits the explanation attached here to the *Ideal Standard* ruling. It seems to indicate a willingness to uphold national regulatory choices judged against

---

[24] Case 193/80 [1981] ECR 3019.   [25] Case 2/74 [1974] ECR 631.
[26] Especially in Case 43/75 *Defrenne* v. *Sabena* [1976] ECR 455.
[27] [1975] OJ L45/19.   [28] Case C–2/90, see 243 above.

primary Community law in a field that was plainly subject to an increasingly complete pattern of secondary legislation. But in *Yves Rocher* the Court boldly ruled against German rules allegedly designed to suppress unfair competition.[29] The Court will not and should not entirely abandon the vigorous application of primary Community law simply because of the rise of practical legislative capacity at Community level. Market integration through judicial decision remains a key feature of the Community map. However, the Court's activity is now pursued in a climate in which the Court is not alone in shaping Community law.

This general perception that the Court can and should show more patience and caution in awaiting legislative activity fails to offer a framework for solving detailed questions. A similar admission was made in the conclusion to Chapter 6 after discussion of the sensitivity that attaches to the role of the European Court in times of regular intergovernmental conferences leading to Treaty revision, where, on some accounts, the Court's energies may require redirection towards consolidation in preference to constitutionalizing.[30] Here, too, much depends on one's perception of where the imprecise margin lies. But, as a general prediction, new advances in the scope of Community 'negative' law will be made only with the support of particularly strong arguments and an assessment of the impact of the legislative background. It should not be forgotten that the relationship between judicial activism and the legislative role is a question for all courts in any democratic structure.[31]

THE COURT AND THE INTERPRETATION OF LEGISLATION

It is plausible that the shadow of legislative activity will act as a brake on some aspects of judicial activism in the European Court. However, this is not to suggest that the spread of Community legislative activity simplifies the Court's role into one of mere application of the solutions chosen by the legislature. The

---

[29] Case C–126/91 *Schutzverbandgegen Unwesen in der Wirtschaft* v. *Y. Rocher GmbH*, judgment of 18 May 1993. See 250 above.　　　　[30] 210 above.

[31] Cf Lord Goff's comments in *Woolwich Building Society* v. *IRC* [1992] 3 All ER 737, Ch. 6, text at n. 51 above.

widening scope of legislative activity brings its own problems to the Community judiciary. Legislation may 'solve' some problems, but it creates others.

This has already been encountered in Chapter 5. Where legislation has been introduced at Community level, a key question of interpretation arises in connection with the demarcation of state and Community competence.[32] The precise scope of the Community rule must be identified; a process which, as a corollary, involves identification of the residual scope of Member-State competence. These issues are especially acute where the Community rule exercises a total pre-emptive effect over national competence. The Court's role in cases in which the scope of Community rules is at stake is distinct from its role in judging the scope of Articles 30–36. However, in so far as the legislation fails clearly to disclose its intended pre-emptive effect, it is scarcely less sensitive.

The scope of the rules contained in secondary legislation which the Court is called on to interpret is remarkably broad. As the law of the EC becomes more multifunctional, more is demanded of the judges of the European Court. One might argue that, even if there is now less need for the Court to break the ground, its task in interpreting the breadth of law that now emanates from the EC is different, but equally daunting. From environmental law to company law, consumer law to culture, the modern judge on the European Court bench is called on to display expertise in a vast range of public- and private-law matters.

One of the more remarkable features of the development of Community law scholarship has been the minimal attention paid to the personalities of the judges. American legal realism has never exerted an impact in Europe that compares with its popularity in the United States, and it had drifted away from the height of fashion even in America by the time that Community law began to evolve in Luxembourg. Perhaps the single collegiate judgment delivered by the European Court has masked the momentum supplied to legal development by the opinions of one or more individual judges. As Community law becomes ever more diverse and more multi-functional, separate, though related, questions about judicial expertise, rather than personality, come to the fore.

---

[32] 141 above.

Little attention has traditionally been paid to the legal background and training of judges appointed to the European Court. Most have been public lawyers or lawyers with expertise in the law of international institutions, broadly construed. That has been sufficient to cover most of Community law throughout most of its existence. But as Community legislation moves ever further into the realms of, for example, private-law, there is a need for private law expertise on the Court. In the absence of such an element, the interpretation of directives such as the Product Liability Directive[33] and the Directive on Unfair Terms in Consumer Contracts,[34] which involve fundamental private-law notions of non-contractual liability and fair dealing, will be severely problematic for the European Court. The quality of decision-making will suffer where an unduly homogeneous set of judges presides over an increasingly heterogeneous Community legal order. The development of a body of judges able and willing to scrutinize matters of economics in the Court of First Instance represents a move towards specialism. The general question arises whether the Community needs a more sophisticated method of selecting its judges. The future of internal market law, in its many nuances, is dependent on clear and effective leadership by the European Court.

FURTHER READING

ALEXANDER, W., Note on Case C–9/93, *Ideal Standard* (1995) 32 *CMLRev*. 327.

BERLIN, D., 'Interactions between the Lawmaker and the Judiciary within the EC' [1992/2] *LIEI* 17.

BRIGHT, C., 'Article 90, Economic Policy and the Duties of Member States' [1993] *ECLR* 263.

CHALMERS, D., 'Repackaging the Internal Market—The Ramifications of the *Keck* Judgment' (1994) 19 *ELRev*. 385.

DAVIES, P., 'Market Integration and Social Policy' (1995) 24 *ILJ* 49.

EHLERMANN, C.-D., 'Managing Monopolies: The Role of the State in Controlling Market Dominance in the European Community' [1993] 2 *ECLR* 61.

---

[33] Dir. 85/374 [1985] OJ L210/29, Ch. 5, n. 33.
[34] Dir. 93/13 [1993] OJ L95/29, Ch. 6, n. 47.

GERBER, D., 'Constitutionalizing the Economy: German Neo-Liberalism, Competition Law and the "New" Europe' (1994) 42 *AJCL* 25.

GORMLEY, L., 'Reasoning Renounced? The Remarkable Judgment in *Keck and Mithouard*' [1994] *Euro. Bus.LRev.* 63.

GYSELEN, L., 'Anti-Competitive State Measures under the EC Treaty: Towards a Substantive Legality Standard' (1993) *ELRev. Competition Law Checklist* 55.

POIARES MADURO, MIGUEL, '*Keck*: The End? The Beginning of the End? or just the End of the Beginning?' (1994) 1 *Irish Jnl of Euro.L* 33.

REICH, N., 'The November Revolution of the European Court of Justice: *Keck, Meng* and *Audi* Revisited' (1994) 31 *CMLRev.* 459.

VAN EMPEL, M., 'The 1992 Programme: Interaction between Legislation and Judiciary' [1992/2] *LIEI* 1.

9

Reshaping the Union

It would contradict the purpose of this book to attempt to
conclude by providing a snapshot summary of the state of the
Community and Union. Much of the book has been devoted to a
depiction of a dynamic entity which develops by solving problems
that lead naturally to the need to address a new set of problems.
Community law cannot be studied as a static set of tidy rules. The
purpose of this short Chapter is to summarize some of the key
tensions that are shaping the evolution of the Community and the
Union.

Under the influence of negative and positive Community law,
markets are altering and so, too, are patterns of regulation. The
application of negative Community trade law achieves market
integration and market deregulation in some circumstances, but in
others negative law alone does not suffice. Elsewhere the
development of positive Community rules serves to integrate
the market through (re)regulation at European level. The creation
of the European market is to be achieved both by removing
Member-State restrictions on integrated cross-border economic
activity (negative law), but also by establishing certain regulatory
measures at transnational level (positive law).

The rationales for the development of positive regulatory laws
and institutional structures at Community level vary. A central
element in the multi-functional nature of Community law and
policy lies in the range of different interests that are served by
Community activity.

Positive law is often associated with the development of an
impulse towards regulation of the market that competes with the
deregulatory ethos of market liberalization driven by negative law.
Positive law tends to be associated with the development of social

protection, broadly interpreted. However, that is part of the picture only. Commercial interests may welcome positive law as a means of clarifying opportunities for constructing an integrated marketing strategy. Once negative law fails to come to the aid of traders—not only because of lawful barriers to trade, but also where it is simply too costly to challenge state practices which might theoretically be unlawful—they may be supportive of positive law, in order to secure Community-wide market access. They may also support Community rule-making in order to secure evenness in standards Community-wide so they are not at a competitive disadvantage compared to traders in other Community states where rules are less strict. Precisely this perception would tend to induce traders to support equalization of enforcement practice so they do not lose out to competitors in states where application of the rules is lax or, at least, is perceived to be lax.

Such perceptions may lead to an insistence by the commercial sector that simple market access may not be enough to create the confidence necessary to pursue an effective internal market strategy. Equalization of competitive conditions through legislative and administrative action will be high on the agenda.

Pressures for positive Community law-making may be driven by several different interest groups. The other side of the coin is that negative law, typically regarded as the instrument of traders, is also properly regarded as beneficial to the individual citizen. Successful market integration is dependent on the abolition of national laws that obstruct enhanced competition and consumer choice. Market deregulation serves to improve the operation of the European market.

Negative law and positive law combine in a complex interrelation to build the market. The detailed question of precisely how much positive law is required remains a intensely controversial issue. Markets are not dependent on states; their existence precedes states. However, in Europe markets have close historical ties to state structures. The growth of a market out of the pre-existing European patchwork implies a necessary diminution in the independent regulatory capacity of national authorities and a necessary increase in rule-making at transnational level. For some, the creation of a European market brings with it a need for even *more* regulation than is required within a single state. For example, one might need laws which deal with the social implications of creating a larger area within which wealth may be maximized but within which distributional inequality is deepened. Such perceptions underlie the Treaty provisions on economic and social cohesion.

Europe is witnessing a rapidly evolving cross-border market, a decline in national regulatory competence (in law and practice), and an ill-shaped development of regulatory structures at European level. Functions such as environmental policy, social policy, consumer protection, and respect for fundamental rights remain the concern of national governments, but the effective discharge of such functions is affected by Community negative law. There is a rise in the profile of positive Community policies in these areas, motivated by the different pressures mentioned above. But the precise shape of Community activity requires a great deal of elaboration.

INSTITUTIONAL IMPLICATIONS OF MARKET INTEGRATION

A persisting tension attaches to the identification of the constitutional basis for building regulatory frameworks at European level. The Treaty pattern of attributed powers, spread unevenly between different provisions, breeds obscurity. The more extensive the power that is potentially wielded at European level, the deeper the concern that there is no European 'state' able to exercise that power in an accountable fashion. For some, that justifies a thoroughly sceptical attitude to accretion in power above national level. The subsidiarity principle reflects some of these concerns. The constitutional sensitivity of the Bundesverfassungsgericht, explained in Chapter 6, also reflects this tendency rigorously to scrutinize the scope of Community competence. However, the same subject matter is capable of provoking a quite different response. The rise of the European market has disabled the Member States from exercising some of the functions normally associated with the regulatory state. This sharpens awareness of the inadequacy of the European 'state', but, from a competing perspective, that places an ever greater urgency on the need to devote attention to the shaping of institutional structures at European level. At least in the sectors where the European market has blossomed, it is only at European level that effective and accountable supervision can be delivered.

Attitudes towards the place of institutional development at Community level continue to diverge sharply among the Member States. At stake is not simply the development of rules at Community level. States have short-term incentives to break the rules and, if this is not effectively controlled, the domino effect will cause the collapse of the system. That perception of a need to secure respect for Community law might be taken to justify phenomena such as Article 171(2), which envisages the imposition of fines on defaulting Member States, and the empowerment of individuals before national courts via the principle of direct effect and the wider notion of state liability under *Francovich*. But does the need to secure compliance justify institution-building at European level?

Subsidiarity is capable of being used as a tool for examining these institutional questions. However, it should immediately be emphasized that subsidiarity, contrary to some interpretations, is in principle as capable of forming a basis for developing Community measures as it is of blocking them. For example, if states seem persistently to fail to comply with their obligations under EC law then subsidiarity in Article 3b points in favour of Community action to put in place legislation and institutions *at Community level*.

In 1992 a committee headed by Peter Sutherland, a former European Commissioner, reported on the management of the internal market. The *Sutherland Report*[1] of 1992 is strongly motivated by the need to achieve effective administrative enforcement of the rules. It portrays 'horizontal' enforcement, between agencies at the same administrative level in different Member States, as efficient and envisages it as essential. National (administrative and judicial) officials should be aware that in the border-free market they apply Community law as part of a pattern of Community-wide responsibilities owed to citizens throughout the internal market. In June 1993 the Commission published *Reinforcing the Effectiveness of the Internal Market* and the

---

[1] *The Internal Market after 1992: Meeting the Challenge* (Report to the EEC Commission by the High Level Group on the Operation of the Internal Market).

accompanying working document *Towards a Strategic Programme for the Internal Market*.[2] This refers to 'a partnership between the Commission and the Member States in the application and the effective management of the rules'. The Commission refined its thoughts in a communication to the Council, *Making the Most of the Internal Market*.[3] Early in 1994 the Commission published a Communication to the Council and the European Parliament on the development of administrative co-operation in the implementation and enforcement of Community legislation in the internal market.[4] This reveals a plan to drive towards a framework for co-operation between Member States and between Commission and Member States.

In the present context, it is striking that the Commission has been careful to present its proposals as inspired by the need to establish and to maintain an integrated market. It has explicitly denied any intention to create new and cumbersome bureaucratic structures. However, these developments touch on the sensitive debate about the relationship between deregulation and reregulation in the evolving market. There is a fragile balance between the strengths of enforcement of Community law through established national procedures and the need for some common, transparent framework at Community level. The Commission's interest in attempting to reduce these matters to 'mere' technical questions of implementation is politically astute, but obscures the fact that implementation of Community rules is a constitutional issue of prime significance. If existing institutional frameworks are judged insufficient, the Member States are invited to move further down the road of empowering European-level institutions. This in turn implies a further redistribution of power away from state level towards Community level.

These are dynamic constitutional processes which are no doubt characteristic of most emergent federations. However, in the Community the redistribution of public functions in the wake of the process of market integration is happening in the absence of any elaborated constitutional blueprint. This absence, in part, explains the persistently unfocused ferocity of much of the debate. Agreeing on a relationship between the European market and the

---

[2] COM(93)256.   [3] COM(93)632.   [4] COM(94)29.

(absence of a) 'European state' represents a major challenge for the future.

THE COURT'S ROLE AS A CONSTITUTIONAL COURT

A consistent theme of this book is that the European Court's role as a constitutional court is in a state of flux. Its lawmaking function is likely to be less overt in future. The realistic prospect of periodic Treaty revision undermines the need and justification for judicial renovation of the Treaty. The enhanced efficacy and democratic accountability of the Community legislature since the entry into force of the Treaty on European Union appear likely to induce a lighter judicial touch when invited to engage in the expansion of the reach of primary Community law. The Court's approach to the development of Community law in general and to its relationship with national courts, in particular, is in the process of undergoing a new period of adjustment.

However, the idea that the Court can now simply 'apply the law' is flawed on several levels. One aspect of the continued need for an active Court lies in the problems caused by supervision of the three-pillar structure created by the Treaty on European Union. Article M of that Treaty indirectly charges the Court with the responsibility of ensuring that developing practice under the two intergovernmental pillars does not diminish the integrity of the Community legal order. In policing the margins of Community activity, the Court is entrusted with a high-profile task that may require boldness where it is confronted by attempts to smuggle matters of EC competence into the hands of the Council/European Council, the predominant institutions of the intergovernmental non-EC EU.

Within the pattern of EC law, the wide scope of legislative activity, in which the Court is called on to perform its interpretative function, will ensure a role for the Court which may come to propel it into ever wider areas than previously.

Most of all, the willingness of the Court to act in defence of the constitutional structure of the Community and the pattern of individual rights arising under it promises lively future conflicts with the political institutions of the Community and, perhaps, even with the Member States when they engage in the process of Treaty revision.

The Court has been subjected to criticism in this book in respect of some of its judgments, but largely for the lack of fully developed reasoning rather than for the outcomes. The spreading influence of the Court's rulings means that the work of the European Court is the subject of increasing scrutiny by national lawyers, some of whom approach rulings from Luxembourg with a degree of scepticism. Now, more than ever, it is incumbent on the European Court to consolidate its position of power by ensuring the delivery of a consistently high quality of legal reasoning. Voices have been raised by politicians and lawyers in criticism of the European Court with increasing frequency in recent years. Hostility towards boldness in the Court will be a self-fulfilling prophecy in such a climate. Although that perception cannot lead the Court to suppose it deserves an immunity from criticism from its supporters, it is appropriate to state the view of this author that the European Court has been an enormously beneficial force in Europe over the last thirty-five years.

It could profitably now allow dissenting judgments. It could build its judgments more firmly and explicitly on the foundations of the Opinions of its Advocates General, who in recent years have been of the highest intellectual quality. Departure from an Advocate General's Opinion should be reasoned. Furthermore, the Court needs to come to terms with the multi-functionalism of Community law and to that end the pattern of appointment to the Court could helpfully be adjusted to secure an appropriate mix of legal expertise. The different chambers of the European Court could more overtly be designed to deal with particular areas of Community law. At the same time, the overall integrity of the Community legal order dictates a need for maintaining institutional links between these chambers. One simple method lies in maintaining the Court on its single site in Luxembourg.

COMPETENCE IN THE COMMUNITY AND THE UNION

Enough space in Chapter 3 was devoted to the tortuous issue of legal base for Community legislation. A brief repetition only: the institutional relationship between the Parliament, the Council, and the Commission would be immeasurably improved by rationalization of the Community's legislative procedures. More important still, such renovation would enhance the transparency of the process and render the potential impact of the 'Community' as an entity affecting and improving the lives of citizens far easier to grasp.

What of competence? A further intransparency resides in the absence of any clear list of what the Community can (and, by implication, cannot) do. The principle of subsidiarity, inserted into the Treaty at Maastricht, was in part designed to address such sensitivities, but it has achieved the very opposite of transparency.

Is there a virtue in attempting to draft a core constitution for the Community? There is an initial attraction in the notion of drawing up a document containing, for example, a list of matters in respect of which the Community is competent; a plan for the principles governing the legislative process; the basic functions of the institutions; the principles of law that are fundamental to the operation of the system; procedures for Treaty revision and admission of new members. It would be necessary in drafting such a document to offer a more precise analysis of the respective scope and functions of the three pillars than is to be found in the Treaty on European Union. This slimmed-down document could then serve as a relatively short, digestible Union constitution. It might prompt the type of reappraisal of the judicial architecture suggested above. A formal constitutional court could deal with cases arising out of the core document. Other types of litigation could be directed away from this 'European Supreme Court'.

Such a codification may ossify the development of the Community legal order and rob the European Court of the flexible power to renovate the system in response to new developments. That, of course, may be interpreted as an advantage, offering relief from the Luxembourg Court's perceived tendencies towards anti-democratic usurpation of power, or it may be regarded as a disadvantage, preparing a gloomy prospect of atrophy at Community level as political intrigue obstructs the deepening of the integrative process and its nourishment of individual rights.

Although questions surrounding the allocation of competence between Community and Member States are likely to remain persistently sensitive in Community law while the Treaty includes no list of competences, fixing the content of such a constitution and such a list would be difficult. There is no litmus test that allows the identification of a constitutional matter. Even were such a list devised, it would not resolve all disputes about its outer limits. The dynamic repositioning of Community competence *vis-à-vis* national competence tracked in Chapter 5 demonstrates the capacity of the institutions to work within the Treaty framework in the absence of tight definitions. Such creative evolution might be jeopardized by an attempt to write a constitution over thirty years after the Court began to lay the foundations of the constitutional order.

It is submitted that a major reason for public resistance to the Community since agreement at Maastricht in December 1991 lies in the impression that the Community is trying to do too much— both in the scope of its activities, and in the power it has been perceived to claim to the exclusion of the Member States. Symptomatic is the false idea, widely thought to have contributed to the 'no' vote in the first Danish referendum in 1992, that Citizenship of the Union replaced Danish citizenship, rather than proving a status additional to it. It is submitted that recognition of the modern reality of shared competence, traced thematically in this book, is capable of providing a means of correcting the misleading impression of an over-ambitious Community that is liable to damage national and local identity. Citizens of the Union should be encouraged to recognize that Community and Union build on the strengths of the Member States and help to support the Member States in areas where international political and economic developments render them weak. The Community and the Union are dependent for much of their strength on the Member States; but the reverse also largely holds true. In the light of this mutuality, the prescription of an evolving shared competence is irresistible. In the light of this preference, the author offers his own conclusion that an attempt to fix a precise list of Community (and, by implication Member-State) competence would miss the point of increasingly intertwining functions.

The reader is invited to continue this complex debate. The author is not about to conclude this book by whisking the blueprint for the future of Europe out of a hat. It is, however, suggested that, whether or not the route of hammering out a short constitutional document is chosen, the indispensable element is transparency. The IGC planned for 1996 will neither succeed, nor deserve to succeed, in winning public support if it is conducted in the manner of the Maastricht negotiations, where openness and accountability found no place on the agenda. Burying differences beneath obscure Treaty provisions characterized both the Single European Act and the Treaty on European Union. Such tactics are doubtless an inevitable part of political manœuvring in international affairs. But the creation of a constitutional order in Europe demands more. The choice of different types of collaborative structures to deal with different types of subject matter is capable of strengthening the patterns of integration—provided the ground-rules governing the different areas are made explicit. Whether the pattern that emerges is based on pillars, concentric circles, or some new metaphor matters less than that it be comprehensible.

Index

European Community (*contd.*):
enlargement
    tensions of 11–14
federal features 187–88
internal market, completion of 15–20
Maastricht Treaty *see* Treaty on European Union
pattern of 23–29
three communities 9–11
transformation into European Union 22–36
Treaty *see* EC Treaty
European Convention on Human Rights 43, 204–5
source of EC law 206
European Council 30, 58
meetings 65
rise to prominence 64–65
Union, position in 58, 64–65
European Court 7, 29, 30, 31, 34
activism *see* judicial activism
Advocate General's Opinions 288
constitutional court, as *see* constitutional court
constitutionalization process 184–87, 191, 210, 220
dissenting judgments 288
Draft EEA agreement, Opinion on 184, 186–87, 212, 220
individual access 194–202
interpretation of legislation *see* legislative interpretation
interpretation of Treaties 7, 190
judges 279–80
judicial review function 189; *see also* judicial review
jurisdiction
    Community competence *see* Community competence
    constitutionality of Community acts 199–200
    non-EC EU pillars 93
lawmaking function 190, 194, 217, 287
legal base, identification of 88–92; *see also* legal base
legal reasoning 288
multi-functionalism of Community law, and 279, 282–84, 288
national courts and 213
national laws, indirect review of 188

reference procedure (Article 177) *see* preliminary reference procedure
Treaty revision 190, 211, 212, 214
Union, position in 58, 79, 93
European Economic Area (EEA) 20–21
Draft agreement—European Court ruling 184, 186–87, 212, 220
European Economic Community (EEC) 9, 11, 23; *see also* European Community
European Free Trade Association (EFTA) 11, 20, 186
EFTA Court 187
European integration
politics and economics of 1–4
European Investment Bank 29
European market 282, 283, 285–5
European Parliament 29, 31, 32, 34, 50, 58, 60
annulment actions
    jurisdiction to bring 191
approval of Commissioners 77
Commission, and
    evolving relationship with 75–78
Committee on Civil Liberties and Internal Affairs 79–80
democratic legitimacy 71, 72, 74, 78, 90
judicial review of acts of 189–91
legislative role 60, 64, 71–75, 191–93
    blocking power 73–4, 86
    conciliation and veto 87–88
    consultation 72
    Single European Act changes 15, 72, 86, 192, 193
    Union Treaty changes 87–88
Single European Act changes 15, 72–72, 86
supervisory role 76–77
Union, position in 58, 78–80, 87
European Social Fund 28
European Union
accountability 79
citizenship *see* Citizenship of the Union
Commission, position of 58
common foreign and security policy 30, 31, 32
competence 56–57
constitution 289–91
    reshaping required 93–94
Court, position of 58, 79

302